KEEPING IN PARADISE

Keeping in Paradise

MY AUTOBIOGRAPHY

JOHN FALLON

WITH DAVID POTTER

BLACK & WHITE PUBLISHING

First published 2015
by Black & White Publishing Ltd
29 Ocean Drive, Edinburgh EH6 6JL

1 3 5 7 9 10 8 6 4 2   15 16 17 18

ISBN   978 1 84502 959 3

A CIP catalogue record for this book is available from the British Library.

Typeset by RefineCatch Limited, Bungay, Suffolk
Printed and bound by Gutenberg Press, Malta

To my father, Patrick Fallon, and my brother, Patrick Fallon, for teaching me the Celtic Way, and to my wife, Esther, and my family for seeing me through thick and thin and helping me come out the other side.

CONTENTS

1

THE EARLY YEARS

The Battle of Britain was raging over the skies of London and Kent on August 16 1940. Unaware of such mighty events, I, John Fallon, was born in Cambuslang, near Dechmont Hill, in the south-east of Glasgow. My father was a six-foot-four coal miner – an oversman, or "gaffer" or foreman – my mother was an ordinary housewife, and I was the fifth of five children, and the fourth boy.

With little concern about the struggle for the future of civilisation going on throughout my early years, I grew up during the Second World War, and in 1945, round about the time that mighty bombs were being dropped on Hiroshima and Nagasaki to end the war, my school career began at St Charles Newton Primary School. I was bright enough, but when it came to the final year, the year of the "quallie", as it was then called, I had already made it clear that I was not interested in an academic career but was content just to get a job and play football.

Football! If Glasgow (and Scotland in general) is obsessed with football now, it was even more so then. There was, of course, the Celtic–Rangers divide, but that was only a part. Four other senior teams existed and thrived in Glasgow – Clyde, Partick Thistle, Queen's Park and Third Lanark – and within a few miles of the city there must have been about ten more – Hamilton, Motherwell,

Albion Rovers, Airdrie and St Mirren, for example. In addition there was Scottish Junior Football, with many strong teams in the Glasgow area, and every two years came the visit of England to play at Hampden in what was simply called "the International". And if you were prepared to save up, you could even go to Wembley to see the International in the year between, a ground where Scotland tended to do quite well in the immediate post-war years. Anyone who did not have at least a passing interest in football in Glasgow did indeed have a few social problems, even though there were other pastimes, like "the pictures" and "the dancing".

There was, of course, also the religious divide. Glasgow had grown up in the nineteenth century, owing its population explosion to two dreadful events of the early nineteenth century. One was the Highland Clearances of the 1820s; the other was the Irish Potato Famine of 1845/46. Both these events were dreadful and devastating to the communities concerned and reflected little credit on the British Empire, which, even if it had not directly set these events in motion, had certainly stood aside and allowed them to happen. Yet there was a beneficiary: the Clydeside city of Glasgow, which built ships and faced the Atlantic Ocean. Glasgow needed labour, and this came from the north of Scotland and from Ireland.

There were always likely to be vast social problems with such a sudden and dramatic influx of people. But the remarkable thing was how well most of these new Glaswegians got on with each other. Glaswegians remain to this day famous for their sociability, sense of humour and ability to help each other in times of distress. In the nineteenth and early twentieth centuries, crammed in appalling housing conditions (unimaginable to this generation, which has been brought up in the Welfare State and with the buttress of the National Health Service), people to a very large extent managed to live together.

But bad housing and evil landlords will always throw up

2

problems. Poverty and desperation, fuelled by drink, stalked the streets. So did crime. Even as late as the 1950s, "razor" crime was common, although Percy Sillitoe, the famous head of the Glasgow police in the 1930s and early 1940s, and the Scottish judicial system brought things under some degree of control. It remained, however, no uncommon sight in the 1960s to find oneself standing beside a man at a football match with a scar from ear to ear, evidence of him having been on the wrong end of a razor attack.

It was against such a background that both streams of Christianity, the Church of Scotland and the Roman Catholic Church, tried to impose some sort of morality and social conscience on their respective flocks. To a very large extent, one would have to concede, they succeeded, but the price was one of exclusiveness. The word "ecumenism" (the unification of Christian Churches) would not have been heard of, and any attempt to bring Churches together – a few brave souls did try – made no headway at all. One was either a Protestant or a Catholic, depending not on anyone's belief but on ethnicity and family considerations. Those who came to Glasgow from the Highlands or other parts of Scotland tended to be Protestants; those who came from Ireland tended to be Roman Catholics. Frequently they lived in the same tenements and they usually, as I have said, got on with each other, but the mark was still there.

It was from this underlying religious divide that the origins of the Celtic v Rangers rivalry sprang. Celtic's origins were undeniably Irish and Catholic, although very early in their history they were happy to employ Protestants as well. Because Celtic were so phenomenally successful, particularly in the Edwardian era – winning six League titles in a row from 1905 until 1910, for example – it was predictable and almost inevitable that a perceived Protestant team would arise to challenge the mighty Irish Catholic side of Jimmy Quinn and Patsy Gallacher. Queen's Park, who insisted on remaining amateur and were forever identified with the rich, merchant, manufacturing middle

3

classes of Glasgow's South Side, were a quaint anachronism by this time, and Third Lanark, Clyde and Partick Thistle had their supports in their areas of Glasgow but were neither ambitious nor rich enough, so the mantle fell on the men in the west of Glasgow, supported by those who worked in the shipyards.

To a certain extent, the carrying of the Protestant torch was wished upon Rangers by the immigration of workers from Ulster after World War One. There was little evidence of sectarian hatred from Rangers before then (although anti-Catholic and anti-Celtic feelings were often apparent at places like St Mirren, Morton and Port Glasgow), but by the 1920s positions were more entrenched. Sadly for the subsequent history of religious intolerance, the Rangers team of the 1920s was an outstandingly good one, with men like Alan Morton, Sandy Archibald, Tommy Cairns and Davie Meiklejohn; therefore more supporters from all over Scotland were attracted by the good football on offer and came to learn, almost as a by-product, all sorts of things about sashes, the Pope and green grassy slopes – which, frankly, they would have been better off not knowing.

Rangers were also able to identify themselves with Scotland. Their colours were blue, which were also Scotland's colours. They supplied many players for the Scottish team – although occasionally men like Bob McPhail would turn awkward and say "no" under pressure from his Ibrox employers – and their supporters would sing Scottish songs like "The Wells of Wearie" and "Loch Lomond", to make themselves the "Scottish" team, as distinct from the alien Irish of Parkhead.

Astonishingly, this division lasted through depressions and wars – if anything, the unemployment of the 1930s made things a great deal worse – and by the time that I grew up and became aware of things, the lines had been drawn. To put it brutally, boys of my background had little choice in what our footballing allegiances were going to be. Occasionally someone might have a liking for Third Lanark or Clyde. They would certainly not support Rangers, and it was simply assumed that he would support Celtic. It was just the way things were. We never questioned it.

The educational system of the time reinforced this. Since 1918, the Roman Catholic Church had been allowed its own schools. Even up to this day they are jealously guarded and protected, although many people now begin to question their value in a society which is endeavouring (with only sporadic success, it must be said) to become non-sectarian. Famously, the question "What school did you go to?" was used by bigoted employers to find out a candidate's religion in Glasgow. Someone from another part of Scotland can say that he went to Forfar Academy or Glenrothes High School without betraying his religion or football team. In the west of Scotland, it becomes immediately obvious.

There was another division in education in my day. The "quallie" or "qualifying" was a sometimes rather brutal exam taken at age twelve in Scotland, after which the sheep were separated from the goats, as head teachers would sometimes rather cruelly put it. I did not pass the quallie, so I went on to St Bride's Junior Secondary School, as distinct from those with the potential for an academic career, who went on to Our Lady's High School, where they could eventually take Highers and possibly go on to university. Very seldom was there any flexibility or even any acknowledgement that a mistake had been made in the quallie. The system was very rigid. But there was no great protest. We accepted things.

This astonishingly paternalistic system would prevail, in both Protestant and Catholic schools, until the late 1960s or early 1970s. It had good points in that high schools were usually very good, and bright working-class boys and girls, if they passed their quallie, had the opportunity to do well in a civilised and academic environment, whereas the junior secondaries, with no great drive or inclinations towards academia, could concentrate on other aspects of education. That was the theory. The problem was that the age of twelve was simply far too early in anyone's life to make a permanent decision on their future, depending on how they did in the quallie.

I owe a great deal to my quallie teacher (the man who taught me in Primary 7), Jimmy Murphy, a man who had had a trial for Celtic a few years previously. John had played in the forward line and in the midfield for the school team, but one day while we were practising I went into goal and saved a couple of Murphy's penalty kicks. After that, I played in the goal for the primary team and I never looked back.

In 1952, I went to St Bride's Junior Secondary School. For the next three years I continued with my obsession with football, this time under the influence of a man called Danny Ward, a man who was himself a great football player and who encouraged me and others all he could. As well as playing for the school team, I started playing for the St Cadoc's Boys Guild team and was very happy playing at that level.

Social change was in the air in the early 1950s. A vigorous Labour government containing the quietly efficient Clement Attlee and the grimly determined Nye Bevan, elected for that very purpose a matter of weeks after the end of the Second World War, nationalised the mines and railways and created the National Health Service. They did this against the background of post-war recovery, something which by its very nature slowed things down, and these reforms would take a long time to work through the system. To his credit, Churchill when he returned to power in 1951 did nothing to dismantle Labour's Welfare State, and slowly throughout the 1950s we saw a gradual improvement in the standard and quality of life of most people.

In the meantime I had started my lifelong love affair with Glasgow Celtic, that most demanding and tantalising of mistresses. It would have been difficult, as we have seen, for anyone from my background not to be "Celtic daft", for they were the team of our culture. Even though the "Irish" had been in Glasgow for over a hundred years in some cases, we still saw ourselves as Irish as well as Scottish. Indeed, the very name Celtic was coined to indicate the bringing together of the two strands of Celtic's support, for the name "Celtic" covers both Scotland and Ireland.

The history and achievements of the club guaranteed that the loyalty of the Glasgow Irish first pledged in the 1890s would remain. The early 1900s and the years of the Great War had seen a great Celtic team, and names like Jimmy McMenemy, Jimmy Quinn and Patsy Gallacher were well known and much spoken about. The 1920s and 1930s had been less successful, but 1938 had seen the winning of the all-Britain Empire Exhibition Trophy, and Kennaway, Hogg, Morrison; Geatons, Lyon, Paterson; Delaney, MacDonald, Crum, Divers and Murphy had sustained the wilting support during the dark years from 1939 to 1945. Even after the war, we all knew who these men were.

While the Battle of Britain was going on, while the Desert Army was driving the Huns (the real ones!) across Africa, and while the D-Day landings changed the face of world history, Celtic had a consistently poor time in the Second World War. Manager Willie Maley "The Man Who Made Celtic" had left the club in acrimonious circumstances in 1940, and the club had never really recovered from that blow. Rangers ruled the roost in the war years, and generally speaking there was little for a Celtic supporter to be happy about in the immediate post-war years either. A win at Dundee in 1948 saved the team from relegation, and general achievement was rarely above the mediocre.

Yet it was not all that bad either. There was, for example, an excellent goalkeeper in Willie Miller (who provided an excellent role model for my young self), and in the middle of all the ordinary players there were a few outstanding ones, like Bobby Evans and Charlie Tully. But the really good thing for Celtic was that their supporters did not desert them. Attendances remained astonishingly high for what was a poor team, on some occasions barely worthy of wearing the famous green and white jerseys or of being associated with the august traditions of the club. But we still stuck by them.

Successes were described as "isolated but spectacular". The Scottish Cup was recaptured for the sixteenth time, in 1951, when Celtic beat Motherwell 1–0 with a John McPhail goal, but we delirious Celtic fans that day who thought that glory was permanently returning were in for a disappointment. Celtic's goalkeeper that day was George Hunter, a grossly underestimated custodian who departed to Swindon Town when he still had a lot to offer the club. He had certainly played a great part in winning the Scottish Cup for Celtic by his heroics in an earlier round at a massively overcrowded Tynecastle. In that febrile atmosphere, he defied Willie Bauld and the rest of the Hearts forwards, with the crowd behind him more or less sitting on his goal net because of severe crushing at the Gorgie Road end of the ground. He also survived a barrage from the talented Raith Rovers team in the semi-final before Celtic narrowly won through. Then in the final itself, Hunter pulled off a couple of fine saves as the desperate Motherwell pressed for a late equaliser.

I very soon became a regular attender at Celtic Park in those days, sometimes walking, sometimes taking a number 17 tram from my home in Cambuslang, and paying my seven pence to get in at the boys' gate at the old Rangers End of the ground before walking round to a suitable vantage point. Often in the morning I had already been at the one-penny matinee performance at the cinema, and seeing Celtic would complete my entertainment for the day. I remember the bitter disappointment of a day when a game against Rangers was postponed because of fog. I had actually reached the stadium when it was announced that the game was off. Fog was a not infrequent occurrence in Glasgow, made worse by all the industrial output from what was still called "the Empire's second city", so the word "smog" was coined to describe it. This was long before clean-air acts and other measures were taken to make life slightly more bearable and a lot more healthy.

In his book *Now You Know About Celtic*, the late Bob Crampsey has a brilliantly evocative description of match day at Celtic Park of that era.

> For those old enough to remember, I hope memories return of the No. 9 Auchenshuggle tramcar wobbling out London Road on the way to the early winter kick-offs of these pre-floodlight times. Of the cries of the optimistic sellers of food. "Fourpence ra meat and cheese sandwidges." Of the tireless vendor and his "Erzi offishal program". Of the twinkling pinpoints of light as the crowd, smokers to a man, lit and constantly re-lit Woodbines, Prize Crop or Capstan Full Strength. Of the days when the reserve side was the Alliance side and the players wore heavy woollen jerseys with lace-up collars and the lace-up boots that, in the famous words of Hugh McIlvanney "chafed you under the armpits", when the T-panel ball became as heavy as lead on a muddy day, needing not only skill but courage to head it and when in a downpour the same heavy woollen jerseys came to weigh a ton.

I can identify with all that.

Celtic had, undeniably, a huge support, but it was a pity for our huge support that there was no great team to watch. For example, 1952 saw an obsession with the flying of the Irish flag in spite of official disapproval and even in defiance of a few SFA edicts – something that was used by the club to rally the support, feeding the Celtic paranoia complex, and (more insidiously) to mask the gross and rather obvious shortcomings of the team. It was not that Celtic did not have good players; it was simply that they failed to produce consistently good performances, and the record was nothing above the ordinary. It was generally agreed that manager Jimmy McGrory, whose playing record for the club in the 1920s and 1930s was second to none, was no great shakes as a manager and that he was in any case too easily influenced by the tyrannical Bob Kelly.

Yet even though the club was going through bad times, it retained the loyalty and love of its support. Younger fans would rapidly tire of the older generation telling them all about Young, Loney and Hay, the rumbustious Jimmy Quinn and the wily Jimmy McMenemy, who rejoiced in the name of "Napoleon". Why, we youngsters would ask, does it not happen now? Why was it that Rangers and Hibs could have such great teams and Celtic didn't? Where were the men like Patsy Gallacher and Tommy McInally, of the previous generation?

But there was, however, the curious business of the Coronation Cup, an all-British tournament to celebrate the coronation of Queen Elizabeth II in 1953. Celtic were lucky even to be offered a place in this tournament, for their League position hardly warranted it, and they had exited the Scottish Cup in a miserable fashion, losing 0–2 to Rangers at Ibrox in the quarter-final. But the tournament was to be held in Glasgow, and Celtic's vast and long-suffering support could hardly be ignored.

Amazingly, Celtic, buoyed up by the inspired purchase of Neil Mochan, first won, in early May 1953, the Glasgow Charity Cup (not in all conscience the greatest tournament in the world but at least a tangible trophy), then turned on the football that they had always been capable of and beat Manchester United and Arsenal to reach the final. Those who felt that the Coronation Cup was meant to be between the two establishment teams of Scotland and England, namely Rangers and Arsenal, were perplexed to discover that the final was between Celtic and Hibs, Scotland's two "Irish" teams, neither of whose supporters had ever been known for their love of the royal family.

My brother and I had the privilege of sitting in the Centre Stand that night, having acquired tickets, which cost the inordinate price of twelve shillings and sixpence (something like sixty-two pence in modern money). My father had known a bookmaker with a leaning towards Rangers. The bookie had bought a couple of tickets in advance, confident that his beloved Rangers would be in the final. When this did not happen – proving that bookies do not always win! – the bookie, a decent bloke, gave the tickets to my father, and my brother and I were in luck. I thus had an excellent view of Jock Stein (without his false teeth) lifting the trophy at the end. Little did I imagine how often and in what circumstances I would meet Jock Stein in the future.

The final was an excellent example of how the most technically gifted team does not always necessarily win football matches. It also proved the value of goalkeeping. Hibs were a fine team, but Celtic won, thanks mainly to a fine defensive display by their rugged but not necessarily talented centre half and captain, Jock Stein, and in particular to a great goalkeeping performance by a man called John Bonnar. At the age of twelve, I must have been very impressed by the calm organisation of that Celtic rearguard, for Bonnar had the game of his life. Well over twenty years later, Willie Ormond, one of the "Famous Five" Hibs forward line and then manager of Scotland, would claim that the biggest heartbreak in his life was not being able to get one past "that bugger Bonnar", as he alliteratively and graphically put it. Once in particular near the end, Ormond fired from the edge of the box, saying to himself, "That's a winner," before to his chagrin seeing Bonnar appear from nowhere to save. I would like to think that I learned my goalkeeping skills from that night.

The season 1953/54 saw Celtic build on that performance with a League and Cup double, and very many talented football players like Bobby Collins, Willie Fernie, Bobby Evans and Charlie Tully all combined to produce the goods under the captaincy of Jock Stein. But sadly any promise of domination was not maintained, with one particular goalkeeping howler losing Celtic the Scottish Cup final of 1955. The same John Bonnar, hero of 1953, failed to grasp a harmless corner kick late in the game and Clyde earned a replay. Jock Stein was still centre half and captain that day, and famously was said to dislike and distrust goalkeepers. It may be that his suspicion and distrust of them dated from that event. It was an awful clanger, and then sadly on a wet Wednesday night, after Chairman Bob Kelly had made the questionable decision to drop Bobby Collins apparently because of a rather undignified shoulder-charging duel with Clyde's goalkeeper in the first game, Clyde won the replay with a solitary goal from Celtic-supporting Tommy Ring. That was painful!

I have my own recollection of that replay. The kick-off was in the early evening, and just to make sure that I didn't miss it, I took the afternoon off school, hoping that I wouldn't be missed. More likely I wasn't all that bothered anyway, because I was far more interested in the destination of the Scottish Cup than I was in my education or indeed the consequences of missing school. Well, I stood in the rain on the uncovered Celtic End (covering at Hampden was still more than ten years away) with a good view of Ring's winner early in the second half and a rather more distant view of McPhail's header near the end, which might just have earned us extra time.

The devastation that accompanies a Celtic Scottish Cup final defeat is one that you really have to experience in order to appreciate what it is like. As I trudged away from Hampden heartbroken and desolate, I suddenly heard a voice call "Fallon!" I looked round. It was my headmaster. "Come and see me tomorrow!" So I was in for a dose of the belt as well as having to cope with a cup final defeat!

I appeared at the heedie's door the following day. "Come in, Fallon." Bracing myself for the inevitable, I was then amazed to hear his tone soften and him saying, "I suppose you're as sick about last night as I am." I nodded. "Very well, you've suffered enough. But just in case anyone is listening and they think I've gone soft, I have to pretend to belt you six times." He then

12

proceeded to hit his desk with his belt six times, then told me to disappear. After that, I would never have a bad word said about him. But the pain of that defeat remained.

2

GROWING UP

The next few years would have made even the most enthusiastic of roller-coaster riders feel a little squeamish. Another Scottish Cup final was lost in a mysteriously disappointing performance against Hearts – it might have been different if Jock Stein had not been injured; then the Scottish League Cup was won, for the first time, on Hallowe'en 1956, just as Great Britain prepared to do battle with Egypt over the Suez Canal; then an appalling goalkeeping performance by Dick Beattie saw Celtic lose a Scottish Cup semi-final in March 1957; and then there was the famous 7–1 victory over Rangers in the Scottish League Cup in October 1957. We didn't know where we were or what to make of it all, but as far as the 7–1 game is concerned, I am proud to say that I was there.

I was, by now, a member of the James Kelly Celtic Supporters' Club of Blantyre. I recall with a great deal of pleasure going round the country to watch Celtic. On one occasion, we travelled to Dundee, watched Celtic in the afternoon and then stayed in Dundee to watch the boxing. This was Scotland v the Golden Gloves at the Caird Hall. The Golden Gloves were the winners of the US tournament of that name for amateur boxers, but such was the strength of amateur boxing in Scotland at that time (particularly in Dundee, from whence sprung Celtic-supporting

Dick McTaggart, who won a gold medal in the Melbourne Olympics of 1956 and another gold in the Commonwealth Games at Cardiff in 1958) that Scotland beat the Americans 10–0! The Golden Gloves also lost to Northern Ireland and Wales but, oddly enough, beat England on that tour.

Trips to Aberdeen involved a twenty-four-hour shift. The bus would leave Blantyre at about six o'clock in the morning. This was necessary, for the roads were not the dual carriageways that they are now and, of course, there was always the need to stop for "refreshments" on the way. After the game, the bus would stay for the evening in Aberdeen (Celtic and Aberdeen supporters enjoyed a very good relationship in those days and there was seldom the slightest hint of trouble in the Granite City) and it would be about midnight before all the "stragglers" were picked up (sometimes literally) and the bus headed south during the night to reach home very early in the morning.

By this time a young lad with flaming red hair, I had left school in 1955, and after working for a spell delivering orders for butchers and other jobs, I was offered an apprenticeship with Foden's diesel trucks as an engineer. Foden's were based in London Road, not all that far away from Celtic Park, and as it happened I was their first apprentice in Scotland. I would serve my time with them and I was still playing Boys Guild football for a team called Halfway on a Saturday. But one day a man called Davie Farquhar approached me while I was playing football in the yard during the lunch break and suggested that I might consider playing for Fauldhouse United, a junior team. My first reaction, according to a quote which I gave to the *Edinburgh Evening Dispatch* about a year later, was that I would rather watch Celtic, but Davie Farquhar was persuasive and I joined Fauldhouse.

Fauldhouse, in the middle of the West Lothian coalfield, is some considerable distance away from Glasgow, although it is on one of the railway lines to Edinburgh. It is by no means a place of

15

scenic beauty, but the people were and are warm-hearted and love their football. Fauldhouse had won the Scottish Junior Cup in 1946, something they are still very proud of. Their opponents in the final were a team called Arthurlie, a name which in 1946 would still have sent a tingle of horror down Celtic spines, for it was the same Arthurlie that had rocked Victorian Scotland by beating Celtic on January 9 1897 in the Scottish Cup. They had since fallen on bad times, hence the reason they were now a junior team, but nevertheless the Celtic community would have been glad to see Fauldhouse beat Arthurlie 2–0 on May 18 1946 at Hampden Park in the Scottish Junior Cup final before an astonishing crowd of over 44,000. Fauldhouse also, unusually for a mining community in Scotland, boasts what was for years a very fine cricket team, which rejoices in the name of Fauldhouse Victoria.

Scottish Junior Football (the word "junior" is misleading, for there are some old gnarled veterans who play at this level) was and remains notoriously tough for anyone, but it is a good place to cut one's teeth in the game. If you can cope with the rough opponents, the sometimes awful pitches and the wild, outlandish, violent and boisterous spectators on a rainy, windy November day, then frankly you can cope with anything. It would be a very brave man who would referee in Scottish Junior Football, and it is definitely a fine way of weeding out those who are simply not brave enough for the senior game. Scottish football is not and never will be a place for "softies". The pitch, for example, at Fauldhouse was not great. I remember it as a red blaze strip with some grass at the side.

I was happy to play for Fauldhouse. My debut was on my eighteenth birthday – 16 August 1958 – against Bathgate. In this game, watched by my father, I must have played well, for I would play for the team for some time, but I had the misfortune to break a fellow's collarbone. This was the centre forward, who was no injured innocent, for he had already subjected me to a few brutal

16

charges – this was the era in which shoulder-charging was still considered to be part of the game – until I found a way to counteract it. I caught the ball, then immediately turned my body so that shoulder met shoulder. On this occasion the centre forward came off worst, and he was carried off with a broken collarbone. I was upset about that.

In reviewing that incident it is important to bear in mind the sometimes brutal nature of charging the goalkeeper. In the 1950s football was very definitely a contact sport, and it was only under the influence of the Europeans that the British associations were eventually persuaded to outlaw shoulder-charging of goalkeepers. In theory there were safeguards – the goalkeeper had to have the ball in his hands, his feet had to be on the ground and the forward had to use his shoulder, not his elbow. In practice it did not always work out like that, and if one consults YouTube to see the English Cup final of 1958, one can see an excellent example of what looks like a brutal foul but was actually, according to the laws of the game, a legitimate goal. This was when Nat Lofthouse of Bolton Wanderers shoulder-charged Harry Gregg of Manchester United for his side's second goal. What is remarkable is the lack of outcry by commentator Kenneth Wolstenholme or anyone else. And if you also consult the 1957 English Cup final, when Peter McParland of Aston Villa "clashed" with Manchester United's Ray Wood, one can see an even worse example of fouling a goalkeeper – amazingly, not punished by the referee. A straight red card would certainly be the result of that incident today.

Clearly the life of a goalkeeper in the 1950s was anything but a cushy number, but shoulder charging was something that was ingrained deep within the psyche of Scottish football. In the old days Jimmy Quinn excelled at the art of "charging", and even the gentlemanly Jimmy McGrory was often much admired for his shoulders, so useful in the art of what was tactfully called "rumbling up" the goalkeeper. Conversely, defenders like Willie

Loney and Peter Johnstone were much praised for their ability to "protect" their own goalkeepers, like Davie Adams and Charlie Shaw, from the brutal assaults of the opposition. Scottish football's reputation for toughness was by no means undeserved. It was no place for shrinking violets.

I clearly must have impressed the Fauldhouse management, for I was given a run in the team. My experiences led to my first encounter with floodlights, then a novelty in Scottish football, and it was a great treat to be allowed to play under them. Floodlights (in their modern form) were first allowed in competitive Scottish football in the mid 1950s, and for a junior to have the opportunity to play under them was considered to be a great achievement. Fauldhouse United played under the auspices of the East of Scotland Junior League, although they were in the western section of that league. On one occasion the eastern section played the western section at Tynecastle, and I was chosen for the western section. Although my team lost, I relished the Tynecastle floodlights. However, I would not always enjoy playing under them. Indeed, in the 1960s some were distinctly poor, and I would single out Falkirk, St Mirren, Kilmarnock and Ibrox for having floodlights that were substandard.

Soon, however, a new dynamic entered the equation of my young life, because I became a "Kelly Kid".

3

A KELLY KID

The "Kelly Kids" were so called because they were a brainchild of Chairman Bob Kelly. They were a deliberate attempt to copy the "Busby Babes" of Manchester United, a phenomenally successful idea from Matt Busby. Manchester United had won the English League of 1955/56 and 1956/57, and who knows where they might have gone had it not been for the aeroplane disaster in the snows of Munich in February 1958?

Kelly's scheme involved enrolling as many talented youngsters as possible and bringing them to Celtic Park for training sessions, without necessarily interfering with their apprenticeships, or university or employment prospects. The sessions would be in the evenings, and those who were considered good enough would, in time, be offered full-time terms. The word used with distressing frequency by the press was "arrive". The Kelly Kids would all "arrive" at the same time, the supporters were told, and the team would then "take off", to continue the travel metaphor. Well, one might argue, that was exactly what happened, but it was a long way down the line and the circumstances were far different from what Mr Kelly envisaged.

In fairness, it has to be said, that the Celtic team of the mid 1950s, although teeming with talent – Willie Fernie, Charlie Tully, Bobby Collins, Bobby Evans, Bertie Peacock – and certainly man for man a great deal better than either Rangers, Hearts or anyone else, had, on rather too many occasions, failed to deliver the goods. Cup finals had been lost; League challenges had faltered on unlikely grounds like Falkirk, St Mirren and Airdrie; there had been an embarrassing ten-year wait for Celtic's first ever win of the Scottish League Cup, and the impression was that although the ability was there, sustained success was a long way away.

It was ironic, therefore, that in the immediate aftermath of what was arguably Celtic's best ever single game Kelly seemed to have decided that changes were necessary. On October 19 1957 Celtic won their second Scottish League Cup in a row by defeating Rangers 7–1 in the final. It made up for a great deal of disappointments, and as we in the Celtic End departed in triumphant delirium that day, the hope was expressed that the corner had been turned, and that Beattie, Donnelly, Fallon, Fernie, Evans, Peacock, Tully, Collins, McPhail, Wilson and Mochan would produce Scottish League titles, Scottish Cups galore and even make an impact on the infant European Cup.

Not so! That team hardly played together again, and was steadily, brick by brick, dismantled in favour of the youth policy. Celtic would not win another domestic honour for seven and a half years, and the frustrations and heartbreaks were intense. It was as if Kelly had said that this team had now done its job and a new one was required. Several players fell out with Kelly and had to be transferred (often, it was claimed, to pay for the new flood-lights), one or two left under a cloud, and some, like Charlie Tully, simply got old. But the whole business was a sorry one – and how Celtic supporters suffered for this colossal piece of asset-stripping, for the laudable youth policy took a long time to develop. Half a century later, Alan Hansen famously said, "You'll never win any-thing with kids." One has to admit that in the context of Celtic in the late 1950s and early 1960s, Alan had a point.

Bob Kelly, or Sir Robert Kelly (he would be knighted in 1969), was the son of Celtic's first great player, James Kelly, who had arrived from Renton virtually at the same time as Celtic were being formed. He found fame while he was with Renton, becoming a Scotland International and twice winner of the Scottish Cup, and was possibly the first player to have the phrase "just like an ordinary man" applied to him. His landlady when he came to live in Glasgow told all her neighbours that he ate his food and drank his tea "just like an ordinary man"!

James Kelly's contribution to Celtic history was immense: that of his son is far more debatable. Precluded from playing football by his withered arm, Bob took a great interest in the administrative side of the club and had been the chairman for several years. No one could deny that he had the interests of the club at heart, and he was certainly very protective of the club's good name, with a laudable insistence on good behaviour from his players, but he was too much of an autocrat to be a positive influence on Celtic. He interfered in team selection – Jimmy McGrory was far too malleable to resist – and his knowledge of how to deal with modern professional football players was sometimes deficient. Four Scottish Cup finals were lost in 1955, 1956, 1961 and 1963, and the common factor as far as Celtic were concerned was a questionable team selection. Bob Kelly was behind all that. Yet he was not without his good points either.

The fostering of youngsters was an excellent idea, and Bob Kelly would always argue that it actually won Celtic the European Cup in 1967. There is an element of truth in that, but it was not quite so simple or easy as Kelly declared, for an awful lot of water, sadly much of it dirty and unpleasant, had to flow under the bridge before that could happen. The trouble was that so much of the youth policy depended on who was running it. For a spell it worked well, when Jock Stein, who had recently retired from playing and captaining the club, was in charge of us. Good players were brought on and encouraged, notably Billy McNeill and Pat Crerand (and I would like to include myself), and although the first team was going through a transitional phase

21

following their magnificent and legendary 7–1 defeat of Rangers in the Scottish League Cup final of October 1957 – they were nowhere at all in the League won by Hearts, and a dismal Scottish Cup exit to Clyde – it was noticeable that the reserve team was doing particularly well.

Indeed, the club needed a good reserve team, for the first team had a dreadful season in 1958/59. Still nowhere in the Scottish League or Scottish League Cup, the team did manage to reach the semi-final of the Scottish Cup, beating Rangers in the process, to the delight of their fans. But at Hampden they appalled their huge support in the 73,885 crowd by collapsing 0–4 to a St Mirren team who, granted, would go on to win the Scottish Cup that year but were no great shakes in their League games. As for Celtic fans that day, "they had folded up both their tents and their tricolours and had stolen sadly and silently away from this harrowing scene half an hour before the finish" according to the *Evening Times*.

And yet the same team seemed to have done the difficult job when they had beaten and outplayed Rangers in an earlier round, the 2–1 scoreline bearing little resemblance to Celtic's superiority. Then in the last League game of the season, Celtic beat potential League winners Hearts, a result which handed the League Championship to Rangers. Little wonder there was so much frustration and bewilderment among the fans. But in 1959 we youngsters in the reserves were winning trophies and showing great promise. By the early 1960s, Celtic reserves would win domestic trebles galore, and I look back on my years with them with a great deal of affection, particularly when we started to play reserve games under the floodlights on a Friday night, thus attracting crowds of close to 10,000 on some occasions. This area of Celtic in those days was very certainly a success.

Trouble came, however, when Jock Stein, an ambitious man, was allowed to go to become manager of Dunfermline Athletic in March 1960. Kelly would always say that this was part of a grand plan for Jock to get experience elsewhere, then return to Celtic to lead the club to glory. Frankly, this is simply not true. Stein himself in a famous TV interview in 1970 hints that his religion might have been a factor (ludicrous to modern eyes, but certainly influential in the 1950s, and possibly even a factor in the departure of Fernie, Collins and Evans), but the simple fact was that Stein wanted to be his own man, aware that under the benign managership of Jimmy McGrory Celtic lacked the necessary aggression and "devil" to earn success. So Stein left us for Dunfermline, beat Celtic in his first game, rescued the Pars from relegation in 1960 and then, on an awful night for Celtic supporters, beat Celtic in the Scottish Cup final of 1961. Once again in this game, it was a goalkeeper who made a difference, for 26 April 1961 was known as "Connachan's Cup final" when Eddie Connachan time and time again denied the eager but inexperienced Celtic forwards. Ironically, Eddie, from Prestonpans in East Lothian, like quite a few of the Dunfermline side, was Celtic daft.

Celtic would thus bitterly regret the departure of Jock Stein, but Dunfermline never looked back, changing status from a small, under-performing provincial club with no history at all (even their nickname, "the Pars", is believed to be a shortened form of "the paralytics", a term of abuse hurled at them by frustrated supporters from the 1920s onwards) into a European power with fine performances against teams like Everton and Valencia to their credit. Before the arrival of Stein, the two teams in Fife had been Raith Rovers and East Fife, with Dunfermline nowhere. Stein changed that. Say what you want about him, he had the power to do such things.

Stein's path and my own had crossed before then, for I joined Celtic as a "Kelly Kid" in December 1958 and very soon began to make a name for myself in the reserves, including on one occasion playing alongside the now ageing and venerable Charlie Tully in a game against Motherwell. Frequently, and to my great delight, my name began to be mentioned as Man of the Match in the *Evening Citizen*'s and the *Evening Times*' reports of games. Reserve games did not, of course, appear prominently, but there was usually a small paragraph which ended with "Man of the Match – J. Fallon, Celtic". Occasionally I was misspelled to be J. Falloon (there had once been an Eddie Falloon who played for Aberdeen) or on another occasion I was called S. Fallon, when the typesetter clearly confused me with Celtic's assistant manager and erstwhile full back Sean.

Sometimes the big press boys would go to a reserve match, if there was nothing else for them to do. Thus Jimmy Brownlie and Jack Harkness, both themselves great Scottish goalkeepers of a bygone age, saw me and mentioned me favourably, as did the recently retired George Young of Rangers (a fine and fair judge of talent, and who had left Ibrox without taking with him any lasting affection for the club). There was also Hugh Taylor, who wrote the magnificent series "The Scottish Football Book", which youngsters loved, and Gair Henderson of the *Evening Times*, a man wrongly accused of pro-Rangers bias and often called "Gers" Henderson.

Thus I was beginning to make myself known in my own little way, but on one occasion I incurred the wrath of Jock Stein and the Celtic establishment – by no means my last contretemps with Big Jock. It concerned Junior Football. I had now left Fauldhouse but was open to offers from elsewhere. The hiring and firing of junior footballers was often a haphazard, last-minute, rushed affair – and often on a match-to-match basis – but there was a rule at Celtic that a Kelly Kid was not allowed to play for a junior team without permission. Normally it would be granted – for how else could a young man learn the ropes? – but I was unaware of the protocol, and when approached by Blantyre Celtic to play a couple of games for them against Bridgeton Waverley and Kirkintilloch Rob Roy, I readily agreed without consulting Celtic, and played well, I thought, on both occasions.

But nothing escaped Big Jock even in the late 1950s, before he became a manager in his own right. He had a wide network of spies and contacts; he read the newspapers avidly; he had, in particular, connections with Blantyre Vics, the rivals of Blantyre Celtic, and one day I found myself facing an uncomfortable interview with the angry youth coach. My defence was that I simply did not know the rule. I was told never to do it again.

Possibly Stein took a dislike to me at this point, and he certainly encouraged me to look elsewhere on one particular occasion, when Falkirk expressed an interest with a view to giving me a trial in a friendly game against Scunthorpe United. I was encouraged by Stein to go and "take some money from them", but I refused to do this, stating that my desire was to play for Celtic, even though it might take some time to reach the first team.

The goalkeeper's spot at Parkhead was now held by Frank Haffey, an effervescent, likeable, bubbly character who was also a good singer, performing Irish favourites like "The Dear Little Shamrock" and "Slattery's Mounted Fut". He had taken over from Dick Beattie, a man about whom rumours refused to go away (he was eventually done for match-fixing when with Portsmouth in 1965) but who was immortalised for his part in the 7–1 defeat of Rangers in the 1957 Scottish League Cup final. Haffey was agile, occasionally spectacular and never dull, although capable of a few howlers. He was a couple of years older than me, and still enjoyed the love and support of the fans, with whom he had built up a rapport. I was aware that Frank would not be easily replaced, even though he did drop some clangers.

Season 1959/60 started badly. In a League Cup section of Airdrie, Raith Rovers and Partick Thistle, most people would have expected Celtic to qualify. In fact we finished third and when the League started lost to Rangers 3–1 at Ibrox on September 5. I had played for the reserves at Parkhead and had distinguished myself, I thought, in a 3–1 win. Those in the know felt that I was good enough to get a run in the first team, but with Haffey still playing well, there was one area in which Celtic did not seem to have a problem, and that was goalkeeping.

The problems lay in the forward line, where there were so many youngsters, full of enthusiasm but with no experience or "street wisdom". But a great deal of the blame has to be laid at the door of the management, who allowed men like Fernie, Collins and (eventually) Evans to go when they all had years left in them. It was said that the club needed money to pay for the new floodlights, which would prove to be spectacularly good in time, but the fans wanted above all else to see a good team on the park.

My big chance came on September 26 1959, when Haffey called off at the last minute and I found myself in the goal for a League game against Clyde at Parkhead. I was not the only debutant that day, for John Curran was also given his debut at right back, and on the left wing, Bertie Auld having called off injured, Tommy Mackle was given a game. In the circumstances, Celtic did well to get a 1–1 draw against Clyde.

It was a lovely day after some recent rain, and the *Evening Times* tells how after only ten seconds Bobby Evans gave me a confidence boost with a pass back. Then, "Two minutes later Fallon showed that the Evans prescription was just what the football doctor ordered with a great and confident save from Herd after he had waded through several Celtic defenders." Referee Bobby Davidson, never the darling of Parkhead, then turned down a Celtic penalty claim before I had another save low down following a corner. Then I had another couple of good moments before half-time, once diving at the feet of a Clyde forward to grab the ball. When Mackle then scored at the other end, my Celtic career was well begun.

Clyde scored in the second half with a shot that I could do little about, and it was generally agreed that the 1–1 draw, an improvement on some recent abject performances, might have been a win if Celtic had had a few more experienced players. But I earned good reports in the Sunday newspapers, and supporters were apparently "beginning to think that a new hero might have arrived in the red-headed Fallon". I certainly felt happy about my game. The team on my debut was Fallon, Curran and Mochan; Smith, Evans and Peacock; Chalmers, Jackson, Conway, Divers and Mackle. It was a respectable, but mediocre, performance from the team, but one would not have predicted that Stephen Chalmers would one day score the goal that brought the European Cup to Britain for the first time.

George Young, the ex-Rangers centre half but also a man renowned for his fairness and gentlemanly behaviour and thus commanding the respect, if not the love, of Celtic fans, was fulsome in his praise, writing in the *News of the World* the following day, "Young John Fallon, taking the place of Frank Haffey in the Celtic goal, started the game off with two cracking saves in the first five minutes. Then he really brought the house down with a brilliant leap and clutch at a Danny Currie shot midway through the second half. Yes, all through the game he was as sure of himself as a veteran. But while young John was turning on all the brilliance, the outfield players from both teams never really got going." Young was also convinced that Celtic should have had at least one penalty from Mr Davidson but had to admit that he had seen better Celtic teams.

It was certainly true that 1959 was no great Celtic team. The previous spring's dreadful 0–4 defeat by St Mirren in the Scottish Cup semi-final had left its mark, and the air of depression, so tangible and visible, had not been dispelled over the past six months. Even the sight of the massive floodlight pylons being erected at the ground failed to convince anyone that happy days were just around the corner. The supporters kept being told that this was only a temporary phenomenon and that in time all the promising youngsters would come good. I was included in the group of "promising youngsters".

I retained my place for the next game at Arbroath. Evans was playing for Scotland in Belfast and Peacock was playing for Northern Ireland in the same game, but the team was hardly weakened, with the deployment of Billy McNeill and John Clark (McNeill had had a few games before but it was the debut for John Clark), and Arbroath were despatched 5–0. At the small, friendly Angus ground, a matter of yards from the North Sea, I had a good game in the opinion of the writer of the *Sporting Post*, Dundee's evening paper, and I delighted some of the support (although I horrified a few as well) with my friendly gestures to them, in particular a "thumbs-up" sign after a good save. One veteran supporter, who had himself been a goalkeeper in Junior Football in his time, asserted that he had never seen Charlie Shaw or John Thomson do that but, under pressure, admitted that I had had a good game.

The following week against Aberdeen at Parkhead, Celtic were leading 1–0 from a dodgy goal, then Aberdeen equalised late in the game and would have won but for two saves from myself, described as "wonderful" by Harry Andrew of the *Scottish Sunday Express*. And then two days after that I was chosen to play in a historic match at Celtic Park. This was the game played on Monday 12 October 1959 against Wolverhampton Wanderers to inaugurate the Celtic Park floodlights before a very good crowd of 45,000.

Wolves were English champions but fielded a weakened team. Even so, they were far too good for the young Celtic team and beat us 2–0. It could have been a lot more, but Wolves had no desire to embarrass their hosts on such a night. John MacKenzie in the *Scottish Daily Express* was impressed by the lights (they were as good and as high as anywhere else in Great Britain) but less so by the Celtic team. Only Bobby Evans and myself ("who stopped half a dozen certs after making one mistake") were given any sort of praise, and the question is posed at the end: "You've got the lights now, Celtic. How about the team?"

It was a valid question, for it seemed that a good team (it was only two years, after all, since the famous 7–1 win over Rangers) had been sacrificed for the floodlights. The tall lights of London Road were a great Glasgow landmark and supporters could instantly see where the ground was, but it would be a long time before there was a team to be proud of. A great deal of unhappiness awaited Celtic and their fans. Past glories were all very well, but supporters needed something going on at the moment if they were to retain their enthusiasm. They didn't come to games to look at floodlights.

Falling gates were a phenomenon of all Scottish football at this time. Society was changing; indeed, in economic terms it was improving. The Conservatives had won the 1959 general election on Harold McMillan's slogan "We've never had it so good", and this was the case. Enlightened Conservative rule, albeit pandering more than a little to the middle classes, had not demolished Labour's National Health Service and welfare state, and wealth was now beginning to trickle slowly down to the working classes. More and more working people could afford the new luxury of the age – the television – and some were contemplating buying a car or even going abroad for their holidays. In such circumstances, traditional working-class pursuits like the cinema and football were under attack.

Football had been slow to spot the signs. Every club now seemed to be keen to build shelters for their fans and to provide better amenities, but by then the damage had been done. Celtic's Jungle, an ugly building like a cowshed with holes in the roof, attracted a great deal of ridicule, but it stayed there until 1966. There had been a shelter built at the Railway or Celtic End of the ground, but it only came halfway down the terracing, and the windows at the back always seemed to be broken. In such circumstances, and particularly in the context of a poor team on

29

the field, going to see Celtic every second Saturday became a less than automatic habit for the "faithful". The attendances were often described as "sparse" for home games, such was the unhappiness at the way things were going. Celtic were always coy about giving the exact attendance, often releasing a figure like 20,000, but that fooled no one. Yet the potential of the club remained enormous.

After my impressive start, I then stayed in the first team until the middle of December 1959. The form of the team was quixotic and mercurial, with some great performances and then a few shoddy ones (as is likely to happen when there are so many youngsters and a haphazard selection policy), but I was consistently well written of in newspaper reports – "the redhead had an outstanding game", "young Fallon stood between Celtic and a real hammering" – and there was real doubt about whether Frank Haffey would ever get his place back.

October 31, in particular, at Easter Road in a 3–3 draw saw me having what was agreed to be a good game. A crowd of 30,000 saw a sadly outclassed Celtic side struggle to get a draw against the talented Hibs side of Joe Baker, Bobby Johnstone and Willie Ormond, and the draw was achieved through the excellence of our defence. Willie Allison in the *Sunday Mail* singled me out under the banner headline "Wonder Fallon Foils Hibs", saying that "Celtic have found a new John Thomson. The keeper they hero-worshipped until his tragic death will, I predict, be succeeded by teenage wonder boy John Fallon". Allison was particularly impressed by one save from Bobby Johnstone in injury time, although he also mentions a few throughout the game from other Hibs forwards.

This game, incidentally, saw an event, insignificant in itself, which may nevertheless have had an effect on my future career. My father and Jock Stein (then still the Celtic reserve-team coach) had an argument about tickets. There may have been a bit of history there in the mining industry, for my father was an "oversman" or a foreman, of whom other miners tended to be jealous, but the whole matter was trivial. Perhaps, however, it was not forgotten in later years!

A 3–3 draw in which the goalkeeper was the star did not say very much for the rest of the Celtic team, who were clearly struggling. Yet everyone seemed convinced that in the "young redhead" there was no problem as far as goalkeeping was concerned. A few days after this game the *Edinburgh Evening Dispatch* did a feature on me as I appeared with the Young Scotland squad at the Turnberry Hotel. At this stage I told them that I did not want a full-time career: "No full-time football for me. I prefer to have a trade behind me and I am still serving my time as a motor mechanic in the Tollcross district of Glasgow. But I work hard at my football too and spend a lot of time practising and working out the best way of 'angling' my goals and making it difficult for forwards to get the ball past me."

The reporter then asked me about the game against Hibs and why I had done so well. He was surprised by the answer: "It was such a smashing game. I just couldn't keep my eyes off it. Standing in goal, you could see every move building up and knew just where the ball was going. It wasn't surprising that I had my eye fixed on the ball all the time and instinctively I just seemed to know just where the shots were going." The reporter then comments on my huge hands (eighteen and a half inches span) and is convinced that I will keep goal for Scotland one day. The reporter thus echoes the feeling of most Scottish football supporters that Celtic had unearthed someone special in John Fallon.

This opinion held good even after a very unfortunate incident at Annfield, the home of Stirling Albion, on November 21 1959. Jack Harkness of the *Sunday Post*, himself the goalkeeper of the Wembley Wizards of 1928, describes it thus: "The Albion equaliser will surely go down as the daftest goal of the season. Bertie Peacock, about 25 yards out, elected to pass back to his goalkeeper.

Bertie's shot was crisp, firm and direct. Fallon came out to collect – then to the consternation of everyone, he slipped. Down he went on his back, and the ball continued on its merry way into the net. No one was to blame for this goal. It was just one of those unfortunate things that happen once in 100 years." Maybe, but it haunted me for some time.

The game ended in a 2–2 draw, yet another disappointing Celtic performance, but then I, while still only a part-time football player, suffered a real piece of bad fortune. I sustained a hip injury at my work at Foden's when a piece of machinery hit me. I played a couple of games against Partick Thistle and Dundee while less than totally fit before losing my place back to Frank Haffey, who had been waiting in the wings, on December 12.

It had been a good run, however, and I had attracted the attention of Scotland Under-23s. I was twice chosen for the squad (the first time after only half a dozen games), although I never earned a game. On one occasion in a friendly game, the Scotland Under-23s beat Scotland 4–0. (This sounds incredible, but Scotland also, ten years previously, had lost to Belfast Celtic after the Irish team had gone out of existence.) On another occasion, I had cause to be grateful to the Scotland selectors who dropped me for the Under-23 International against England at Ibrox on March 2 1960. My place went to Adam Blacklaw, the huge Aberdonian then playing for Burnley, but, although Scotland earned a 4–4 draw with Denis Law outstanding, poor Adam had a dreadful game, conceding three to Jimmy Greaves and one to George Eastham. How would I have coped with Jimmy Greaves, I wonder?

The team of the year that season were Hearts, who won the League and the League Cup. Celtic lost to them on January 2 1960, and as we had also lost to Rangers the day before, it would be a fair comment that the decade of the 1960s (those incredible ten years!) did not start well for Celtic. Indeed, the 1960 season finished dreadfully for Celtic, losing 1–4 to Rangers in the Scottish Cup semi-final replay after a reasonable performance in the first game. Frank Haffey, however, played for Scotland v England at Hampden and saved a penalty. He was given a rest by Celtic after that and I was given a run in a few meaningless League games and the Glasgow Charity Cup. The semi-final of this light-hearted competition, now clearly on its last legs, was against Rangers. It ended 1–1 (and then Rangers won the toss to play in the final), but I was injured in an accidental collision with Alec Scott and was thus unable to prevent Rangers scoring.

I thus missed out on the end-of-season tour to Ireland. I was disappointed at that, especially as I thought I had recovered, but the team sailed without me. Then one afternoon Celtic back-room man John McAlindon suddenly appeared on my doorstep to tell me to get to Ireland on the overnight boat from the Broomielaw, for Celtic had an injury crisis in Ireland. My father went with me as far as the Broomielaw. The purser was an old friend of his and I was given a first-class cabin, even though the main Celtic party had travelled, as normal, in second-class accommodation. Mr Kelly, a man not normally given to extravagance, later reluctantly paid for the first-class cabin. I played several games on that tour – at Derry City, Dalymount Park and Limerick before returning to Scotland along with everyone else in second-class accommodation.

Thus ended my first full season as a Celtic player. I had had a good run and made everyone sit up and take notice, but it was probably just as well that Haffey returned when he did, thus giving me some more time to practise my craft in the reserves. The next season, 1960/61, was one of the most frustrating and heartbreaking of Celtic's history. Celtic were nowhere in the League, but in the Glasgow Cup, the League Cup and the Scottish Cup the team had seemed to be in with more than a chance of glory before being found wanting when we needed to be at our best. I, though still mainly in the reserves, shared in the agony of it all. I was also, as you shall discover, the victim of one of the craziest decisions of football selection history.

4

STILL LEARNING

The 1960/61 season had started with two victories over Rangers, one in the Glasgow Cup and one in the League Cup. The League Cup victory had been at the cost of a broken toe to Frank Haffey, so I was brought in for an extended run of ten games. The League Cup section was this year an all-Glasgow one of Celtic, Rangers, Partick Thistle and Third Lanark. I came into the team at the halfway stage of the section with the form good, supporters optimistic and John Hughes in particular making an impressive beginning to his Celtic career. When Celtic beat Third Lanark 3–1 at Cathkin, with myself having a good game in goal, things looked rosy, but then we blew up badly, losing to Partick Thistle and then, tragically, to Rangers at Parkhead in the final game on September 3 – the game in which the Celtic inferiority complex of the early 1960s, as far as Rangers were concerned, was born.

The rain was heavy, but Celtic scored first through Chalmers within the first five minutes and for the rest of the first half remained well on top, with me being able to deal competently with anything that came my way. The team left the field to the cheers of the Celtic End, who kept asking for "Seven! Seven! Seven!" As Cyril Horne put it in the *Glasgow Herald*, Rangers' chances of victory looked "as dismal as the weather". But then we collapsed like a pack of cards in the second half, and although

I was blameless for either of the goals, I felt totally depressed and heartbroken, as my young teammates, particularly in the forward line, were unable to raise their game.

Disillusion and pessimism now stalked Parkhead. The following week, when the two teams met again in the League, the self-destruct button had been well and truly pressed: the team took the field expecting to be beaten after throwing everything away in the League Cup, and Celtic went down 1–5. I have to hold my hands up and admit that I was by no means blameless on this occasion, but in truth Celtic had thrown in the towel long before half-time in a way that shocked and distressed their supporters, with the *Evening Times* carrying the banner headline of "Celtic Not in the Same Street".

These were the bitter fruits of a youth policy which was ill-thought-out and not implemented properly. Of the team that went down to Rangers 1–5, only Bertie Peacock could in any way be described as experienced. We others were youngsters. Youngsters need to be encouraged, cosseted, made a fuss of, told they are good and encouraged to accept a reverse for what it is, and that "there is another game next week". This emphatically did not happen at Celtic Park in 1960, now that Jock Stein had gone to Dunfermline. The young players were left, to a large extent, to their own resources. Some would eventually make it, others remained "promising" and others failed to make any impact at all – and they were now up against an efficient and brutal Rangers team.

Normally such hammerings take a long time to recover from (the 1988 1–5 defeat at Ibrox took several years) and this one was no exception. Celtic went the next four games without scoring a goal. I was still in the side for the Glasgow Cup final against Partick Thistle on Monday, September 26. This might have given Celtic some sort of a boost and a kick-start to the season, but once again the team created chances, scorned them and then folded to two late goals, plunging their supporters into all kinds of misery.

All this, however, hardly explains the brainstorm of Chairman Bob Kelly on Saturday, October 1 1960. After a week of sustained (and deserved) criticism from fans, the team headed to Airdrie. The bus left Celtic Park at the appropriate time, with myself on board, looking forward to the game and hoping that it would allow us to get back on track. There was the usual players' banter, but there was also a grim determination to improve on some shockers of late. As we passed Monklands Hospital, Bob Kelly spotted the cover goalkeeper Willie Goldie standing at a bus stop, Celtic scarf round his neck, clearly going to the game as a supporter. The reserves had no game that day. Kelly was impressed by this sort of commitment and ordered the bus driver to stop and to give the player a lift.

Amidst much laughter – "Who's this young hooligan?" and "Can ye no' afford the bus fare, Willie?" – the overwhelmed and slightly embarrassed Goldie got on. The bus arrived at Broomfield, and after a walk to inspect the pitch and the goalmouths I returned with some other players to the dressing room to get ready for the game. There, to my astonishment, I saw that my boots had been removed from the place where the goalkeeper's jersey was, and discovered that Willie Goldie, who had set out for this game as a supporter, was going to play instead. No one seemed to have thought to tell me or even considered how I might feel to lose my place in such circumstances!

This was cruel on me, but was even worse for Willie Goldie. The poor lad was not in any way prepared, either physically or emotionally, and it will come as no surprise to discover that before half-time he gave away two goals "like free soap coupons", in the words of one reporter, and the team continued its abysmal run by losing 0–2 to an Airdrie team who would struggle to avoid relegation that season. Goldie never played again for Celtic, and the following week, Frank Haffey returned and displaced me for the rest of the season.

The Goldie incident was appalling, and it took some time

before the support realised what had actually happened that day. It says a great deal about the shambles that Celtic were in at this time of their history. It also must have made the media wonder just what exactly was going on. Jock Stein, now with Dunfermline, for all his dictatorial approach to the game, including his sometimes insensitive treatment of fringe players, would never have done anything quite as mad as that. But, for me, depression had to be ignored and it was back to the reserve side. I worked hard and played consistently well for the reserves, once again earning plaudits and good press reports. The first team themselves slowly rallied and by New Year 1961 began to show a little improvement, thanks mainly to the return from Middlesbrough of the "auld heid" in Willie Fernie, who, many thought, should never have been allowed to go in the first place.

A Cup run was put together, the highlights being a good win at Falkirk (never an easy place for Celtic) and two great games against Hibs, with Celtic equalising late at Parkhead, then scoring in extra time in the Easter Road replay. Playing in goal for Hibs on those occasions was a veteran called Ronnie Simpson, who had won two English Cup medals with Newcastle United in 1952 and 1955. He still was good enough to play for Hibs, but it was beginning to appear that perhaps his best days were behind him.

Celtic, however, buoyed up by our late, extra-time win over Hibs in the replay, and with Rangers and Hearts now out of the Scottish Cup, were installed as favourites. There followed an excellent 4–0 beating of Airdrie in the semi-final. This set up a final against Dunfermline Athletic, a team who had never even played in a Scottish Cup final, let alone won the trophy, and who, although they had come far under Jock Stein, still seemed well below the revived Celtic, whose supporters were now nourishing hopes of a return to the glory days in Celtic's favourite trophy, the Scottish Cup. But those supporters and players who remembered Jock Stein were cautious.

One recalls the atmosphere in the Celtic community in the

build-up to this game. The disasters of the late summer and the early autumn of 1960 had not exactly been forgotten about, but they were laid aside for a moment as everyone geared themselves up for the final on April 22 at Hampden, where it was almost taken for granted that there would be green and white ribbons round the Cup yet again after the trophy's longest absence (if one ignored the war years) from Celtic Park in the twentieth century. The team had improved immeasurably over the winter and the support would surely carry Celtic through. I remained as keen a Celtic fan as anyone and could only look on in envy at Frank Haffey, who would have the job, and wish him well.

But before that happened, Haffey found himself picked to play for Scotland against England for the second year running, this time at Wembley. Billy McNeill was chosen as well for his International debut, and Pat Crerand and I went to London to cheer them on. It was my first visit to Wembley, and it was a dreadful experience to sit there enduring all sorts of abuse from England and Rangers fans as the team crashed 3–9.

Haffey, who had waved to his friends in the crowd at the start of the game, was never quite the same man again. Losing nine goals was bad enough, but when the Rangers section of the Scottish fans turned on him it became too much. He feigned insouciance to the extent that he sometimes seemed to milk the occasion, allowing himself, for example, to be photographed on a railway platform with the number 9 above his head, but inside, Frank was hurting.

Haffey played next week in the Scottish Cup final – a 0–0 draw before a crowd of 113,618. It was, in truth, a poor final, which either team might have won if the forwards had taken their chances. But then I suddenly found myself told to stand by for the replay, for Haffey had apparently picked up an injury. One can readily imagine my feelings as the fateful Wednesday night of April 26 1961 approached. I had not played for the first team since well before New Year, and I might now be called upon to turn out in a Scottish Cup final at Hampden, tasked with protecting the goal in Celtic's biggest game since the 7–1 defeat of Rangers in 1957.

But this was, we must recall, the era of the mad Celtic management of Bob Kelly, with manager Jimmy McGrory, one of nature's gentlemen and not cut out for the rough and tumble of the job, having little real say in what was going on. All sorts of funny things were going on at Celtic Park that very week: the transfer of Bertie Auld (who might have won the replay, one feels, but was *persona non grata* with Bob Kelly) to Birmingham City was in progress, and Bertie Peacock, still technically the club captain, was allowed to play in a friendly for Northern Ireland instead of a Scottish Cup final. Then Jim Kennedy, the left back, went down with appendicitis. Kelly refused, even at that late stage, to recall Bertie Peacock, and Celtic had to give a debut game to young Willie O'Neill at left back. In these circumstances, the loss of the vastly experienced Bertie Peacock was badly missed. Granted, O'Neill was indeed a full back, but the defence could surely have been rejigged to give the influential, experienced and still vastly talented Peacock a game.

As far as I was concerned, I went to Celtic Park that afternoon of April 26 fully expecting to be told that I was playing in the final, but in the event Haffey declared himself happy and fit enough to play at Hampden. I was then told to go to Tynecastle to play for the reserves. I was disappointed, naturally, but I thus missed one of Celtic's worst ever horror shows. The fault lay in poor finishing rather than defending, but Haffey was certainly culpable for the second of Dunfermline's goals in the 2–0 defeat.

I played for the reserves in the 6–3 win in Edinburgh, and later heard the news and sighed. I then returned to Glasgow to a devastated Parkhead, then went out virtually on my own to Ferrari's restaurant for what should have been a celebration. I personally had some sort of consolation, for the reserve team, with Bertie Auld playing what would be his last game for the club, won the Reserve League that night, but this was scant comfort for the rest of the dispirited support. It was another huge disappointment.

Supporters went around in a state of shock for the rest of the summer. I was still, of course, a part-timer, and that suited me at the moment. Retained for the 1961/62 season, I turned up for my weeknight training and played for the reserves all through the 1961/62 season. But I did question my future when, at the start of the season, Frank Haffey was injured and was now generally suffering from a lack of self-confidence (in spite of his brash and happy exterior) after his Wembley debacle. He never played for Scotland again, and there were those, even a few in the team, who questioned Haffey's right to a Celtic spot after Dunfermline's second goal in the cup final. However, the Celtic first-team spot was given to Frank Connor for a few games, while I stayed in the reserves.

In fact, I didn't play a single game in 1961/62 for the first team. It was actually a better season for Celtic than many they had had. The Rangers complex was not quite so pronounced, with two respectable draws: Rangers were lucky to get a late equaliser at Ibrox, and the draw at Parkhead in April was highly significant in the destination of the League title, which went, deservedly, to Dundee that year. Celtic had even been talked about as League challengers but let themselves down badly with away defeats to teams like Falkirk, Stirling Albion and Airdrie, and a shocking home defeat to Raith Rovers at a now deserted Parkhead on the same dull day as Rangers were winning the Scottish Cup a mile away, at Hampden. Yet there had been some good games as well, with form in December particularly impressive.

If the players let themselves down badly in the League, it was nothing like the way in which the supporters disgraced the club as the team exited from the two domestic tournaments. The Fair City of Perth was subjected to some dreadful hooliganism ("Perth's worst pasting since the Jacobite rebellions", according to one newspaper) in August after the team lost in the League Cup there. The railway station in particular was a dangerous place that night, and a supporter recalls the sight of a man with a boy and a girl bedecked in St Johnstone scarves cowering in the entrance to the waiting room as the green and white savages went past. It was difficult to identify with Celtic in any way that night.

And then at Ibrox in the Scottish Cup semi-final the team put on a curious and mysteriously lacklustre display. It seemed to hint at internal dissension (caused, apparently, by dissatisfaction at captain Dunky MacKay's decision to play against the wind after he won the toss) and they were 0–3 down to an incredulous St Mirren before half-time. When a second-half fightback failed to materialise, some supporters invaded the park in a vain attempt to earn a replay. They failed, of course, for Celtic's directors conceded the tie even before the teams came back, but it was a disturbing indication of the depth of feeling among the frustrated and angry support. And, frankly, the Celtic management really had to take a share of the blame. They were not the hooligans, but they were the cause of the hooligans. It is never a good idea to frustrate such a large section of Scottish society.

I could only watch this from the sidelines, of course, and was to a certain extent surprised at still being retained as a part-timer at the end of the season. By this time I was a married man, having married Esther Daley, whom I had been going out with for some time, on Monday, March 5 1962 (just before Lent, for the priest would not marry anyone after Ash Wednesday). It has proved, more than fifty years later, to have been an enduring and successful union, with five children born to it – Thomas in 1962, John James in 1964, Brian in 1965 (in circumstances which we will hear about later), Stephen in 1966 and the only girl, Elaine, in 1968.

Season 1962/63 saw me still playing as a part-timer but unable to break into the team. In truth, Haffey was playing very well most of the time and missed only two games that season. I played in one of them but not in the other – another remarkable piece of team selection on a par with the Willie Goldie incident of 1960. The team started the season well but could not score in a gnawingly frustrating 0–0 draw at Tannadice Park to earn a place in the League Cup quarter-final. In the following week at Parkhead in the League, they missed a penalty kick against Rangers to obey the apparently immutable law of fate that Celtic are not allowed to beat Rangers even when given the chance. Mediocrity then followed.

The game in which I played was a remarkable one, however. It was, in fact, Celtic's first trip on competitive business to Europe, the Spanish city of Valencia on the eastern Mediterranean coastline, on September 26 in what was then called the Inter-Cities Fairs Cup (the forerunner of what is now the Europa League). I was delighted to be selected to go on the trip as the substitute goalkeeper. In fact, it seemed like a couple of days' holiday in the warm Spanish sun, infinitely preferable to the dreich Scottish autumn.

But the trip, as I recall, was a shambles. The hotel, some twelve miles out of Valencia, had some rooms which were flooded, scorpions and other insects were everywhere and the hotel swimming pool had a few dead rats in it. Clearly the Spanish tourist industry was still in its infancy and had a good bit to go yet, but this was Franco's Spain and complaints were not exactly encouraged. The hosts had put on a reception and offered the Celtic players some paella, which looked so disgusting that hardly anyone dared touch it. On the afternoon of the game, at siesta time, those who were playing were told to go to bed to rest while the rest of the party, myself included, sat in the hotel lounge, talking to journalists like John McPhail and Davie Allister, and other reserves.

Suddenly the team doctor came down and said that Haffey

had just had an asthma attack. This may have been brought about by the poor conditions of the hotel, but whatever the cause, I suddenly found myself in the team for the game that night. I was hardly in the best state of mental preparation, not having played a first-team game for well over a season, and now finding myself in the Mestalla Stadium with 40,000 hysterical Spaniards shouting at me! But I felt I played well enough even though the team went down 2–4, having been totally overrun by the Spaniards. I recall two things – being pelted with oranges and seeing for the first time a ball being bent in flight, something that did not happen with the big, old-fashioned, heavy brown Scottish ball with laces. Being pelted with oranges was bad, though, and it did not help to discover than Rangers, also in Spain that night in Seville, received similar and indeed worse treatment.

Haffey recovered in time for Saturday's game at the far more civilised venue of Kirkcaldy, and I never played again in the first team all season. It was a dreadful season for Celtic, with a 0–4 defeat to Rangers on New Year's Day at Ibrox being the catalyst for the departure of Pat Crerand. There was then a long spell of frozen weather which meant that Celtic did not play a competitive game in the month of February, and then there was the cataclysmic Scottish Cup final replay in which the whole Celtic End, virtually of one accord, turned round and walked out as they went down 0–3 to Rangers. But perhaps what really summed up the incompetence and woolly thinking of the Celtic management was the night of the second leg against Valencia at Parkhead in October. Bobby Craig, by no means a household name, was signed from Sheffield Wednesday that day and virtually stepped off a train to play at Parkhead that night. The move, not surprisingly, was hardly a success.

I did well to miss all that, but I was annoyed to miss one particular game at Kilmarnock on a Wednesday night in late March. Celtic, by now well out of the League race (if they had ever been in it), were keeping themselves for an important

Scottish Cup quarter-final against St Mirren at Love Street. A few players were rested and a young redhead called Jimmy Johnstone was handed his debut, as was a Glasgow University student called John Cushley. When I heard that Haffey was also getting a rest, I hoped for a game myself, but the goalkeeping place was given to a young unknown called Dick Madden.

The reason for this was bizarre. Madden's father (well known to me, and a fellow citizen of Blantyre) had recently won a considerable amount of money on the football pools, when the football pools were a big thing. (They have since been replaced by the National Lottery as the carrot of wealth for impoverished families.) Bob Kelly thought that for this reason Madden's son Richard would be sufficiently full of confidence to play in Celtic's goal at Kilmarnock that night. Maybe his dad was lucky with the pools, but his son was less fortunate in the Rugby Park goal, for Celtic went down 0–6 to a ruthlessly determined Kilmarnock side who still nourished vague and unlikely hopes for the League Championship. For the second time, as with the Willie Goldie incident of three years previously, a hunch of Bob Kelly had worked to the detriment of the team and of myself.

It was a dark night for Celtic but no darker than the rest of that dreadful season. Celtic fans began to wonder if there would ever be any end to their horrors. "The dark anguish of my soul" it has been named by some Celtic historians, with the Scottish Cup final replay of May 15 1963 being the one event that seemed to symbolise the belief that it was all preordained and that Celtic were not meant to beat Rangers. The annoying thing was that Rangers, as they proved in their repeated European forays, which ended in tears, were not all that good. Better management would have produced better results for Celtic.

5

1963 – THE BREAKTHROUGH AND GOING FULL-TIME

In 1963, Celtic were at a low point. It should have been a great celebration of our seventy-five years of history, but this anniversary was in fact hardly mentioned, for 1963 saw Celtic in the doldrums (as, funnily enough, they had been also in 1913, after twenty-five years of existence). The Scottish Cup final replay on May 15 had surely been Celtic's worst ever, as we went down 0–3 to a Rangers side who quite clearly eased off rather than vindictively wreak revenge for the 7–1 of 1957, and Hampden had seen the astonishing sight of the Celtic End emptying with well over twenty minutes to go.

English journalists sat and stared in astonishment at such a massive protest. The Celtic End itself was full of an eerie silence as people jostled past each other to get out. There was no dignity; there was no self-respect; there was not even much in the way of anger. A few hurled curses and obscenities at those who had led us into it; a few blamed it all on Pat Crerand, who had left us for Manchester United a few months earlier; a few shouted defiantly at the triumphalist enemy; but most scurried homewards to their trains and buses, almost glad that the nightmare was now over.

But there was more to it than just one bad game. There was the feeling that Celtic were not allowed, as it were, by some sort of malevolent destiny to beat Rangers and, worse than that, the feeling that the chairman and directors of the club did not seem to care – or at least did not seem to care to the extent of spending money to build a better side. The air of gloom that hung over that sadly neglected ground was tangible. Even the word "Paradise" seemed a cruel mockery, as was the pathetic repetition by the fans of "Seven! Seven! Seven!" to commemorate their 7–1 beating of Rangers in 1957: a victory glorious in itself but, in a historical context, in "splendid isolation". Besides, 1957 was receding further and further away. Yet Chairman Bob Kelly kept telling everyone that the Kelly Kids would come through in the same way that the Busby Babes had come through in England.

Ah yes, the Busby Babes. But they had been supplemented of late by a Kelly Kid, one Pat Crerand, by some distance the best passer of a ball that Scottish football had seen for some time. Ten days after Celtic's Hampden cataclysm, Crerand won the FA Cup with Manchester United, an occurrence which rubbed salt into the festering wounds of Celtic fans. The parallels between 1948 and 1963 were clear. Celtic had sold the great Jimmy Delaney to Manchester United in 1946. In 1948, the price was paid when Manchester United won the English Cup, and Celtic were almost relegated. It was a vicious penalty that had to be paid for asset stripping, or what would now be called "downsizing".

Jimmy McGrory was at the centre of all this. It was difficult for Celtic fans to get angry with James Edward McGrory, arguably the greatest Celt of them all, with his 550 goals between 1923 and 1937. He was the ideal ambassador for the club, pipe in mouth, talking benignly to reporters and members of the public, some of whom were overwhelmed in the presence of this gentle and clearly lovable man. He had a particularly good memory and could recall supporters of thirty years previous whom he had met for possibly half an hour. They were all so thrilled when he gave them a smile and a nod of his famous head.

But Jimmy was simply not cut out for the cut and thrust of

46

management and the nasty side of the game. Clearly Jock Stein would relish all this in years to come, but Jimmy McGrory would always see the good in people. He was a great friend and confidant to his players, but he was no manager. Managers have to be ruthless and even brutal at times. They cannot always be Mr Nice Guy. Sadly that was exactly what the great Jimmy McGrory was.

That, of course, was only half the problem. The real problem, as everyone knew, was that Celtic was being run not by Jimmy McGrory but by the stern, firm but occasionally quixotic chairman Bob Kelly. McGrory was little more than a "glorified office boy" (in the words of one veteran fan), and he was also a good shield, for Kelly could always hide behind him, knowing that no one would hurl stones, literally or metaphorically, at Jimmy McGrory. And as long as this state of affairs prevailed, there was no end in sight to the inept direction of the club in the hands of the statesmanlike, political, opinionated but ultimately pernicious Bob Kelly. His word at Celtic Park was law. He had had his moments. He won his point about the flying of the Irish flag at Celtic Park in 1952, the floodlights were impressive, and he deserves a little credit for occasions like the 7–1 of 1957, the Coronation Cup in 1953 and the Scottish League and Cup double in 1954. But these successes had not been sustained. And when Fernie, Collins and Evans were offloaded far too early, it took a long time for replacements to come through.

Perhaps the most frequent and at the same time most valid criticism was that Celtic would not spend money and buy players. Scotland teemed with talent – the national side in the early 1960s was a more than respectable force in world football – and Celtic appeared, to the casual observer, to have a great advantage over Rangers in that Rangers refused to sign Roman Catholics while Celtic's broad-based selection policy allowed them to welcome players of all faiths. Celtic therefore had a theoretical head start over Rangers – but what use was it if Celtic refused to buy players? Rangers, on the other hand, were very happy to sign men like Ian McMillan from Airdrie, Jim Baxter from Raith Rovers and George McLean from St Mirren, all of whom would have done a great job for Celtic. In addition, when a provincial team like Dundee, with a fraction of Celtic's support and resources, could reach the semi-final of the European Cup, what excuse was there for Celtic not winning anything in Scotland?

It was certainly not down to any lack of money. Celtic's attendances, although they had dropped a little in comparison with those of the successful Rangers, were still high, and there seemed no reason to believe that a little investment on the playing side would not have yielded great results in terms of cup final appearances, interesting and thrilling League races and, increasingly more important in the early 1960s, the riches of Europe. It was puzzling that Mr Kelly never saw that, and there did not seem to be any way for the support to get through to him.

There was, simply, in 1963 no apparent hope. Supporters, particularly older ones, tried to reassure the younger ones with statements like, "They'll come again," but Rangers were rampant, and Celtic's management was half-hearted and feckless. Celtic did, however, sign one player. But the announcement of a signing called Paddy Turner, an Eire International who had played sporadically for Morton, to boost the forward line was hardly a huge encouragement in summer 1963 to supporters already distressed by the news that Celtic were drawn in the same League Cup section as Rangers and that Rangers would open the season at Parkhead on August 10. Time would tell that Paddy Turner was a major flop.

So summer 1963 – a gloriously sunny one with the West Indies cricket team in England, a growing scandal developing about the Conservative Secretary of State for War John Profumo and his relationship with a lady called Christine Keeler, and the ever-present, raucous Beatles forever blaring out of the ubiquitous portable radios – was full of apprehension for Celtic fans. But where there was life, there was hope, and we frequently reminded ourselves of the classical myth of Pandora's Box whereby all the evils of the world were released . . . but there was also hope.

So where could I fit into all this? As a Celtic supporter first, I was naturally distressed at the goings-on, but what chance was there of a first-team place? Frank Haffey was still the man in possession of the spot. He was a curious character whose many goalmouth howlers were forgiven by his personality, antics such as conducting the Celtic choir, by his talking to supporters even during the game at grounds like Tannadice Park and Tynecastle when the goal was close enough to the spectators to make this possible, by his regular and willing appearances at supporters' functions, and by his recording of songs. He was a fine singer, but his goalkeeping was astonishingly inconsistent.

He was immortalised by the 9–3 Scotland defeat at Wembley. Rangers fans, frankly, enjoyed that and kept chanting about how bad he was, conveniently forgetting that Shearer and Caldow were the full backs. Rangers fans now, in the twenty-first century, often give little impression of being bothered about Scotland; if anything, the stress is on the Union between England and Scotland. It was different in 1961. Rangers supplied the bulk of the Scottish team and, indeed, of the Scottish fans. They were not slow to turn on Celtic players playing for Scotland and even on the occasional Anglo-Scot, if he were suspected of going to the wrong place on a Sunday.

Frank had had a poor game that Wembley day in 1961, but people forget that he had saved a penalty the previous year in 1960 at Hampden for Scotland, and had had many fine performances for Celtic. But he was badly at fault in the Scottish Cup final replay of 1961 against Dunfermline, conceding an appalling late goal when Celtic were still in with a slight chance, and both fans and teammates had turned on him, some fans disgracing themselves with the hurling of missiles in frustration and anger.

Yet he kept his place in the Celtic team, beating off a challenge from Frank Connor in 1961/62 (not me!), and in the first game of the 1963 Scottish Cup final was in inspirational form, fending off the determined Rangers challenges that rainy May day in the second half in front of our own fans at the King's Park End. Headlines like "Fantastic Frank" and "Franktastic" and "Heavenly Haffey" appeared in the press the next day, and oh! how different life would have been if Celtic had managed to snatch a winner late in the game. We almost did, but then, the team having earned a little respectability, the management went mad yet again and rearranged the forward line to disastrous effect for the replayed final that awful May evening, the scars of which over fifty years later still remain.

Thus, with me still a part-timer, we come to the start of the 1963/64 season with three defeats to Rangers in the first month – something that more or less killed the season before it started and proved that the pre-season qualms were totally justified. There was also an astounding game against Third Lanark when Celtic were four goals up within the first quarter of an hour but conceded three before half-time and another immediately after, and the remaining forty minutes were played out in an unnatural silence as both teams had clearly shot their bolt. On one occasion, on the same day that Rangers were winning the League Cup against Morton at Hampden, Celtic put nine goals past Airdrie, and Frank Haffey could have made it ten but missed a penalty. The things that were happening at Parkhead were absolutely crazy.

In the midst of all this, I was suddenly given a first-team game on October 5 against Jock Stein's Dunfermline at Celtic Park when Frank Haffey reported ill with influenza. Such was my lack of confidence and lack of match practice that I was a bag of nerves and did not have a good game, making two blunders early on.

However, I was able to recover and saved a goal, albeit in a rather undignified fashion. Celtic then went two goals up, but the Pars came back, and with me still not feeling very confident, Stein's side earned a 2–2 draw.

The *Evening Times* gives the crowd as low as 4,000 at ten minutes before kick-off. There were probably more than that (eventually it was claimed that 17,000 showed up) but it was still a poor turnout, and the disgruntled fans were not slow to make their feelings known to us. They had been quite encouraging when the team were ahead, but the atmosphere changed when Dunfermline equalised and, indeed, almost won at the end. We had not won a domestic game since the last day of August, and I was not exempt from the barracking, even though I had not really been part of it all. Worse still was the stony silence as both Dunfermline goals went in, with only Jock Stein's cry of acclaim, supplemented by those of the busload of Fife supporters, being heard.

Slowly things began to improve in that autumn of 1963, however. I was now back in the reserves, but the team and the supporters were given a boost when Rangers exited the European Cup with a hammering from Real Madrid – something which said a great deal about how indifferent a side Rangers really were – while Celtic themselves made a modest start to their own European campaign. (It was one of life's ironies that that 0–3 Scottish Cup final disaster had qualified us for the European Cup Winners' Cup.)

We beat Basle on an atrocious night at Parkhead on the same night that Rangers were going down 0–6 to Real Madrid in the Bernabéu. The fortunes of the two Glasgow sides are, of course, intermingled, however much anyone tries to deny it, and Rangers' misfortune worked to Celtic's advantage. Celtic fans now fell in love with Real Madrid. There was good reason for this, for it had been at Hampden that Real Madrid had played their best ever game in the European Cup final of 1960. Then Real had played a friendly at Celtic Park in September 1962 and had earned the approbation of the support. Now the Celtic fans even changed a line in "The Soldiers' Song" in their honour with the Irish phrase *bearna baoghal* (which no one understood anyway) now becoming, for a spell "the Bernabéu".

Events in London took over the public attention for a spell, for Harold Macmillan resigned due to ill health as prime minister and then, amazingly, was replaced by an even more aristocratic anachronism called Sir Alec Douglas-Home – without even a leadership contest. Even the Conservatives themselves questioned this method of doing things, while Celtic fans began to ask similar questions about whether it would ever be possible to get rid of Bob Kelly. There had been a street demonstration against him in August but the rebels were dispersed by the Glasgow police, and frankly the fans were so disheartened about goings-on that they now gave the impression of accepting everything.

However, now that we were in October, things looked a little better. There was a good victory at Tannadice Park, and Mr Kelly had even agreed to meet the Supporters Association. There was a full and frank exchange of views, with a few clichés like "We're all in this together" emanating. Then suddenly, as autumn gave way to winter, Celtic not only began to win but also to play well, with the "Cel-tic!" chant followed by three handclaps beginning to make a welcome reappearance. It could be an awe-inspiring phenomenon at a full Celtic Park.

It was at this time that I at last got a break and the decision was made to include me. In a sense, the decision was forced on the Celtic management, for Haffey sustained a nasty ankle injury in a Glasgow Cup tie at Firhill on Monday, November 11 against Partick Thistle, but the decision might have been coming anyway because Haffey's erratic performances were becoming a liability to an improving side, while I was consistently earning good reports in the reserves. Frank's career would effectively come to an end and he would soon emigrate to Australia, but for me it was the green light.

My first game in what would be an extended run in the team was at Easter Road against Hibs on November 16. Easter Road was a favourite ground of mine and I felt I did well in the game. It was a 1–1 draw, after which I never looked back. The *Sunday Post* talks about what a rough game it was but singles out for praise the two goalkeepers, young John Fallon of Celtic and (ironically, in view of later events) Ronnie Simpson of Hibs: "Ronnie in fact brought the house down with two wonder diving saves from cracker-jack shots by wee Jimmy Johnstone. And young John Fallon had to do a miraculous leap to tip over a Baxter thunderbolt which had ricocheted inwards off a defender."

But my position was still somewhat tenuous, for it appears that Jimmy McGrory was not there at Easter Road that day, having gone instead to Dens Park to see Pat Liney, Dundee's reserve goalkeeper, who had now lost his place for the Dens Parkers. Pat had played a glorious part in their Scottish League triumph in 1962, which had included a crucial penalty save in their penultimate game. Bert Slater, however, was now in the Dundee goal. But Alec Young, writing in the *Daily Mail*, assured everyone that "John Fallon's display against Hibs did not suggest a goal-keeping crisis at Parkhead" – the clear implication being that if Haffey had still been in the team, there might have been. In any case, nothing came of the interest in Pat Liney, and I was in the team, deciding now to take a gamble and go full-time.

Months later, in April 1964, Jack Harkness in the *Sunday Post* did a feature on me in the context of how well I had done that season. The headline was "The Celt Who Grabbed His Last Chance" and the piece said that nine months ago, in autumn 1963, I was a "futureless, forgotten man". But I told Harkness:

The difference this time was that deep down I knew it was my last chance to make good with Celtic. It was obvious that the club didn't have a lot of faith in me – as soon as Frank was injured, they started looking at other keepers. So I really got stuck in. I took time off work and became a full-timer on part-time wages. It was a gamble, but it paid off. After only two or three games, the club called off their search for a keeper. Then I got another break – the Cup Winners' Cup. Celtic had to play me in the early round, for even if they had signed a new man, they couldn't have played him because of the registration difficulties. Well, the team put up a good show and I got the chance to settle in. For weeks, although I lived on my nerves, I always had the feeling that one slip and I'd be out. Nowadays I'm more relaxed – although I know only too well that Frank Haffey is only too ready to step in any time. A lot of people have said to me that I'm playing better than ever before. Honestly, I don't see it that way. I reckon that, for a long time, I played just as well in the reserves. But of course most of the fans don't see you then. Certainly since the club put me on a full-time contract, I have sharpened up a bit. But I don't feel that I have suddenly become a new man or anything like that.

Harkness then wished me all the best in the upcoming European Cup Winners' Cup semi-final.

What I am talking about here is the same feeling that any actor, amateur or professional, will feel when he goes on stage. It is usually a good thing to be nervous. The trick is not letting it get out of control, but to focus and to concentrate. Along with nervous energy will also come adrenaline. This is clearly what happened with me here. The sense that it was now or never galvanised me into action, and I had a really great season for Celtic, eventually proving to my doubters, in the boardroom and on the terracings, that I could do it.

But returning to November 1963 and the steady improvement

in the team, a spectacular 5–0 thrashing of Kilmarnock on November 23 (when everyone was still trying to come to terms with the assassination of President John F. Kennedy the night before) was followed by creditable draws at Dundee and Hearts and good wins over St Johnstone, Motherwell and Queen of the South, with me feeling more and more comfortable at the back and gaining the odd word of praise from the press for a good save or, better still, not being mentioned at all – always a good thing for a goalkeeper. Indeed, I benefitted from having a good defence in front of me, with McNeill, now the captain, well in control of most situations and particularly good in the air. There were also full backs Ian Young, who could tackle ferociously, and Tommy Gemmell, accident-prone but always cheery and determined, now beginning to stop the leaking of goals.

It was round about this time that I made my decision to go full-time. It was, as I said, a gamble, for I was a competent diesel mechanic, even, according to the *Celtic View* a couple of years later, with promotion prospects. But that would have involved me travelling to Sierra Leone, and I felt that I would at least give full-time football a go, even for a spell being prepared to do so on part-time wages, if necessary. I could always return to being a mechanic.

What really lit up Celtic and our support in the latter part of 1963 was the great European Cup Winners' Cup success against a then unknown team called Dinamo Zagreb in what was then called Yugoslavia. The name meant nothing to anyone in Scotland at the time, but the first leg at Celtic Park was considered big enough for STV to offer to beam the second half live. Amazingly, for the 1960s, Celtic agreed, with Mr Kelly's moral-high-ground stance of "no live football on TV lest it affect attendances" taking a bit of a knock, as money spoke, on this occasion at least, rather more loudly than principles.

Thus, over 42,000 at Parkhead on December 4 and considerably more on black-and-white TVs (which one had to put on five minutes before the start of a programme to allow it to warm up) saw a fine Celtic performance as we routed the Yugoslavs 3–0, and it should have been more. I did all that was asked of me and I can't remember being all that troubled, as Steve Chalmers scored two first-half goals and John Hughes one in the second half.

It was a fine performance and contributed greatly to the sales of the new Celtic song which was being marketed for that Christmas. It went along the lines of "There's Fallon, Young and Gemmell, they proudly wear the green, Clark, McNeill and Kennedy, the best there's ever been, Jim Johnstone, Murdoch, Chalmers, John Divers and John Hughes – and 50,000 Celtic fans who proudly sing the news – that it's Celtic, Celtic, that's the team for me ..." Amazingly, that song, over fifty years later, retains its popularity, even though four of that team are sadly no longer with us.

But there was still the second leg to be played. It took place in Zagreb on a cold December day a week later, with an early kick-off in front of a minuscule crowd. The pitch was frozen and had to be heavily sanded. Indeed, it was felt that it was touch and go whether the game would go ahead, but it did and we had to defend in this surreal atmosphere with not a Celtic supporter in sight, other than the directors, the reserves and a few Scottish journalists. But I was in top form that day, and I had to be! Celtic went ahead following a through ball from Chalmers and a fine shot from Bobby Murdoch, but then we were forced back for all the second half. Two goals were conceded, but that was all – and we eased through, to the great relief of their fans back home, who heard the glad tidings on the BBC News on radio and TV.

Thus Christmas was spent on a high. I was delighted that I had made the team and the clear indication was that Celtic were beginning to go places. Gair Henderson of the *Evening Times* (still commonly referred to as "Gers" Henderson, but prepared to back a good Celtic side as well) enthused about the team and predicted that we were about to take off, and every Celtic supporter was upbeat about how well we were doing. It seemed the corner had been turned, and the Kelly Kids (including myself, of course) had at last "arrived". They were meant to have arrived several times before then, of course, but this time it looked real. On midwinter's day the side beat a classy and determined Motherwell team 2–1 at Parkhead, a game in which "Fallon added to his growing and glowing reputation", according to the *Scottish Daily Express*. Two days later Partick Thistle were beaten in the Glasgow Cup, and then on December 28 we travelled to Palmerston Park, Dumfries, to beat Queen of the South 2–0.

There was, however, one major fly in the ointment: Rangers, who were due to come to Celtic Park on New Year's Day. I had played in Old Firm games before – without having many happy memories of them, particularly the 5–1 defeat in September 1960 – but this one was big, for it was Celtic's great opportunity to show the world, Rangers and, more importantly, ourselves that we were now a force to be reckoned with, that we had to be taken seriously. A win would have set down a marker that we were definitely back in the League race. The credibility of the good work of the last two months of 1963 was at stake.

The weather was fine and dry for New Year's Day, and Celtic opened brightly, with me rarely called into action. In twenty minutes, Celtic were denied by referee Willie Syme as clear a penalty as one is ever likely to see when Chalmers was brought down by Ron McKinnon. The BBC TV highlights that evening showed clearly what a dreadful decision it was, the press the following day were unanimously in agreement that a penalty should have been awarded, and Alec Cameron in the *Scottish Daily Mail* even claimed that McKinnon "faced Chalmers and clearly showed what he himself thought of the tackle – by apologising to the Celt". Things were hardly helped by the repeated rumours of Willie Syme having Rangers sympathies, but it was no penalty, as the crowd looked on in amazement and the Rangers End heaved a sigh of relief. But Celtic then pressed and pressed, and the pressure even intensified after half-time when the teams turned round and Celtic began to attack the goal behind which the desperate green and white hordes were thronged.

But there seemed, yet again, to be a law that Celtic in 1964 must forever frustrate their fans. Chances continued to be scorned as the forwards hesitated and lacked belief in themselves – on one occasion John Divers had a clear chance on goal but dithered and the ball was taken off him – and then the inevitable happened as Rangers, ruthless, disciplined and confident, ran up and scored the only goal of the game: Miller found a ball on the edge of the box, wheeled round and gave me no chance. Celtic, although we still had twenty-five minutes to go, knew somehow that we had blown it. More chances came, but belief was lacking and a sense of fatalism, visible and tangible, descended over the Celtic End. The game finished a travesty of Celtic 0 Rangers 1. The *Glasgow Herald* the following day talks of "the success that might have been for Celtic, and if there had been any justice, would have been".

Yet it was part of a pattern of that season, when Celtic faced Rangers five times and lost five times. Each of these games had the same template, whether it was myself in the goal or Frank. Celtic started well but could not capitalise, then Rangers got the goal and were always professional enough to hold on. The sad thing, however, was the all-pervasive and ominous depression that settled over the Celtic End whenever Rangers got a lead. Of course, on the field we were aware of it. It was like a Thomas Hardy novel, with the omnipresence of fatalism. It was as if they knew that there was to be no way back. Being "the better side" counted for nothing, and neither did clichés like "a moral victory" or "a travesty of a scoreline". Celtic simply lacked conviction and belief in ourselves whenever we saw the Rangers jerseys.

New Year's Day was painful, even though I myself felt that I had had a good game. Indeed, the whole defence had little to reproach themselves for. Every Celtic supporter shared the agony, and once again the team took it on the chin. Predictably, following the heartbreak of New Year's Day and with clouds of gloom hanging over the support, the January 2 game at Cathkin against Third Lanark was drawn. But for a couple of fine saves from myself towards the end of the first half, the team might have been defeated.

But then on January 4 hangovers were dispelled as the team came roaring back with a 7–0 demolition of Falkirk. This proved that there was no real problem with the forward line and that the problem lay in the minds of the players. A Scottish Cup win over Eyemouth, which was actually my first ever Scottish Cup tie in over five years of being at Celtic, followed, and then came a League victory over St Mirren, before the game that had all of Scotland talking about it: the Scottish Cup tie at Greenock against Morton, who were having a remarkable season.

The *Celtic Supporters Handbook* for season 1964/65, in its review of the previous season, talks gleefully about this game and "the laughable spectacle of the good people of Greenock, from the Provost downwards, being brainwashed by the press into believing that they were bound to beat Celtic in the Scottish Cup tie". There was more than a little truth in all that, for the Press, the *Scottish Daily Express* in particular, spearheaded by a man called John MacKenzie, the self-styled "Voice of Football", went into overdrive in what seemed to be a deliberate attempt to unsettle us before the game to be played on the birthday of Robbie Burns, January 25 1964.

Morton fans did have cause for optimism. Their team were running away with the Second Division and were as yet still unbeaten in the League. They had even reached the final of the Scottish League Cup, when a similar campaign had been orchestrated in the press in their honour, but, after a respectable first half, they had subsided to a 0–5 defeat to Rangers. They were well led by their manager Hal Stewart, and in Allan McGraw they had a free-scoring centre forward. With the game being at Cappielow, one of the grounds in Scotland where the crowd were almost on top of the players, and in a shipbuilding area where anti-Celtic feelings were said to prevail, there could hardly have been more hype – helped by the fact that it was possibly the only interesting Scottish Cup tie to be played that day, for Rangers were at home to the Borders team called Duns.

In view of the incident in the game involving myself, it is worth stressing the tension. There had been trouble at this ground before when Celtic went there, not least in 1922 when Celtic had won the League at that ground in the middle of the Irish Troubles at that time. In the late 1940s and the early 1950s, before Morton were relegated and when Celtic had a nasty support, Greenock and Falkirk were the grounds where bad behaviour could almost be guaranteed. Greenock is by no means the most salubrious of towns in Scotland, as distinct from the considerably more snobby and fashionable Gourock, and there were strong Celtic and Rangers factions in the Tail of the Bank area.

The weather was good for January. If anything, it had been a milder January than normal and, it being Greenock, there had been a considerable amount of rainfall. The game kicked off at a frantic pace in spite of the heavy ground, with both goalkeepers, myself in particular, in the thick of the action, having at least two good saves. Morton were kicking towards the smaller end where all the Celtic fans were congregated, whereas the other end had a mixture of both factions. It was Morton who scored first, through McGraw, who unfortunately for Morton injured himself in so doing. I had no chance with that one and earned a certain amount of praise for mopping up several subsequent goalmouth scrimmages as the Ton pressed to go further ahead. We looked to be on the ropes, but Morton's success had come too early for them. John Hughes, the subject of as many arguments on supporters' buses in the 1960s as Georgios Samaras was in the early twenty-first century, suddenly picked up a ball in midfield, charged to the Morton goal, beating at least three defenders, and crashed home a brilliant equaliser. It was the kind of goal that Yogi was capable of, but how seldom did we see it!

Delirium and mayhem now reigned among the Celtic supporters, and then just on half-time, when things were getting "towsy" (the famous word of the late Arthur Montford of STV, himself a self-confessed Morton supporter) on the field as several players were booked, we were awarded a penalty kick. Bobby Murdoch could hardly have made a worse job. To the distress of all in green and white, he fired the ball yards wide. Half-time and 1–1.

But the second half saw Celtic in command. With McNeill in inspired form, and wing halves Clark and Kennedy taking a grip on proceedings, Celtic surged forward. Charlie Gallagher (a late replacement for the injured John Divers) scored direct from a corner kick, and then Jimmy Johnstone hit a third goal as Celtic finished well on top. It was a good victory for us, and the faithful began to be optimistic about their team again. There was still the Rangers complex, but Celtic were, after all, still in two tournaments – the Scottish Cup and the European Cup Winners' Cup.

The matter should have ended there, but there were repercussions, not least for myself. One was when a Morton director, motivated, it would appear, by sheer disappointment and pique, decided to go public on saying that Celtic were a rough and dirty team. This was nonsense, for Morton gave as good as they got in what was an entertaining, competitive and typically Scottish game well refereed by the experienced Tom "Tiny" Wharton. The other was an incident involving my good self, not really noticed at the time, nor made much of until the Monday.

Immediately after Celtic had scored their third goal, I turned to the fans behind me (a mixture in those pre-segregated days but predominantly Celtic fans) and raised my arms in triumph. This did not seem to be all that heinous an offence, and I, being a Celtic supporter, did such things (once, you will remember, doing the thumbs-up gesture to fans at Arbroath), but on this occasion a policeman, one Sergeant Eoghain Robertson, motivated possibly not so much by sectarian prejudice as by a desire for promotion, told me to stop doing that and to get on with the game. The press made much of it and had some fine photographs of myself and the policeman.

Even Mr Kelly the chairman, clearly still needing some street credibility in the eyes of Celtic supporters, spoke out on this one in my favour. Such over-zealous policing did little to counteract the widely held belief that policemen, particularly in places like Greenock, were irreconcilably anti-Celtic and shook hands with each other at promotion interviews in funny ways. But there was a certain levity about it as well. A policeman had overreacted, but I got on with the game and Celtic were in the next round of the Scottish Cup, to play Airdrie. There always is something rather ridiculous about pompous policemen making a public fool of themselves, and we had a good laugh about it.

I was quoted in the *Scottish Daily Express*: "There was quite a bit of barracking but I never shouted at the crowd or did anything to rouse them. The one thing I did was wave to the Celtic fans after each one of our three goals. I certainly had no intention of niggling the Morton fans." Indeed, no Morton fans seemed to have been niggled; it was just the feathers of a rather too officious member of the constabulary being ruffled.

Before the next round of the Cup, however, there were two League games. One was a disappointing 0–1 defeat at Dunfermline (in which Celtic played well and deserved more), but the other was a very good 3–0 win at Pittodrie. It was a good day made all the better by the camaraderie of both supporters and players on the train. Some players feel nervous before a game and don't wish to talk to fans, but I feel that fans are vital. It is not often that

I agree with Big Jock, but when he said that they were the "life's blood" of the game, he was surely correct.

It is interesting, incidentally, to reflect a little on the parsimonious nature of the Celtic management at this point. Nowadays the team will travel by luxury coach to Aberdeen the day before the game and stay in a luxury hotel. In 1964 it was cheap second-class travel on the normal service train, leaving Buchanan Street Station at 10 a.m. for a 3 p.m. kick-off. The good thing about that, of course, was that we were travelling along with our supporters and there was a certain feeling of common purpose and being in it together.

The train stopped at Stonehaven and a couple of earnest young lads with the red and white scarves of Aberdeen boarded the train. I engaged them in conversation (they are the "life's blood" too) and the two boys, who did not recognise me, must have wondered who the genial redhead was who seemed to know so much about football and Celtic. They would not believe the Celtic supporters who told them that this chap was Celtic's goalkeeper!

The two Aberdeen boys would not have enjoyed the game. The redhead did indeed turn out to be Celtic's goalkeeper and he had a quietly efficient afternoon as Celtic won 3–0, a goal from Divers on the edge of the box being the highlight. My best moment was a spectacular save from Aberdeen's Don Kerrigan just at the end of the first half. At Aberdeen station after the game, I saw the fans again, including the two young Dons supporters, and took great delight in relaying the glad news to them from Charlie Gallagher's transistor radio that St Mirren had beaten Rangers 3–2.

Celtic then beat Airdrie twice, once in the Scottish Cup and once in the Scottish League, neither game causing me any great concern, in that I dealt comfortably with everything that came my way as the team won 4–1 at Parkhead in the Scottish Cup and 2–0 at Broomfield in the League. In between them there had been a game against Dundee United at Celtic Park when the team had played terribly and I was called into action on many occasions for a few saves, before Steve Chalmers got the only goal of the game.

Then on Leap Year's Day 1964, Celtic beat East Stirlingshire 5–2. 'Shire had put up a plucky display earlier in the season at Firs Park, but this was simple "shooting practice" for Celtic, in the words of the *Evening Citizen*, before the Celtic defence relaxed and allowed them two goals, one at the end of each half. I was vexed about that, for I was beginning to cherish the idea of "clean sheets". It seemed that Celtic had hit top form just at the right time of the season, for two quarter-finals of cups awaited in early March. One was the second leg (Celtic were 1–0 up from the first leg) against Slovan Bratislava in the European Cup Winners' Cup on Wednesday, March 4, and the other was, fatefully, against Rangers in the Scottish Cup three days later on Saturday, March 7.

I played "impeccably" (according to the *Scottish Daily Record*) in both games against Slovan Bratislava. The game at Parkhead on the last Wednesday of February, before the East Stirlingshire game, had been hugely frustrating for the massive Celtic support, with only a 1–0 lead (and that from a Bobby Murdoch penalty) to show for a huge amount of pressure. It would be fair to say that we flew to Czechoslovakia in an apprehensive state of mind, expecting a drubbing and then having to come back to face Rangers at Ibrox in a Scottish Cup quarter-final on the Saturday. It was also true to say that Celtic fans would have settled for a defeat in Central Europe in return for a win on the Saturday. In fact, the opposite happened.

The *Glasgow Herald* singles me out for a great save halfway through the first half in Bratislava, when I dived to the right to keep out a splendid shot from Ivan Hrdlička, as Celtic, with McNeill outstanding (as was Jim Kennedy, who had just recovered from a flu bug), coped well with the Slovan pressure. But it was still only a fragile 1–0 lead that Celtic had from Parkhead, and although half-time at 0–0 brought some welcome respite, there were still forty-five long minutes to go through before a semi-final place could be achieved.

Back home, I was later told, crowds gathered outside newspaper offices for news of the 1.30 p.m. kick-off (there was no radio or television coverage from the parochial, amateurish BBC or STV) and now and again a sympathetic worker from the newspaper would lean out a window and shout things like, "Still 0–0. Fallon's had another save," before triumphant cheers from Celtic sympathisers within the building would indicate that John Hughes had scored late in the game and that Celtic had gone through 2–0 on aggregate. For the rest of the nation, eventually a grudging BBC News bulletin on the radio included the result at the end.

It was one of the few nights in the early 1960s that there was "dancing in the streets of the Gorbals", as had famously happened on the nights of the Coronation Cup and the 7–1 triumphs of the 1950s. True, it was on a lesser scale than in the past, but the following night, when we came home, Celtic Park was opened to allow the fans to greet the team who had made their mark on Europe in a particularly satisfying way, the main attribute (as the press unanimously stated) being superior fitness. Supporters now had a spring in their step, for their team was making Europe sit up and take notice. What made things all the sweeter was the fact that Rangers had long since exited from the European Cup, and that Celtic were enjoying the attention of being "our only representative in Europe".

But as we all revelled in the return to Celtic Park to be greeted by a modest but joyous crowd, there was a niggling thought at the back of our minds. We still had Rangers on Saturday. Newspaper opinion was divided about whether we would benefit from being on a high after our deserved triumph or whether we would be jaded, as distinct from Rangers, who would be rested after a week's leisure. In addition, there was the complex about Rangers, who had already beaten us four times this season, admittedly needing an increasing amount of luck to do so, and, moreover, the game was at Ibrox, where Rangers would have more supporters and where they would feel at home in the psychological battle that Old Firm games always were. On the other hand, things had to change some time, and we were definitely due a break from Lady Luck. We certainly approached the game with confidence.

The *Weekly News* on the Friday before the game had an article written by Peter Black entitled "The Whipping Boy of Parkhead Makes Good", which said that I had a personal score to settle with Rangers, for I was the goalkeeper in September 1960 when the team lost to Rangers twice in successive weeks, 1–2 and 1–5, and "rightly or wrongly, John has always felt that the fans held him responsible". My wife Esther, then heavily pregnant, was quoted as saying that the Ibrox game would be a chance to "get back the fans' regard", and Peter Black says that the Parkhead management gave me a vote of confidence by not giving me a free transfer in April 1962, when I half expected one, and then earlier this season when they upgraded me to full-time status.

The Ibrox match programme for that day contains a famous Freudian slip. It claims that the match was to be played on March 7 1694 rather than 1964. Clearly the Ibrox typesetter was thinking of historical events played out at in the 1690s in Ireland, such as the Battle of the Boyne, and the proofreader failed to pick it up. The Celtic End that day was convinced that it was no error.

The game was played in fine crisp spring weather – it had been a mild winter, with very few match postponements – in front of an all-ticket crowd of 95,000, according to some press reports. A late rush for Celtic End tickets, following the euphoria of Wednesday night, guaranteed that Celtic supporters would not be completely outnumbered. Our team was a surprise – Bobby Murdoch was in at right half in place of the injured John Clark and Jimmy Johnstone was at inside right with Frank Brogan on the right wing. It was strange, but it seemed to be a winner in

Celtic's whirlwind start as Johnstone quite clearly won the battle of the Jimmies, getting the better of his direct opponent Jim Baxter.

Before that, there had been a strange sight. Normally in the 1960s the teams came out separately to the cheers of their supporters and the boos of their opponents. Old Firm games were an exception, for, in a laudable attempt to promote sportsmanship, the two teams came out together. On this occasion, Rangers came out first, lined up in a guard of honour and clapped us onto the field. This was because of our triumph in Bratislava and the move reflected credit on Rangers – although one suspects that it did not have the wholehearted support of some of their fans. It was much praised in the press. But was it all psychological warfare?

Celtic started off playing towards our own supporters, and took the game by the throat. For the first half-hour we were the better team – but then again, in all our previous games against Rangers this year, we had started off with a bang – and with a bit of luck might have been ahead. But Rangers slowly fought back, and with half-time approaching forced a rare corner on the left. There then followed a moment which would haunt me.

The *Evening Times* states: "Wilson took the kick, Fallon palmed the ball in the air and Forrest headed into the roof of the neat." In my defence, I was being hampered by the attentions of several other Rangers forwards, but the consensus of opinion at the distant Celtic End, from where you did not get the best of views, was that I should have clutched the ball. It was unfortunate for all sorts of reasons, not least because the half-time whistle came soon after, and it was Rangers who now trotted off with a spring in their step. Our heads were down, and it was no coincidence that police dived into the Celtic End to take away a couple of desperados during the half-time interval. An athletics event was being held in a praiseworthy but vain attempt to distract the crowd, but Celtic fans were pessimistic.

Yet this Celtic team had mental strength, did it not? We had come back from beating top European competition in midweek against the odds. This would be a greater test, however. Who knew? An early goal and we would be back in it. And an early goal did come – but it was for Rangers. This time I was blameless. It was a very fine goal indeed (albeit not appreciated at the Celtic End) scored by Willie Henderson, who beat a couple of defenders and hammered home from the edge of the penalty box, giving me no chance. A more determined challenge from the still raw and callow Tommy Gemmell might have made all the difference, but Rangers were now 2–0 up.

The game now petered out. Forty minutes still remained, but Celtic were clearly affected by fatigue. However, more potent was the psychological aura of Rangers, whose supporters chanted "Easy! Easy!" and whose players simply passed the ball around. Celtic, having no one on the field to rally them, no midfield general, failed to raise our game to meet the challenge. A Celtic goal would have made a huge difference, but it did not happen and Rangers finished 2–0 on top. Celtic had fallen, once again, to the Rangers complex. The *Evening Citizen* had as its headline: "Rangers Clap Celtic On, then Spank 'Em".

I, like the rest of the Celtic players and supporters, was devastated. I was no mercenary professional as far as Celtic were concerned. When the team lost, I was as hurt as everyone on the terracings. It was all very well to rationalise and to say that there were some very good players in the team and that all was needed was just a little luck. That one would not wash, for we had heard it all before. Indeed, we would hear it again. Nor would Celtic supporters like to admit, true though it was, that Rangers were a very good side, at least in Scotland. It may have been one of the best in their history, but that cuts little ice with those who feel (correctly) that whatever Rangers do, Celtic can also do.

But there was still some balm of Gilead. On the domestic front, Esther duly gave birth to our second son, John James, on

March 10, and if anything can stop someone from moping about their own misfortunes, it would be the domestic upheaval involved in the birth of a baby. But in any case, the football season was not quite over. There was something else in which Celtic were still involved, and it would occupy a great deal of newspaper space for the rest of the season.

6

A EUROPEAN MISADVENTURE

European success really would make the world sit up and pay attention, but one would have to qualify that by saying that it was not the European Cup. It was the European Cup Winners' Cup, and Celtic were only there courtesy of Rangers, who of course had beaten us in last year's cup final. Nevertheless, it would be something. No Scottish team had ever won that trophy (Rangers had lost in the final in 1961) and only one English team, Tottenham Hotspur, last year on the same night as the dreadful Scottish Cup final replay, had achieved that feat.

The cup draw on March 25 threw up Celtic against MTK Budapest. It might have been Olympique Lyon or Sporting Lisbon, but Celtic were paired against the little-known Eastern Europeans. However, they were Hungarians, and Hungarian football still inspired some awe in Scottish hearts following the phenomenally good Hungarian national sides of Ferenc Puskás, Nándor Hidegkuti and Sándor Kocsis of ten years previously. Yet Celtic, now out of all Scottish competitions, had nothing to lose.

Domestic form now went haywire, as often happens in the wake of a defeat from Rangers and when there is not really very much at stake. March 14 and 28 saw fine wins, 5–0 against Hibs and 4–0 at Motherwell. The trouble was that there was a 0–4 hammering in between – inexplicable and irrational – to

70

Kilmarnock, who, like ourselves, had blown the Scottish League. There was, however, one moment of triumph, albeit a muted one. On Wednesday, March 25 in front of a poor crowd of 13,500, we won a trophy when we defeated Second Division Clyde 2–0 in the Glasgow Cup final. The time was when a Glasgow Cup triumph would have been a great thing, but the *Scottish Daily Express* was more than a little underwhelming in its report of the game. Davie Allister does not mention me at all but shows a picture of the team with the Glasgow Cup. It was at least something, and Second Division Clyde had defeated Rangers in a previous round. Chalmers and Divers scored for Celtic.

A poor crowd then saw Celtic on April Fool's Day (a Wednesday night) beat Scottish Cup finalists Dundee 2–1 with a fine late rally after well over an hour of incompetence, and then Celtic went to St Johnstone in Perth on the first Saturday in April. We played absolute rubbish and were deservedly getting the bird from the unhappy travelling support, but I at least gave them something to cheer about with a last-minute penalty save from "Buck" McCarry, something that helped to gain us entry into next season's Inter-Cities Fairs Cup. Another dreadful team performance followed in the last League game of the domestic season, a dismal 1–1 draw with Hearts on April 18 before a crowd which would surely have been bigger than the 18,000 if either team had lived up to their pedigree. But by that time we had other fish to fry.

The previous week in the rain at Hampden, Scotland had beaten England 1–0, and McNeill and Kennedy had both played honourable parts. The country was thus on a high, and when MTK Budapest came to Parkhead on Wednesday, 15 April, we found themselves enjoying the support of quite a few Scottish fans who would not normally follow Celtic. The extremists didn't, of course, but the press certainly did, and it was a pity that no agreement was reached to put the game on TV. Both channels, BBC and STV, showed highlight programmes, but there was no live transmission.

This was a pity, for 51,000 at Parkhead saw a magnificent attacking Celtic performance and a great 3–0 victory which should have been more. Jimmy Johnstone scored once and Steve Chalmers twice in an exhilarating display of Celtic at their best. It would be a mistake, however, to think that I had a quiet night. Not so! The *Glasgow Herald* talks about "two magnificent and timely saves from Takács and Bodor", and the truth was that MTK were an asset to the already high credentials of Hungarian football. But they were simply overwhelmed by the "determination, relentless aggression and pace" of the Celtic machine. (We had even been training that very afternoon.) Everyone thought 3–0 was a good score and confidently predicted that we would be in the final on May 13.

John McPhail (admittedly not the most unbiased of journalists, for he had been a Celtic star a decade previously) in the *Scottish Daily Record* has a headline of "Celtic the Great" and singles out Stevie Chalmers for his two goals and myself for my two saves. Gair Henderson of the *Evening Times* even went so far as to say that this was a lesson to all of Europe, and that no 4-2-4 system (associated in 1964 with defensive football) could cope with old-fashioned Scottish football as played by Steve Chalmers and Jimmy Johnstone. Even the BBC in England was impressed, with men like David Coleman and Kenneth Wolstenholme making complimentary remarks about Celtic. Of all the great European nights at Celtic Park that we would see in the late 1960s, this one was the forerunner. Supporters were mightily impressed and sang the praises of their men for days afterwards but also asked themselves the question why their favourites couldn't turn it on like this in domestic competitions against Rangers.

The two weeks between April 15 and April 29 were spent in increasing euphoria, and the support began to make plans for attending the final in Brussels, even speculating about whether our opponents would be Sporting Lisbon or Olympique Lyon. Sporting Lisbon wore green and white striped jerseys as well, so if it were them, what colours would we wear? How much was it to fly? Could we go by train? Or even bus? Would the game be on TV? All these things were much discussed with gusto by the support, who did not even entertain the possibility of defeat, even though the grim precedent was pointed out of how Manchester United had blown a 3–0 lead in similar circumstances to Sporting Lisbon. Sean Fallon in particular kept mentioning this to us, but no one seemed to play attention to Sean's warning.

So where did it all go wrong? Two psychological factors entered the equation, one well thought out by our opponents and one totally irrational. First, MTK twigged that Celtic's defensive game might not be as good as their attacking game. Research had been done on the defeats to Rangers that season and the miserable 0–4 capitulation to Kilmarnock. Quite deliberately, MTK played up how good Celtic had been, singling out the little redhead called Jimmy Johnstone whom the Hungarians would love and compare with Puskás. His talents must be given full rein in Budapest, said the MTK chairman in his frequent phone calls to Mr Kelly, thanking him for his Scottish hospitality, talking about a future close relationship between the two teams with pre-season friendlies and so on. Mr Kelly swallowed all this and, nothing if not naïve, decided to continue Celtic's attacking policy. "The people of Budapest must get the opportunity to see Jimmy Johnstone," said the MTK chairman. It was an ambush. Jock Stein would have been considerably less gullible and accommodating.

The other factor was the irrational one, and one which can only really be understood in the context of Glasgow. On the Saturday before Celtic flew out, Rangers beat Dundee 3–1 in the Scottish Cup final, giving them the domestic treble. It was, one has to admit, deserved, and the press went into overdrive about Rangers and how good they were, mentioning, as if in passing, that Rangers had beaten Celtic five times this season and that they had now won the Scottish Cup eighteen times to Celtic's seventeen. Jim Baxter, John Greig and Willie Henderson dominated the press and the TV, and Celtic were not only pushed to the side but also were constantly, if indirectly, reminded of their own shortcomings.

It would, of course, be going too far to say that this was a deliberate ploy by a mystic, Masonic conspiracy to unsettle Celtic. Some supporters thought these things, and still do, but the Scottish press would have loved a Scottish team in a European final, simply because it would have sold newspapers. Yet it cannot be denied that the Scottish press does show its true colours when Rangers are successful, and this does have its effect on other teams.

It must also be remembered that this was still a young Celtic team, easily affected by what they read in newspapers. Tensions ran high on the aeroplane as we listened to Jimmy Johnstone's neurotic whingings about possibly crashing over the Alps, and several others were frightened about what we were letting themselves in for in this unknown land where less than eight years previously the Russians had brutally repressed a populist uprising. Was it not also the home of Dracula? Bob Kelly did not deign to talk to his players to reassure them, and Jimmy McGrory, who should have been geeing everyone up, sat back with a glass of sherry and reminisced about the great days of 1931. There was also the all-pervasive and seemingly irreversible phenomenon, ever-present and almost tangible and seen in Argentina, for example, in 1978: this is what we must call Scottish self-destruction.

The hotel was not great; some pointless sightseeing trips were arranged; training facilities were limited. A reception at the British Embassy, stiff and formal, the night before was not really what footballers needed, nor were the flowers presented in great quantity at the airport. Eventually we were allowed to train on the pitch of the Nep Stadium on the morning of the game, but the atmosphere was laid back and casual. I was amazed at how run-down a stadium the Nep was. Like most people who were young in the 1950s, I had been bedazzled by everything "Hungarian". I had taken an afternoon off school to watch TV on that famous day in 1953 when Hungary had beaten England 6–3, then recalled how they beat them again, this time 7–1 in Hungary in 1954, but the great days of Hungarian football had passed (to a large extent crushed by brutal Russian repression after the 1956 rebellion) and the Nep stadium was now underfunded, neglected and almost derelict. This was Communist dictatorship.

Only 10,000 turned up at the stadium, such was the apparent pessimism of the Hungarian fans. The game might have been on TV, but again Scottish arrogance (or, more likely, parsimony) turned down the opportunity, although there were limited broadcasting facilities with regular "score flashes" and progress reports.

Questions would be asked after the game of the referee Dimitris Wlachojanis of Austria, who disallowed two apparently good goals from Hughes and Johnstone and tended to favour MTK in his decisions. Much was later made of the fact that the referee appeared at the post-match banquet flanked by two beautiful young women, but it must be stressed that the main cause was our naivety in not expecting anything other, in an Eastern European country in 1964, than a bent referee. The referee was Austrian; the opposition were Hungarian. These two countries had once formed the Austro-Hungarian Empire and were still very friendly with each other. Even more than that, it was totally naïve folly to play an open attacking game and leave me exposed as the full backs surged forward, without the psychological effect of the Parkhead crowd behind us.

In addition, the Hungarians had the great Károly Sándor playing for them. He had been recovering from injury and had not played at Parkhead. He had earned seventy-five caps for Hungary, some of them with members of the really great Magyar side which had reached the World Cup final ten years previously. He himself had played in the World Cup finals of 1958 and 1962.

He was a vastly experienced forward and would make a telling difference.

We were 0–1 down in eleven minutes, and that was the score at half-time. That could be coped with, even though doubts were beginning to be expressed about the referee, but then early in the second half Tommy Gemmell handled in the penalty box and MTK converted. With the self-destruct button now well and truly pressed, we then conceded another two goals, to the horror and agony of all those listening to the primitive, intermittent radio coverage at home. I could do little with any of the goals, and I felt it could have been a lot more if I had not made a few good saves.

It was no end of a lesson. In future years Celtic would learn from that, but in the meantime, I, who was generally regarded to have had a good game in spite of the loss of four goals, was devastated. Yet I had come far in the past year. I was playing for the club that I loved and my domestic life was also settled and happy. Now established as the Celtic goalkeeper and regularly putting in fine displays, I was happy with life. My rival Frank Haffey, who for the past few years had been the talk of Glasgow and Scotland, now disappeared from scene and would eventually go to Swindon Town and then Australia.

The season may have ended disappointingly for Celtic and their many fans, but for myself, life had rarely been better. On July 11 1964, George Aitken of the *Evening Citizen* did a feature on me in a series entitled "The Soccer Greats of 1964" in which he tells of a transfer request before the big breakthrough came, but Jimmy McGrory, in typically kindly and compassionate fashion, had advised me to "bide my time". I also stressed my friendship with Frank Haffey and stated that the friendly rivalry was good for the club. It being the summer, I also said that I was doing a lot of "Beat the Goalie" appearances for fetes but was looking forward for the new season to meet again friendly rivals like Jimmy Miller of Rangers and Tommy White of Hearts. I recall doing the interview with George Aitken in my Blantyre home with four-month-old John cradled in my arms and saying that I had to be on my game all the time to prevent eighteen-month-old Tommy doing a wrecking job in my house. But I was clearly relishing the thought of the new season.

I was now twenty-three, with a great future ahead of me, I hoped. There was even talk of a Scottish cap, and there was also, in spite of everything, a feeling that Celtic might well be on the way back. So we were, but 1964/65 was to prove a remarkable season.

7

A BRIGHT START

Summer 1964 was a funny one for Celtic and our supporters. Hope always sprang eternal, as they said, but the previous season had finished so disastrously in Budapest that it was hard to get sanguine. Rangers were an ever-present factor in our psyche as well. The aura of invincibility was still there, as was the arrogance and the swagger. Conversely for Celtic there was the feeling, irrational but real in the minds of supporters, that it was never going to happen and that Celtic were fated never to beat Rangers. The annoying thing too was that, as Real Madrid had proved so convincingly, Rangers were not all that good.

There was, of course, Jim Baxter, who in some ways typified the confidence of Rangers. Those who knew him in his youth and in the days when he played for Raith Rovers talk highly of him and deny that there was any big-headedness about him. Off the field, he was friendly with Celtic players, but whenever he put on a Rangers jersey, arrogance and confidence surrounded him. And he could play.

But he was only one player. There were other Rangers players who were good but not great, and one often felt that if Celtic could only unearth a player of Baxter's ilk, he might be counteracted. Bobby Murdoch would in time become that type of player, but at the moment he was an ordinary inside forward, even though a few more intelligent supporters, like the perceptive fanzine *The Shamrock*, remarked that Bobby would make a brilliant right half. The other gnawing annoyance about Baxter was that Celtic had had someone who was just as good, but supine management and possibly sheer greed had allowed Pat Crerand to go to Manchester United.

Baxter's Achilles heel, it was said, was indiscipline off the field. That had been the problem with Crerand as well, according to Mr Kelly, and certainly if the stories about the Celtic dressing room at Ibrox on New Year's Day 1963 were anything like true (Crerand was reputed to have been on the point of refusing to play after a dressing down from Sean Fallon), then action had to be taken against Crerand for such inexcusable insubordination. But transferring him out of the club was possibly going a bit too far. Rangers worked harder to hold on to Baxter, and as winners of the treble in 1964, their decision seemed to be justified.

There was almost a desire among some fans in summer 1964 that the season would never start. We were enjoying the summer talking about golf and tennis and cricket. The weather was fine, and it was nice to be without that sinking feeling gnawing at your vitals, which grows and grows in intensity the closer you get to a Celtic game. The more important a game, the greater it is. Celtic fans of more recent years in the twenty-first century have experienced at least some success; 1964 had seen none, and it is difficult for those who were not alive then to appreciate what we are talking about. We players felt similarly. One or two of us made noises about wanting away from it, expressing a desire to go to Tottenham Hotspur or Manchester City, for example, where the pressures were not so strong. Some were even thinking of emigrating to Australia. On the other hand, Celtic meant an awful lot, and the new season was beckoning.

The price of admission had been raised to four shillings from three, but that was no problem, for business was booming in 1964. The Beatles were rocking, and the baby boomer (born during the war and immediately after) generation were now coming to manhood and womanhood. Slums were beginning to disappear and prosperity was in the air. Things were looking good for the Labour Party of Harold Wilson. A general election was not far away, when the benign but decadent aristocracy of the Tories must surely be swept away. But what about that other constant worry and concern – Glasgow Celtic?

It was a relief when the League Cup draw was made and Celtic were not, that year, paired with Rangers. Partick Thistle, Kilmarnock and Hearts were the opposition – difficult enough, in all conscience, but not impossible. The season opened on a roasting-hot day at Parkhead against Partick Thistle before 40,000 spectators. I wore all green and was considered to be one of the few successes of that day, which ended in a feckless 0–0 draw, with Celtic well deserving of the slow handclapping and boos that punctuated the air. Billy McNeill was good and I had a few decent saves at the end to prevent a defeat, but the faithful trudged homewards in depression, their moods in total contrast to the lovely weather.

Gair Henderson in the *Evening Times* talked about me showing "why Frank Haffey is playing reserve football" with four great saves within five minutes of each other at the start of the second half. My opposite number in the Partick Thistle goal was ex-Ranger George Niven, who also had a great game, even earning a few cheers from a reluctant Celtic crowd for some great acrobatics, but good goalkeeping was all there was at Parkhead that day, and the *Evening Times* had the ominous headline "Season Dons Light Blue" – a clever but depressing play on words to indicate that Rangers had thumped Aberdeen 4–0 at Ibrox, on the other side of the city.

Even on the Monday, Gair Henderson was still singing my praises:

> Some of Fallon's saves were in the superlative class, but it was his routine work that impressed me most. Every

goalkeeper can pull off the miracle save now and again, but great goalkeepers are judged by the mistakes they do not make. Fallon never looked like giving away a goal as all the Thistle favourites will corroborate. There was not one "untidy" moment on his goal line. When he went for a ball he got it with both hands . . . when he clutched it to his chest, it might have been stuck to his jersey with glue . . . and when he went up for a high ball, no opponent could get near it. The Celtic fans, counting their blessings in an afternoon of misery, marked down Fallon.

But the same *Evening Times* contained a remarkable story. In what seemed like an amateurish attempt to stave off serious supporter discontent, Celtic had suddenly announced over the weekend that they were interested in Alfredo Di Stéfano, the ageing star of Real Madrid. A party consisting of a director, Jimmy McGrory, and reserve centre half John Cushley (who had just graduated in French and Spanish) flew to Spain to talk to the great man. It was laughable. Cushley managed to speak to him once over the telephone, but the communications were difficult. Spanish telephones were antiquated and underfunded, and Di Stéfano had an Argentinian accent which was difficult to understand, but in any case, the bottom line was that although he loved Scotland and Scottish football fans, Di Stéfano was not really very interested in coming to Scotland.

What were we players to make of this? Some would not have welcomed the appearance of this prima donna, for he would have been a threat to their place; others felt that it would at least galvanise the support; but most, including myself, thought that it was a stunt, the sort of thing that Stein might have pulled in later years with the express intention of keeping Rangers off the back pages. However, in this case it lacked any real purpose or thought.

But one way or another it had an effect on the team and suddenly, at the most unlikely of venues, Celtic turned it on.

Tynecastle was a bogey ground in the early 1960s, but the Wednesday after the Partick Thistle game saw a great 3–0 win, to the astonishment of those who had seen the stodgy performance on the Saturday. An impressive victory over Kilmarnock followed, then Partick Thistle and Hearts again were put to the sword, and suddenly we were the team of the early season. Chalmers was among the goals, as was Murdoch, and the defence of Fallon, Young and Gemmell was looking very, very solid. We were now working together. Supporters were now almost beginning to look forward to the visit of Rangers in the League on September 5.

But before that, Celtic had to go on a fateful trip to Kilmarnock. It was a dead game, for it was the last fixture of the League Cup section, which Celtic had now won. But Kilmarnock, managed by Willie Waddell, were in no mood to let matters drop. They had been well beaten by us in the first fixture at Parkhead. Killie won on this day at Rugby Park, but that was not the point. Celtic supporters and players were more concerned about the stretchering-off of Billy McNeill and Bobby Murdoch: both of whom, McNeill in particular, would be out of action for some time. This would have disastrous consequences for the emergent Celtic team. I remain convinced that Killie, urged on by a small but nasty support, were out to get Celtic that day, and I would single out one player in particular for his actions.

Peter Hendry of the *Evening Times* has an interesting take in this game. He blames it all on two shoulder charges by Ronnie Hamilton on me. In both cases referee Alistair McKenzie gave a free kick, and this caused such resentment among the Kilmarnock players that "liberty became licence". Some Celtic players were by no means guiltless either, it has to be said, but the nine men of Celtic deserved a great deal of credit for their performance.

I myself was singled out by the press for some fine saves, but that was the only good news that day. It reminded the *Glasgow Herald* of a "bull fight", and the reporter says that the referee would even have been justified in abandoning the game. Indeed, at one point referee McKenzie called together Kilmarnock captain Frank Beattie and our deputy captain Jim Kennedy (after McNeill had been carried off) to warn them of just that possibility. The Celtic supporters did not take very kindly to such brutality, and it was a long time before relationships between the supporters of both teams (Ayrshire was in any case often perceived as a Rangers-supporting area) approached anything like normal.

So Celtic had to face our first Old Firm game of the season without two of our better players. Cushley, McNeill's deputy at centre half, was adequate, but he was not McNeill, lacking Billy's sheer class, and although Bobby Murdoch had not yet reached the heights that he would reach in Jock Stein's time, he was still a big loss for Celtic. Young Jim Brogan was drafted in. Yet I would enjoy this game as one of the best of my life.

It rained on September 5 – that constant rain that seems to happen only in Glasgow, yet is accepted as part of Glasgow life and culture. Rangers had been involved in Europe the Wednesday before, but that was no excuse for them. They were simply beaten to the ball every time, and although I had a couple of good saves near the end of the first half, Celtic were seldom in any kind of trouble. Suddenly the Celtic team had developed a hunger, an edge and even a certain degree of confidence.

The final score was 3–1, but it should have been at least two more. A great individual John Hughes goal, in which he ran the length of the Rangers half to score, was disallowed for a mysterious infringement on the halfway line. Then Charlie Gallagher missed a penalty which hit the post and eventually bounced out of play on the other side of the park. All this was in the early stages of the game, but then Chalmers scored a great header near half-time before Chalmers and Hughes scored another two in front of Celtic's deliriously happy supporters in the second half. One of the goals was a mis-hit trundle which went between Billy Ritchie's legs. At the far end, I had some sympathy for my opposite numbers – goalkeepers do tend to stick up for each other and Billy was a decent bloke – but I was also swept up in the ecstatic mayhem which enveloped Parkhead. I wonder what the great Billy Wright, then manager of Arsenal and reputed to be considering tabling a big money offer for Jim Baxter, made of the passion of it all.

It was a great deal more than a victory; it was even a great deal more than an Old Firm victory. It was the release of a tension that had built up for over four years, since Celtic had last beaten Rangers in a Scottish competition. The horrors of the past few years had not been forgotten or even forgiven – that could never happen – but they had at least been put to one side for a moment, and the psychological barrier had been broken. Celtic could beat Rangers. Small wonder that the newspapers on the Monday were now beginning to say that there was talk down Parkhead way of a League and Cup double.

George Aitken in the *Evening Citizen* said that Celtic were "a team and a half" and quoted me as having said before the start of the season that although it would be nice to have a run in the Inter-Cities Fairs Cup, I would settle for a win against Rangers. Well, said Aitken, now that Celtic had crossed that hurdle, there was no reason not to believe that they could win the League and play in next season's European Cup. I was described as an "impressive figure" and other members of the team were similarly praised.

It was probably at times like this, however, that Celtic suffered from the lack of a good manager. As unbridled optimism abounded, what was needed was someone like Jock Stein or Martin O'Neill to calm everyone down, to dampen any superfluous enthusiasm and to inject a note of realism into the proceedings. The season, after all, had only just begun.

As it happened, before the flush of victory had died down the team were in trouble. We travelled to Methil on the Wednesday night to play East Fife in the first leg of the quarter-final of the Scottish League Cup. The time was, not all that many years previously, when the black and golds from that unlikely provenance of one of the most run-down parts of Scotland, were a force in the land. They had won the Scottish League Cup in 1947/48, 1949/50 and 1953/54, but by 1964 they were a mediocre Second Division side – and yet they beat Celtic 0–2. The *Glasgow Herald* was in no doubt where the problem was – "Fallon was capable in goals, but there was no outstanding Celtic forward".

Oh dear, we were back to square one. Saturday seemed like an illusion. The damage, however, was repaired in the second leg when Celtic scored early, took the game by the scruff of the neck and hammered the hapless Fifers 6–0 before a crowd of 32,000 at Parkhead. In this game I found myself singled out for praise for one particularly spectacular save. Bobby Maitland of the *Evening Citizen* of Thursday, September 10 praised Celtic for their fine performance but added:

> Yet my memory of the night was the one and only save by Celtic keeper John Fallon. It was just before the interval. Celtic were 3–0 up, having overhauled the Fifers, who were two goals ahead from the first leg. For once East Fife had opened up the Parkhead defence. Centre forward George Christie in front of goal smashed the ball against the crossbar. Out came the rebound to Bobby Broome, whose flashing header looked a goal all the way. Then Fallon, with a swallow-like leap, glided through the air and held the ball with his capable hands. Surely one of the greatest saves ever seen at Parkhead for a long time. It earned John the biggest cheer of the night and a chant from the followers "We want Fall-on".

This was in stark contrast to the luckless Andrew Kruzycki in the East Fife goal, who more or less palmed the first goal into his net and generally had a poor game. His confidence had been shot to pieces, apparently, by barracking from opposition fans, all too obvious at small Second Division grounds like Forfar, Montrose and East Fife themselves. At Forfar a few weeks previously he had been visibly upset when the loudspeaker announcer could not pronounce his name correctly, and then he was subjected to a tirade of abuse from one local yokel in particular. I sought him out after the game and commiserated. I was aware that it was the easiest thing in the world to lose confidence.

But the scare at East Fife brought some collateral damage in the shape of two feckless draws against Clyde and Dundee United and then a dismal 4–2 hammering at Tynecastle to Hearts. The good that the win over Rangers had brought was already totally dissipated three weeks later. There was indeed a "long, long trail a-winding into the land of my dreams", as John McCormack would have sung in the First World War. The 1964/65 League campaign would be an unmitigated disaster, and it all started, after some brief illusory success, in the month of September.

But progress was made on other fronts. A brutal Portuguese team called Leixões, who had little football skill but loads of aggression in other respects, were dispatched in the Inter-Cities Fairs Cup. The *Scottish Sunday Express* tells how I played this game wearing gloves made by Mrs Helen Haffey for her husband. They were specially made with stippled rubber strips (of the kind one gets on table tennis bats) sewn onto the palms, and now that Frank was about to leave Celtic Park, he gave them to me. If any further proof was needed that there was a goalkeepers' union at Celtic Park, it came when Ronnie Simpson, who had now joined the club, travelled with me to the game, sitting beside me on the plane and then at half-time having a long talk with me about what he saw as the strong points of Leixões.

I had my own moment of satisfaction as well when I was chosen to be part of the Scotland pool for the World Cup qualifier against Finland on October 21. In the event I didn't play, for Campbell Forsyth of Kilmarnock was between the posts for Scotland's comfortable 3–1 win, but it was nice to be part of the squad, and it was a sign of the growing esteem in which I was held.

I was back at Hampden three days later, on October 24, for Celtic had reached the final of the Scottish League Cup, winning a fine tussle against Morton at Ibrox in the semi-final on Tuesday, September 29. A crowd of over 54,000 saw a good Celtic defensive performance against a Morton team who did not give up after Lennox and Gallagher scored. This was evidenced by the fact that the newspapers tended to pick out defender John Clark and myself as the men who saw Celtic into their first League Cup final since the glorious 7–1 game of 1957.

But the following night, Rangers also reached the League Cup final. They did so in extra time against a desperately unlucky Dundee United side. Some called it professionalism, others (even some of their own supporters) were less charitable, but Rangers were yet again the opponents in a game which mattered. They had not been playing well – they had suffered some fallout from their defeat at Parkhead – earning some abuse from their own fans, but they seemed to have the ability to win when they had to.

How would this League Cup final go? It was my first ever cup final, and it would be a lie to deny that I was very excited. Murdoch was now back, but we were still without McNeill, and, with all due respect to the capable Cushley, Billy was badly missed. We lacked mainly McNeill's command in the air and his ability to radiate confidence and reassurance. On the other hand, we had beaten Rangers in the rain in September without McNeill. Could we draw on that and win the trophy that the fans so craved? Or would the old Celtic self-destruct button be pressed yet again? Would the old belief that this was the way things had to be hold sway? Would Celtic allow themselves to beat Rangers? Most supporters agreed that the team which Celtic really had to beat were Celtic themselves.

The week before the League Cup final, things had changed in another sphere, for Harold Wilson's Labour Party had won the general election, winning in Glasgow by their usual mammoth majorities. This was a source of great joy to the Celtic faithful, for it ended thirteen years of Tory rule. Could the same thing happen on the football field? Could the green flag fly in football as well as the red one in politics?

Sadly, no. The Scottish League Cup final of October 24 1964 was one of the most painful in my sixty-odd years of following, watching and playing for the club, all the more so because Celtic could have won it – and should have won it. Quite clearly we were the better team in the first half when attacking the end behind which our own supporters stood in great numbers, and Celtic should have killed the game before half-time. I stood a lonely figure at the far end as Jimmy Johnstone missed an open goal. Murdoch was a shade slow to get to a cross ball, and referee Mr Phillips, normally highly regarded, refused a blatant penalty kick when Johnstone was brought down by Davie Provan. Rangers rode their luck and then began to string together a few attacks, forcing me to come more into the action and to make a few fine saves.

But at half-time the songs from the Mount Florida End were louder, for they felt that they were on top, as the Celtic End, while impressed with the play of some of our men, began to feel that the moment had passed and that the death wish was about to take over. So it proved. I recall vividly, as do so many veteran supporters behind my goal that day, how Cushley was pulled out of position twice to allow the hitherto underperforming Jim Forrest to score. In between the two goals, Celtic claimed unconvincingly that a ball had crossed the line at the other end, and then with the damage done and the Celtic End already emptying, Jimmy Johnstone pulled one back.

The last twenty minutes are often described as the best twenty minutes of Old Firm football of all time. Celtic fans are not so charitable. The team certainly threw everything at it, exchanging wingers at one stage and Rangers countering this move by exchanging full backs, but the final result for myself and the Celtic fans was not so much disappointment as sheer disillusion and despair. Somehow the victory in September in the rain at Parkhead made it all the worse. Celtic had shown that day that they could defeat Rangers, but only, apparently, on an isolated occasion.

Yet when the full-time whistle blew, there was nothing for it but to shake hands with the Rangers players and collect the losers' medals. There is nothing quite like the feeling of defeat in a cup final. It is so disillusioning and crushingly disappointing. For the fans, this was just one defeat too many. Many would now walk away, for the desolation was total and the pain unbearable. As the goalkeeper I felt I had nothing to reproach myself for, but the supporter in me was as devastated as anyone.

8

THE DARK ANGUISH OF OUR SOUL

Yet in some ways this had to happen. Things had to get worse, a lot worse, before they got better. A 2–5 defeat at Kilmarnock in midweek followed – another painful one, for Kilmarnock really needed to be beaten after that nasty game earlier in the season – and then the game against Airdrie at Celtic Park began with fewer than 5,000 present. The crowd swelled to 10,000 by half-time and the team did limp to a 2–1 win, but the predominant word that one heard, amidst all the slow handclapping and the catcalling, was "finished".

A year previously, when the team was doing badly and caving in to Rangers, there had been demonstrations in London Road. This time, there was not even the enthusiasm to do that. Tellingly, the crowd began to talk about horse racing and English football. Clearly Mr Kelly would not relinquish command, even though it was obvious to anyone that the team was heading for disaster. The *Sunday Post* had a story of a supporter telling of the dream he had of the good ship SS *Celtic* heading for the rocks and the captain saying, "Don't Worry! Everything will be all right!"

I would not have been human if I had not been affected by all this. The team now went into free fall with a shocking 0–3 defeat at Muirton Park, Perth. The incredulous St Johnstone players were visibly unable to comprehend how they were three goals up before half-time. I have to say that I had a bad game that day, misjudging the second goal, which I thought was going past, and not looking too clever for the other goals either. The thin Celtic support in the gathering November gloom began to mutter even about those of us who had hitherto been spared such vituperation. "I havenae missed a gemme for years, but I'm no' comin' back" was a common refrain.

I also shipped a couple of goals in a game against Dundee on November 14, but, in all fairness, I could hardly be blamed for them, because the game should never have been played. Or if it had started, it should have been abandoned, for it was played in torrential rain with not a little thunder and lightning, as three bulbs on the floodlight pylons were knocked out of action by the strong wind. There was something symbolic about the small crowd that day as they huddled together under the Jungle roof (such as it was) or the Railway End enclosure with the broken windows. Celtic were clearly sinking and it was almost as if, in the thunder and lightning, the good Lord had decided that enough was enough – "and the elect were gathered together", as the Bible would put it. Was this the end of Celtic?

Fortunately, such apocalyptical thinking did not come to pass, but Dundee won 2–0. Incidentally, that game saw the debut of a man called Hugh Maxwell, signed the day before. Supporters would have been forgiven for wondering who he was. He had played for Falkirk and had hardly set the heather on fire. (Against his old team Falkirk the following week, he scored within ten seconds of the start – but that was virtually the sum total of his achievement for Celtic.) Yet opposing Celtic that day was a man called Alan Gilzean, currently in a long dispute with Dundee about his contract. He had scored the winner for Scotland last April at Hampden against England, and it is hard to believe that he could not have done a good job for Celtic. It was also hard to believe that Celtic could not have afforded him – and this was one of the things that supporters found hard to understand or accept. The money, after all, was there. It did not need to be like this.

I felt particularly harshly treated when I found myself dropped for the next game – a trip to Barcelona in the Inter-Cities Fairs Cup. Considering events some fifty years later, this was an amazingly low-key affair, but it reflected the supporters' lack of confidence or even interest in any overseas adventure by the club. I was particularly hurt by the way in which I discovered that I had been dropped. It was at the airport when awaiting for our baggage when Alec Cameron ("Candid Cameron" of the *Daily Record*) said to my namesake Sean, technically the assistant manager but de facto running the team, in a voice loud enough so that I could overhear, "I suppose Simpson must be playing because of his experience." That was hurtful, but once again a piece of man-management (or the lack of it) which reflected no credit on those running the club in those days. For a man who had already lost his place in bizarre circumstances to Willie Goldie and Dick Madden, this was another body blow.

At least on this occasion, I lost my place to someone credible. My replacement was Ronnie Simpson, a man whose career had seemed to be over several times and who had arrived anonymously at Parkhead a couple of months previously. He was the son of Jimmy Simpson, the centre half of Rangers in the 1930s. Celtic were actually his third Glasgow team – for he had already played for Queen's Park and Third Lanark – but his great days had been for Newcastle United, with whom he had won English Cup medals in 1952 and 1955. While with Queen's Park he had actually played for Great Britain in the Olympic Games. After losing his place at Newcastle, he had then gone to Hibs and played well enough for a while but then experienced the horrors with them, and reputedly did not get on with the Hibs manager of 1964, Jock Stein. This was apparently because of a dispute in which Simpson had asked if he could play part-time rather than full-time and had received an angry response. Stein had little compunction about offloading him to Celtic, but at the time it had looked very much as if Simpson was merely here to cover for injuries until he retired at the end of the season. He was thirty-four when he joined Celtic.

Simpson played in Barcelona and held his place after that for several games until mid-January. I thus missed the real horrors of midwinter 1964/65 – the feckless defeat to Dunfermline the week before Christmas (the winner being scored by a hitherto under-performing centre forward called Alex Ferguson), which really threatened Celtic's credibility in the eyes of their support. Amazingly, 10,000 diehards turned up on a cold Boxing Day to see Celtic at least beat someone, as John Hughes, wearing sandshoes, scored twice to defeat Motherwell.

Then came the horrendous New Year's Day at Ibrox when Celtic were actually the better team but Jimmy Johnstone got sent off before half-time for having a go at Therolf Beck (who was by no means innocent himself and recovered instantly). Then, just when we thought things couldn't get any worse, Bobby Murdoch ballooned a penalty kick over the crossbar. This had followed a credible fight by the ten men of Celtic, but there was a glazed fatalism in the eyes of the Celtic support that day – a look that reminded a Second World War veteran of the shattered remnants of Rommel's Afrika Korps surrendering in their thousands to the British Eighth Army at Cape Bon in 1943.

There followed a 1–1 draw against Clyde punctuated by boos, and a miserable defeat at Tannadice Park in which Celtic were described as having a "one-man forward line" in John Hughes. We were on our knees, but at least, after a spell in the reserves, I was brought back for the next game against the strong Hearts at Parkhead, and Celtic at last made a credible signing in the return of Bertie Auld from Birmingham. Bertie would claim in later years that Jock Stein (still technically manager of Hibs at the time) had a part to play in his return, but the fans knew nothing about it. Similarly, it looks, in retrospect, as if I was brought back to play against Hearts on January 16 by Sean Fallon, who knew that Stein, who would be arriving soon, would not approve of Ronnie Simpson.

Celtic fans were still unimpressed. The crowd for what was potentially a great game was given as 21,000, and the Hearts fans, for the first time in their history, came close to outnumbering the Celtic fans at Parkhead, even feeling bold enough to "invade" the Jungle in the search of some shelter from the incessant Glasgow rain. It was hardly a wise choice, for the Jungle's roof was full of holes. My start could hardly have been worse when a cross ball cannoned off my knee and went into the net. Celtic fans, by now inured to disappointment and heartbreak, shrugged their shoulders and said things like, "When you are down, you stay down." We did fight back, however, and Tommy Gemmell scored a good goal, but Hearts scored again before half-time and, in spite of strong Celtic pressure, held out for a 2–1 win.

I was at least back in the first team, and the following week there was a distinct improvement as we earned a draw at Morton. Celtic, with the new left-wing combination of Lennox and Auld combining brilliantly, were 3–1 up at one point but lost two late goals to Morton and might have even lost another one had the referee not blown for full-time when the ball was in mid-air, heading for my goal. It was, nevertheless, a better performance from Celtic.

The following day, the Sunday, saw the death of Sir Winston Churchill, who had been ill for some time. He had, in the past, been no friend of Ireland, the miners or the working classes, and his First World War career had included the ghastly campaign of Gallipoli, for which he had been directly responsible. But he had saved Europe from slavery to Adolf Hitler, and for this he was given a grudging respect.

His funeral was on the following Saturday, January 30, and a few hours after the service in London, and round about the same time as he was being laid to rest at Bladon, near Blenheim Palace,

Celtic took on Aberdeen on a frosty day at Parkhead before a meagre crowd of 14,000. No supporter could have predicted the events that were to unfold in the next twenty-four hours, but there was a new urgency and enthusiasm about Celtic. In the first place, I had one of the quietest games of my career. I had one save from Dons cult hero Ernie Winchester, but apart from that I was virtually a spectator as Celtic, who had dropped Jimmy Johnstone and brought back Steve Chalmers on the right wing, went on the rampage and beat a normally respectable Aberdeen side 8–0, with John Hughes in his now trademark sandshoes scoring five of them. Amazingly, on January 30, it was Celtic's first win of 1965.

Clearly something was in the air. We all knew that something was going to happen soon, but we didn't quite know what. In truth, we might have guessed. It is always darkest, they say, before the dawn. There are times, even in the most desperate of days, when things go your way, and it was almost as if Rangers too realised that something was up, for they went down 0–1 to Hibs at a snowy Easter Road that same day. And it was from Easter Road that the great news came the following day, for it was announced that Jock Stein, currently manager of Hibs, from March 8 (for Hibs insisted on him serving his notice) would become manager of Celtic.

"Now is the winter of our discontent / Made glorious summer by this sun from York" is a famous quote from *Richard III*. Never could it have been more appropriate to Celtic and their supporters as January gave way to February. There was suddenly a spring in the step of everyone, newspapers began to talk about Celtic, and their awesome potential and the future suddenly seemed to be full of possibilities. A few journalists, who should have known better, made an issue of Stein's religion. Mr Kelly, apparently, himself thought that this was a significant point, hence, possibly, his reluctance to appoint Stein earlier, but the matter was treated by the supporters with the contempt it deserved. Celtic supporters and players could not have cared less about anyone's religion. It was success on the field that was craved.

The arrival of a new manager is always an exciting yet worrying time for players and, to a lesser extent, fans. A player will know that the manager will have his ideas, which may or may not include him. He will almost certainly want to bring in new players, and that might be a threat to one particular player's place in the team. All a player can do is work on his game and try to impress. I, of course, knew what I was getting in Jock Stein. We had worked together from 1958 until 1960. Did Jock like me? Would he keep me in the team? What would the future now hold for John Fallon, a man who had, by and large, enjoyed a certain amount of success since breaking into the team a year past November? For a man with two young children and another imminent, the future was full of uncertainties. All I could do was prove myself worthy.

9

A HYMN FOR THE DAWN OF THE FREE

No one could mistake the excitement that was in the air, as the sleeping Celtic giant showed distinct signs of waking up. The Scottish Cup of 1965 was targeted. (There was nothing else left, for the appalling form in November and December had killed any chance of doing well in the Scottish League.) It was therefore crucial that Celtic should stay in the Cup until Stein arrived. Three difficult cup ties had to be negotiated. St Mirren at Love Street (always a tricky one) was the first one, on February 6. Conditions were hard on a pitch that was rapidly thawing, and the game had to be delayed by ten minutes to allow in the mass of resurgent, revivalist, revanchist Celtic fans. Some parts of the ground were dangerously overcrowded, but they saw a real, old-fashioned cup tie, with myself called upon twice to make what the *Evening Times* calls "suicide dives" to make saves. Chalmers opened the scoring early in the second half, and then Lennox scored twice near the end to give us a somewhat flattering but nonetheless still deserved 3–0 victory.

The following week, in a now pointless League match, the born-again Celts thumped St Mirren once more, but a tougher nut needed to be cracked at Hampden when we were drawn to play Second Division Queen's Park on February 20. At least it was a visit to Hampden! On a tolerably pleasant early spring day,

Celtic amazed the 31,000 fans by appearing in an all-green strip and then appalled them by playing a dreadful game of football, needing my services several times before Bobby Lennox eventually broke through for Celtic and put us into the quarter-finals.

Now enter Kilmarnock. There was, of course, a history this season. Twice Celtic had gone down at Rugby Park – once in the League Cup game which had seen the serious injuries to Billy McNeill and Bobby Murdoch, and then in a deserved thrashing immediately after the League Cup final when we were demoralised and, frankly, beaten before we started. The resistance had been pitiful. Kilmarnock now came to Celtic Park on two successive Saturdays. The first game, a League one, was mundane, a 2–0 win with a goal in each half in a match which never rose above the ordinary, although I did earn a certain amount of praise for a couple of good saves from a strong Kilmarnock side, who were still going for the League Championship.

It was even (prematurely) described as a "fatal blow" to Kilmarnock's League Championship chances. The League this year was far more interesting than normal. Celtic were already also-rans, and Rangers had also shown signs of struggling after Jim Baxter had broken his leg in a European game in December, but Kilmarnock, Dunfermline and the two Edinburgh teams, Hearts and Hibs, were all doing well. Celtic fans, self-absorbed as always in the fortunes of their own team, were less aware of the exciting race for the Championship.

The next week in the quarter-final of the Scottish Cup was totally different. This game, so pivotal to Celtic's season and their future, took place on Saturday, March 6 1965, only after the pitch had passed a morning inspection. By the time that the 47,000 crowd assembled, the ground was bathed in sunshine and the snow and ice had gone, but although it was nice and bright it was still just a little too cold to be described as spring. There were so many subplots to this game. There was the ill feeling caused by the game in August in the background; there was the general dislike of Willie Waddell, ex-Ranger and now Kilmarnock's manager; there was the undeniable fact that Kilmarnock, although beaten last week, were still a very good team; but all that paled into insignificance compared to the desire of the Celtic crowd and players to win the Scottish Cup and the knowledge that Jock Stein was to arrive on Monday.

There was even more to it than that. On that very day in Edinburgh, Rangers were playing their Scottish Cup quarter-final at Hibs, in Stein's last game there, and Rangers, who had been knocked out of the European Cup on Wednesday, were welcoming back Jim Baxter after his leg-break. The Celtic v Kilmarnock game was at Celtic Park and it was Jimmy McGrory's last game as manager (he had been in position since 1945). He would stay at Celtic Park but in the honorary position of public relations officer. He had managed only two teams since retiring as a player in 1937, and the other was Kilmarnock. Some supporters with really long memories recalled that in 1938, McGrory, after only a handful of games as Kilmarnock manager, had put the talented but complacent Celtic side out of the Scottish Cup. March 6 1965 was also the last game that Celtic would ever play in their reserve strip of white with green sleeves (just like Hibs, but in reverse). It was quite an occasion, and quite a game.

We won 3–2, with goals from Bobby Lennox in the first half, then Bertie Auld and John Hughes in the second against two from Jackie McInally of Kilmarnock. It might have been a different story had I not been in top form. Several times I dived at the feet of Kilmarnock forwards and had at least four or five good saves. Celtic had looked secure at 3–1 ahead, but Kilmarnock then pulled one back. The result was in doubt until the final whistle, but Celtic showed real character to come through this game and we left the field to great cheers from our supporters. Peter Hendry in the *Evening Times* on the Monday predicted that Celtic's lean years were over, for there was a team of "skill, determination and confidence" in place there. And the Big Man had not even arrived yet.

And the good news did not stop there, for transistor radios, that crackling new menace of the age, which took considerable patience to listen to and had an infuriating habit of breaking up as the commentator got excited, told the crowd that Hibs had scored a late goal against Rangers and that Rangers were therefore out of the Scottish Cup. Even before he arrived, Jock Stein had an effect.

When Stein did arrive on the Monday (it was Tuesday before he met all us players) those of us who had been expecting instant success were to be disappointed. As far as the League campaign was concerned, inconsistency was the order of the day. We lost to Hibs at Parkhead, then beat them at Easter Road. We thumped Airdrie, then blew up at home to St Johnstone, who thus, to their total incredulity, registered a League double against Celtic. ("I see now why I am here," growled Jock Stein in the wake of that game.) A good game at Dens Park saw an entertaining 3–3 draw, but a 6–2 defeat at Falkirk was one of the club's worst ever performances. Several players were put in their place – Tommy Gemmell was told that although an occasional foray upfield was in order he was in the team as a defender, and Bertie Auld was told not to take the rise out of his fellow professionals by showing off to the crowd.

I did not feel that I particularly distinguished myself in any of these games, but I think I sensed that my place was comparatively safe until the end of the season at least, for, given the ill-concealed dislike and distrust between Jock Stein and Ronnie Simpson, there was no real alternative goalkeeper to myself. I knew therefore that unless I did something horrific in goal I had a chance of playing in the Scottish Cup final, providing the team could get the better of Motherwell in the semi-final.

The game mentioned between Celtic and Hibs at Parkhead

was interesting, and a revealing one about the psyche of Jock Stein. It was played on a Monday night (Monday being a common night for football in the 1960s, for Tuesday and Thursday tended to be "overtime" nights) on March 22, and Hibs, with men like Peter Cormack, Neil Martin, Pat Quinn, Willie Hamilton and Pat Stanton on board, simply swept us aside with devastating football to lead 4–2 at half-time. Only a determined defensive performance (with myself given credit for several outstanding saves) throughout the second half kept the scoreline the same. It would have been no injustice had Hibs put another four past Celtic.

We trudged off, fully expecting a round of the guns from Jock. Some of us had already experienced his wrath, and it had not been a pleasant experience, but on this occasion Stein simply got all the men together and said very quietly that the way Hibs played that night was the way that football should be played, and that that was the way that we would be playing in a few weeks' time. Of course, Stein had every right to say that, for until a few weeks ago he had been the manager of Hibs. But his prophecy came true some sixteen days later, on April 7, when we went to Easter Road. With a few subtle changes, notably the deployment of Bertie Auld in the middle of the field, we beat that same Hibs team 4–0, as brilliant at Easter Road as Hibs had been at Parkhead. It was probably that day which marked the end of Hibs challenge for the Scottish League Championship, and as they were now also out of the Scottish Cup, having lost in the semi-final against Dunfermline, Hibs' woes were manifold.

The truth was that, as far as Celtic were concerned, League games did not matter, and Stein used them to try out players and ideas with a view to the future, but in the shorter term the Scottish Cup of 1965 was dominating everyone's thinking. One idea that did emerge at this time – and it was a winner – was the deployment of Bobby Murdoch, at that time an inconsistent and under-performing inside forward, in the position of right half. Within a year of that happening, Murdoch was recognised as world class and everyone had forgotten about Pat Crerand. All this time I was left alone in the goal. My only rival was Ronnie Simpson, and although Ronnie trained conscientiously, was treated with respect by Stein and was surprisingly retained at the end of the season, it was still clear that the two men, Stein and Simpson, simply did not get along – at least not at this stage of their lives.

But I cultivated Simpson, with whom I shared goalkeeping "secrets" like how the modern trend of a winger running to the dead-ball line and cutting it back was a greater danger than the high ball, plus the danger involved in having too many defenders in front of the goalkeeper, whose view could thus be impaired. There was always a "goalkeepers' union" between all goalkeepers. On one famous occasion in the late 1920s, Celtic were playing Hearts, and as daylight was likely to be a problem, the players did not go off the field at the interval but stayed on and someone brought them their tea. The crowd then saw Willie Maley ranting at his Celtic team and the Hearts equivalent Willie McCartney doing the same with his team, while the two goalkeepers, Jack Harkness and John Thomson, sat together, the greatest of friends, albeit rivals for a Scottish cap, drinking their tea and discussing the art of goalkeeping.

I would always go out of my way to talk to the opposing goalkeeper after a game and, having got on well with Frank Haffey in the past, now forged a good relationship with Simpson, even though we were clearly rivals. Both of us were naturally sociable and friendly, and I realised that I could learn a great deal from this man, who had twice, in 1952 and 1955, won English cup medals with Newcastle United, so we sat together on the team bus and discussed goalkeeping. We could also exchange confidences in lowered voices about Jock Stein! It is important to stress, however, that I never felt that my place was in any real doubt, for I was, I thought, playing well enough.

The really important game in the month of March was, of

course, the semi-final against Motherwell, on March 27. It was a windy spring day, with intermittent showers of rain now and again, at Hampden before a crowd of over 50,000, and it was a tough game with future Celtic star Joe McBride taking advantage of a hesitant McNeill to score twice for Motherwell in the first half. On neither occasion did I cover myself in glory, for on the first occasion, according to Gair Henderson of the *Evening Times*: "as Fallon came out and dived, [McBride] hit the ball under his body and jumped for joy as, half stopped by the goalkeeper, the ball rolled nearer and nearer to the line and then into the back of the net."

The second goal was a fierce drive from McBride, which I though I did well to get my body in the way of, but the ball rebounded to Joe, and Motherwell, who had just conceded an equalising goal to Celtic, were back ahead. Motherwell went in at half-time with their fans' cheers ringing in their ears and Celtic fans were wondering whether, Jock Stein or no Jock Stein, there was some sort of hoodoo about the Scottish Cup. It was ironic as well that Motherwell's star performer was centre half Pat Delaney, son of the great Celtic legend Jimmy Delaney.

Fortunately, Bertie Auld organised the rescue in the second half, scoring a penalty kick and leading Celtic with a verve and panache that made us all realise just what we had missed in those years when he was with Birmingham City. A late "winner" was chalked off for offside, but it was only a postponement of the triumph. In the replay on Wednesday night, the last day in March, with Steve Chalmers back for Jimmy Johnstone, who had been struggling with an injury and who had not yet really impressed Jock Stein in any case, Celtic were simply too good for Motherwell – so good, in fact, that the following day's *Evening Times* states that "Fallon and the other Celtic defenders could have taken turns at nipping in for a cup of tea!" Shades of what they used to say about Davie Adams and Charlie Shaw in the old days!

Defeating Motherwell was a relief, but the focus was now very definitely on the Scottish Cup final. It was to be played at Hampden on April 24 against, ironically enough, Dunfermline Athletic. They had beaten Hibs in the other semi-final and, with Stein as manager, had inflicted so much woe on Celtic and their supporters in the 1961 Scottish Cup final. It was easy to detect the rising excitement in Celtic circles. Were the wilderness years about to end at last? Had we discovered the messiah who was to lead us to the promised land? More mundanely, next year would we be able to talk about football without being drowned out by the naysayers? Could we at last see a trophy draped in green and white ribbons?

For myself, there was the additional complication of Esther being pregnant and due to give birth round about the day of the cup final. For the other supporters and players there was the worry that the team was, frankly, not doing very well. The games that had been played did not really matter, but it would have been nice to have had a few more wins under our belt. Billy McNeill, now back to fitness and form, had played and played well in the Scotland v England International at Wembley, a 2–2 draw – a result, funnily enough, looked upon as a failure, for Scotland had won the last three Internationals against England. But on the Wednesday after, Celtic, without McNeill, had collapsed woefully at Falkirk, that old bogey ground, and then the week before the final, a minuscule crowd watched our last home game against Partick Thistle, a feckless 1–2 defeat.

That particular performance sealed the fate of Jim Kennedy and Jimmy Johnstone, at least for this season. Kennedy was possibly past his best, but the decision to drop Jimmy Johnstone in favour of Steve Chalmers on the right wing proved that Stein was Celtic manager material. It was not necessarily a popular decision, for even in Johnstone's early days Celtic supporters identified with and loved "wee Jimmy", who could dazzle opponents and delight admirers. But Stein felt that he was not

104

yet ready and that in any case there would be more need for the pace of Chalmers on the right wing. Perhaps Jock saw too much of the Charlie Tully in Jimmy Johnstone, it being well known that Jock had not always approved of Tully's antics, preferring a more direct approach (though Jock and Charlie eventually became firm friends). John Hughes would be in the centre, Bobby Lennox on the left, and Bertie Auld and Charlie Gallagher would patrol the middle along with Bobby Murdoch.

We players naturally were anxious about our long-term future, but for the fans there was now the feeling that, even if Celtic lost in the final, Celtic now had the manager who would rebuild the club over the next few years. The *Evening Citizen*'s pre-match edition (the "Cellic Souvenir Speshul" trumpeted by the ubiquitous newspaper sellers at Central Station and Mount Florida Station) said, "Even if by some unkind quirk of fate, the Scottish Cup is not tonight wearing green and white ribbons, the future for Celtic looks good." It then hinted darkly that some players who assumed themselves to be "built-in with the bricks" had better not make too many assumptions about whether they would still be there in a few years' time.

Over 108,000 attended Hampden on that bright spring day. Phrases like "Celtic's day of destiny" were not an exaggeration in the minds of the support, who recalled previous cup final heartbreaks (four of them) since the last Scottish Cup triumph of 1954, now an astonishing eleven years ago. One recalls the desperate words of one supporter, "We'll forgive everything, Cellic, everything, if ye's jist win the day"; the stone-cold sober, middle-aged man with the collar, tie and soft hat (probably a banker, a teacher or a lawyer during the week) slumped over a hedge in relief after it was all over in Aitkenhead Road, telling everyone, "I couldn't have stood it, if we'd loast the day"; the faces of delight on the youngsters who had never seen this before; and the words of the RAF veteran who had played his part in liberating Europe (Italy in particular) twenty years before, telling

105

everyone that he had never seen anything like this. Sitting in the cafeteria of Lewis's Polytechnic having one's tea of mince and chips and fearing that it was all a dream and that suddenly you were going to wake up was reported as a frequent phenomenon. This day was indeed the day on which history looked down on Celtic.

A young fan, on his day trip to Glasgow, bought a record that day from Lewis's Polytechnic in Argyle Street which had a line "with a hymn for the dawn of the free". No lyric was ever more appropriate. Before that day Celtic could not win anything and their supporters freely used words like "finished" and "betrayal"; after that day they couldn't stop winning. One recalled the words of Sir Winston Churchill about the Battle of El Alamein: "Before El Alamein we never had a victory; after El Alamein we never had a defeat."

It was not quite as simple as all that, but for the rest of the 1960s, Celtic won every Scottish League, every Scottish League Cup and lost only two Scottish Cups. Earlier that season there had been a pop song by a group called Herman's Hermits with the lyrics, "Something tells me I'm in for something good." So we were. I was there at the start of all this. I am proud of that.

The details of this game are etched on every Celtic heart. Down 1–2 at the interval (my concentration for the second goal was distracted by a freak loudspeaker announcement after Bertie Auld had equalised, and John McLaughlin scored from a free kick), half-time was spent in the deepest recesses of introspection. But this was a real Celtic team, and Bobby Lennox and Bertie Auld combined to put Celtic back in it early in the second half. Then came my own great moment, when I saved a shot from Alex Edwards which might well have won the day for the Pars. Gair Henderson of the *Evening Times* describes it thus: "Fallon made the save of the match – a brilliant leap to his right at a rising shot from Edwards. The ball looked as though it had beaten the keeper, and it was actually behind him but not over the line when

106

he made his brilliant save". A hunt for the Scottish Cup final 1965 on YouTube will confirm Henderson's impression. Deservedly, I felt, applause rang out from the Celtic End behind me, but there was still a cup to be won.

In truth, it was one of the better cup finals, with action raging from end to end, but the longer that eventful second half wore on, the more often Celtic found themselves in the Dunfermline half of the field. Nine minutes remained: Lennox forced a corner, Gallagher took it and Billy McNeill propelled Celtic to glory. Some books like to imply that that was that, and everyone knew that Celtic would win, with the more prescient even forecasting that they could win the European Cup two years from now. That was far from the case. Dunfermline were a far better team than that, and it was hands to the pumps for everyone, as the supporters behind the goal consulted watches in a state of unbelievable tension and (unashamedly) prayed. I just wanted that final whistle to go, and for the ball to stay away from me. What they say about your life passing before your eyes is true . . . but referee Hugh Phillips eventually pointed to the stand. John Milton had written poems called *Paradise Lost* and *Paradise Regained*. A young fan would write about these poems in his Higher English exam a few days later, knowing exactly what he was talking about.

I swung on my bar. Had it been Wembley a few years later the bar might have broken, but fortunately it held firm and I had my Scottish Cup medal, something that I had to keep staring at to prove it was real. The Scottish Cup was draped in green and white ribbons for the first time in eleven years. Harry Andrew of the *Scottish Daily Express* put it brilliantly when he said, "The exile in the wilderness is over. Parkhead is Paradise once more." Waverley in the *Daily Record* waxed lyrical about the "Bhoys' Old Magic", comparing the current team with men like Patsy Gallacher, Peter Wilson and Tommy McInally, but he also struck a note of realism when he said that Dunfermline were men "of stout heart. After the second equaliser, [Dunfermline] put on the pressure and but for some fine goalkeeping by John Fallon, plus a bit of luck, might have taken the lead for a third time." The *Sunday Post*, in a play on Bertie Auld's name, talked about "Auld Lang Syne".

Hardly anyone in the Celtic community noticed that Kilmarnock won the Scottish League that day. They had to win 2–0 at Tynecastle to do so, and did just that, thus ushering in a prolonged period of gloom for the men of the capital. Kilmarnock, who had done little to endear themselves to Celtic and their fans that season, were nevertheless worthy winners, having come so close on many other occasions, and some Celtic fans felt magnanimous enough to congratulate some young Killie fans whom they met in Glasgow on their way back to Ayrshire.

There were several postscripts to that season. The first was that Esther was taken from the celebration at the Central Hotel to the hospital to give birth to Brian the following day; the second was that Celtic went to Dunfermline on the following Wednesday and, with a significantly different team, went down 1–5 in the last, meaningless League game of the season; and the third was that Celtic, with the strain now off them, went on to win the Glasgow Cup as well, beating Rangers in the process. We were lucky to beat Rangers, who, even from my viewpoint that first Friday night immediately after the Liberation Day of the Scottish Cup final, looked the better side. But was not that even more proof that the tide had turned? Celtic, the worse team, winning! But in 1964, the worse team had more often than not won as well. The whirligigs of time had indeed brought in their revenge.

The Glasgow Cup was duly won in a one-sided game against Queen's Park at Hampden on May 11. It might have been easy for Stein to say that it was "just" Queen's Park and "just" the Glasgow Cup, but he insisted that Billy McNeill and John Hughes should delay their joining the Scotland squad so that they could play in this game. With Bertie Auld in fantastic form, the score was 5–0, Celtic having scored in thirty seconds. I was virtually a spectator as Celtic turned on "a relentless display of attacking and enterprising football" to the delight of the 17,000 crowd and the approval of the press and even veteran referee Willie Brittle, who apparently expressed his appreciation for such a great performance. I had one save to make, and it was a difficult one as well, from Queen's Park's Jimmy Stewart in the early stages. Otherwise I enjoyed a quiet evening.

Celtic fans in the crowd sang "Happy Days Are Here Again" and "Take My Hand, I'm A Stranger in Paradise". This was because jokes went round Scotland about the latter song, originally sung by Nelson Eddy in *Kismet* but now sung by the Scottish Cup on her first arrival at Celtic Park for eleven years. The grand old lady now had company in the equally venerable Glasgow Cup, won for the second time in a row by Celtic.

Things would never be quite the same again, and I was there at the start of the glory days. Like the rest of the supporters, I walked on air all that summer of 1965.

10

THE GLORY DAYS OF 1965/66

Celtic and I lived on a high in summer 1965. There was, of course, a new baby called Brian in the house as a permanent reminder of the great day in the Scottish Cup final. Three boys kept me and Esther busy, but there seemed little doubt that things had changed permanently for Celtic and their fans as well that day of April 24.

Not only was there a Scottish Cup decked in green and white ribbons to show off – won eighteen times now, and again equal to Rangers, who had overtaken Celtic in 1964 – and think about on nights when one couldn't sleep because of children wakening and crying, but also the whole atmosphere at Parkhead was upbeat, with Jock Stein making a determined effort to seize the moral high ground on everything to do with football, and to take every opportunity to get Celtic into the newspapers. He himself had been approached to take temporary charge of Scotland for a couple of World Cup qualifying fixtures. He gladly did this but made it clear that he was not interested in the post on a permanent basis. He was to be the manager of Celtic, not Scotland, and the way that this was handled suggested, subliminally, that Celtic were now to be Scotland's number one club, and of course that, in times of emergency, Scotland would naturally turn to Celtic, rather than to anyone else, for help.

Stein realised correctly that there was no real bias in Scotland's Press against Celtic, however much his supporters were convinced that that was the case. Or, if there was any bias, it was his responsibility to do something about it. Journalists like Gair Henderson and John MacKenzie might have been born as Rangers supporters, but they were in the business of selling newspapers and Celtic's support was at least as large as that of Rangers, and potentially a great deal larger.

Stein twigged that the real problem was the lack of constant copy, which the press needed and thrived upon, particularly in the quieter summer months. Pre-season training open days were therefore held at Parkhead. The press and TV were invited, and everyone was given loads of tea, coffee and biscuits, and the result was that in July 1965 the word "Celtic" screamed at fans every time you opened your newspaper. We happily gave interviews and were seen doing the 100-yard sprint, jumping through hoops (literally) and even playing the odd game of football with each other. It is well documented that before the arrival of Stein, training tended to consist of running round the track. Little wonder that so many players hated training and avoided it as much as they could. Neil Mochan's arrival as trainer pre-dated Stein and he made some difference, but now, under Stein, training became fun. Billy McNeill would say in later years that everyone suddenly enjoyed going to training, and the press saw that this was the case. Suddenly everybody started talking about Celtic. The result too was that, under the stern but fair regime of Neil Mochan, Celtic suddenly had some very fit young men.

Celtic also entered the media themselves with the launch of the *Celtic View*, the first newspaper of its kind in the world. It was small and cheap but a key factor in keeping the support onside. The first edition symbolically and potently contained a picture of our team with the Scottish Cup. So I am in the very first edition! An attempt was made to eradicate hooliganism from the

111

support – something that became immediately necessary after some disgraceful goings-on at Sunderland in a pre-season friendly. Joe McBride had been signed from Motherwell and a couple of young Brazilians were invited to train at Celtic Park with a view to signing.

One wonders about the last item. They were called Ayrton Inacio and Marco di Sousa and would be joined in time by another two called Jorge Farah and Fernando Consul. It was not an age in which Brazilians came to Scotland very often, but there was still the magic associated with the word "Brazil" from those who had seen Didi, Vavá, Garrincha and Pelé in the Swedish World Cup of 1958. But not all Brazilians were like Pelé, and one wonders how these young lads would have coped with a fierce Scottish winter, hard pitches, different referees and brutal defenders – if indeed Stein was seriously interested in signing them. None of the four of them ever played a first-team game and it may have been a publicity stunt, designed to gain even more newspaper space. In this respect it was like the Di Stéfano interlude of last year, but far more cleverly handled. They were nice guys as well, those Brazilians.

In the game where the supporters had disgraced themselves at Sunderland – the throwing of an orange at Jim Baxter, who had now joined them from Rangers (on one famous occasion David Coleman on BBC Grandstand said "Jim Baxter of Celtic"!), did at least have a funny side to it, but breaking windows, wrecking pubs and street fights with the all too willing Mackems didn't – Celtic had won 5–0. This was something that raised eyebrows outside Scotland and was welcomed by Celtic supporters everywhere, for not only did Sunderland have Jim Baxter, but also Ian McColl, ex-Rangers, had now left his post with Scotland to become their manager. That day at Roker Park I had little to do other than worry about the crowd. The problem was that a pre-season friendly was just that – of little real, lasting importance.

The season itself did not get off to the start predicted by so many of the support. Drawn in a tough League Cup section with Dundee, Dundee United and Motherwell, we started badly with a disappointing 1–2 defeat at Tannadice on a hot day in front of a huge and very disappointed Celtic support (arguably the biggest Celtic support ever seen in Dundee). Then, a week later, we went down to Dundee at Parkhead, and I have to hold my hands up and say that I might have done better with one of the goals. Even the game in between, a 1–0 win over Motherwell at Parkhead, had looked laborious and pedestrian.

Things did not look good, but in those days a League game was played between the two halves of the League Cup fixtures. By sheer chance, Celtic were back at Tannadice Park, and on this occasion the team really turned it on and hit the Taysiders 4–0 in an astonishingly good performance which, although no one realised it at the time, was the first game of nine Scottish League titles in a row. I had a quiet night, although I was lucky to avoid being seriously injured by a few coins hurled from the Shed End by an idiotic faction of Dundee United's support – normally a decent and docile lot but sadly brainwashed by the local press into thinking that their team were better than they were. Örjan Persson, Dundee United's left winger, who later joined Rangers, was sent off that night by referee Bobby Davidson.

Using this game as a springboard, Celtic then won the next three games to qualify for the League Cup quarter-finals. The last game of the section was at Dens Park and was characterised by one of the best goals ever seen at the venerable old ground. It was scored by John Hughes, and no goalkeeper on earth could have stopped it. Even from the far end, it looked good. But Dundee fought well and I was called upon to make a few good saves. As the qualifying section finished with Celtic triumphant, I had every right to feel happy about myself. I had made a few mistakes – all goalkeepers do – but I wasn't under any real threat for my position, for there was only the cheerful and supportive veteran

113

Ronnie Simpson and a young Irishman called Jack Kennedy. I was not really prepared for what was to come.

Stein, not always taciturn when he talked about Jimmy Johnstone, for example, said little about goalkeeping. I felt I was generally popular enough with the supporters. But the catalyst for my fall from grace seemed to be the game at Ibrox on September 18, allied with the fact that Ronnie had an outstanding game in the reserve fixture at Parkhead on the same day. The game at Ibrox was much played up by the media and led to the gates at the Celtic End being closed with thousands left outside and everyone suspecting a dastardly plot by Rangers to keep Celtic fans out.

I still feel that I was blamed unfairly by Stein for Celtic's defeat. Stein often felt the need for a scapegoat, and I fitted the bill. I did not have the best of games at Ibrox, it is true, but there were other reasons for Celtic's defeat. It was Tommy Gemmell who was mainly responsible for the first goal, and the second was a penalty conceded by a clumsy and unnecessary barge by Billy McNeill on Jim Forrest. And in any case, Celtic were hampered by the loss of Joe McBride, Ian Young looked distinctly out of form, and to cap it all, Billy McNeill was badly injured and could only limp about ineffectively on the wing in the second half. (The following season, substitutes would be allowed in Scotland, and this game proved the need for them.)

This game was a huge disappointment, but it was not the terminal disaster that it was portrayed as in some quarters. It has always been the case that too much emphasis is laid on games against Rangers, but as Jock Stein himself never tired of pointing out, you get two points for beating Partick Thistle and St Johnstone, just the same as you get for beating Rangers. Celtic at this stage were halfway through their League Cup quarter-final against Raith Rovers. We had already walloped the hapless Fifers 8–1 at Stark's Park and for the second leg, with the tie well won, Stein felt entitled to give a few fringe men a game. The young

Irishman Jack Kennedy thus played against Raith Rovers at Celtic Park in a 4–0 win before a small crowd.

But then a large Celtic crowd turned up at Parkhead on Saturday, 25 September 1965 to see Aberdeen – and found Ronnie Simpson in goal. Some of the morning newspapers had predicted that, but a few others had speculated on whether a long chat between George Farm, the manager of Raith Rovers, and Jock Stein after the game on Wednesday night had been about a possible transfer of Simpson to Kirkcaldy, where he would get a chance in the first team. But Simpson appeared in the Celtic goal against Aberdeen, and enjoyed a very quiet afternoon, for Celtic decided to turn it on and to hammer the Dons 7–1. He was injured at one point when an over-zealous Aberdeen forward tried to kick the ball out of his hands, but otherwise had a good game.

And Ronnie then stayed in the position for a long, long time. As far as I was concerned, I had now lost my place as first-team goalkeeper. I watched the game that day. Jack Kennedy had gone with the reserves to Pittodrie. I was naturally disappointed and possibly even a little perplexed about this turn of events, but I made a point of wishing Simpson well and seeking him out afterwards to congratulate him. He always did that sort of thing with me.

It would be fair to say that, at the start, Celtic fans had mixed feelings about Ronnie. The fact that his father, Jimmy, had played for Rangers was mentioned by some, but the main objection seemed to be that Ronnie, now approaching his thirty-fifth birthday, was simply too old. In addition, in his few games last season, admittedly at the low ebb of Celtic's fortunes, he had not impressed, and although everyone admired and respected him for his glorious past with Newcastle United (he is still to this day revered on Tyneside) and Hibs, he was not felt to be the best choice for Celtic's goal. In addition, rumours persisted – there are no such things as secrets in Glasgow – that Stein still did not like him and that the feeling was mutual.

But Ronnie would soon win over both the fans and Jock Stein, particularly after the League Cup final a month later, in which his experience was so vital. One remembers vividly the last few minutes of this fraught game when Simpson, in front of 50,000 desperate Celtic fans and behind some panicky defenders (even the normally cool Billy McNeill gave indications that he was beginning to lose it), punched one fist into the other, pointed, gestured and generally took a grip of the situation, which might have been lost as the frantic Rangers threw everything at Celtic. Simpson became a Celtic legend that day. His father, it was said, watching from the stand, changed sides that day as well!

But where did this leave me? On the day that Ronnie took over against Aberdeen, it was Jack Kennedy who went with the reserves to Pittodrie. This was only natural, because the reserve team is there to develop youngsters and give them a chance, but my future began to look grim, especially when Ronnie began to play so well. But on October 16, when Simpson failed to pass a fitness test for a shoulder injury before a game at Brockville (a very exciting 4–3 win, as it turned out), I was drafted in, while Kennedy stayed at Parkhead to play for the reserves. I was thus not entirely out of the picture, and it showed that when pushed Stein would still go for the experience of myself, if he needed a replacement, rather than the unproven Kennedy.

My reaction to my replacement by Simpson was a muted one. Whatever my private feelings may have been about unfair treatment, there was a distinct lack of tantrums, transfer requests and quotes to newspapers with melodramatic stuff like "my career is at the crossroads" and so on. Instead, Ronnie and I became even closer friends, sitting beside each other on the team bus and comparing notes. I was bright enough to realise that Ronnie had a lifetime of experience (including the rare distinction of having played for Great Britain at the Olympic Games of 1948) and there was a great deal that I could learn from him. Moreover, I was still with Celtic, and that was where I wanted to be. It was the team I loved. There was the financial question as well. Even though I was not playing with the firsts, I was still earning enough money. So I gritted my teeth and bided my time.

Another side of me, I would like to think, came out as well. This was John Fallon the Celtic supporter. I loved to go with the team to watch the game and to be on hand if anything happened. As I have said, substitutes were not yet allowed in Scottish football, and there was always the chance that Ronnie might trip coming off the bus or injure himself in the warm-up session, or "shooting-in" as it was called, before the start of the game. Moreover, Stein may not have liked me, for reasons that are hard to discover or analyse: maybe because of the time when I played for Blantyre Celtic without his permission, or maybe because of an argument he once had with my father, or maybe because he simply didn't understand goalkeepers. But he recognised that my cheerful redheaded presence was a positive influence on the bus, the train or the dressing room. I was a good diplomat, talking to the opposition goalkeeper, the referee and other players, and generally did the image of Celtic a great deal of good.

I was also determined not to cause trouble. Cliques and conspiracies abound in every walk of life, not least professional football, and it was by no means uncommon for a player on the fringes of the starting eleven to whisper and bitch about the manager, thereby unsettling other players. I was emphatically not like that. There are many pictures of me cheering the team on from the stand or the bench, even being delighted at the successes of my rival Ronnie Simpson.

Round about Christmastime 1965, both the *Celtic View* and the *Scottish Daily Express* worried out loud about my future, especially as Celtic now had four goalkeepers, with Bent Martin arriving for a month's trial. I had to admit that I was a bit worried, as I couldn't even rely on getting a game for the reserves, because I was sharing that job with Jack Kennedy.

As far as the playing side of season 1965/66 was concerned,

that was about as good as it got for me in the first team. I watched as Celtic, playing some fine football, won two trophies out of four and were distinctly unlucky in the other two. The two won were the Scottish League and the Scottish League Cup, and the real hard luck came in the European Cup Winners' Cup and the Scottish Cup. The Cup Winners' Cup game against Liverpool would have been won if more goals had been scored at Celtic Park. As it was, a perfectly good Lennox goal was disallowed for offside near the end of the Anfield game, triggering a rather shameful outburst of hooliganism and bottle-throwing, which obscured the real injustice done to Celtic that night.

The Scottish Cup final went to a replay after a rather dull 0–0 draw, and the replay was little better. I could not be at that game, for I was playing for the reserves in a 7–0 beating of St Mirren at Celtic Park that night, but I was kept in touch with what was happening. The teams were evenly matched, but it was Rangers who won the day with a late Kai Johansen strike from outside the box. Perhaps this highlighted a weakness in Ronnie's goalkeeping, in that it was believed that he was not so good at saving from a distance; this was something that I felt I was better at. The important thing about that goal, as far as the future was concerned, was that Stein was able to capitalise on it.

Stein knew that Johansen was no great goalscorer. It would be unfair to class his strike in the 1966 Scottish Cup final as a total fluke, but it was certainly one of these strikes which sometimes work for you and sometimes don't. Stein also twigged that Johansen would never be able to resist the pressure from the Rangers terracings to try it again and would therefore come up more often than he should, on the off chance of an opportunity. This would leave only the ponderous John Greig to cope with the rapier thrusts of the speedy Bobby Lennox. Lennox became a prolific goalscorer against Rangers.

As far as Stein's relations with his goalkeepers were concerned, the press tried hard to drive a wedge between Simpson and Stein

118

on the basis of their previous (supposedly) poor relationship at Hibs. A more unscrupulous character than myself might have tried to exploit this to his own advantage, but I pointedly refused to do so. Ronnie was my friend, and I distrusted Stein, who could be charming and supportive sometimes but considerably less so on other occasions. As it happened, Stein realised that there was not, in any case, any great problem in the goalkeeping department (there were, in truth, very few problems in any aspect of this great team) and left Simpson to it. A feeling of mutual respect, if not exactly affection, gradually developed between Stein and his goalkeepers.

I felt that I had a dilemma. I was a professional football player, and it was only natural for me to want to play first-team football, even if it meant moving to England or playing for another Scottish club. But on the other hand, I was secure enough where I was. I loved Celtic, I was still well enough paid even when not in the first team, and I had a young family. Besides, I never knew when I was going to get my place back. Simpson, born in 1930, a good ten years before most of the other players, including myself, could not go on forever. Or could he?

But then a great thing happened for Celtic and myself when we went on tour to Bermuda, the United States and Canada between May 12 and June 12 1966. Eleven games were played, and Celtic came back undefeated. It was deliberately arranged as a long tour so that players could get to know each other better, and good accommodation and travel arrangements were insisted on. We beat Tottenham Hotspur twice, drew with them the other time we played them, drew with Bologna and Bayern Munich, and beat Atlas of Mexico and the local opposition in the other games, usually by large scores.

It was light-hearted stuff, most of the time. Jim Craig didn't go because he had his finals in dentistry at Glasgow University, and Ian Young and Jimmy Johnstone came home early to get married. Newspapers carried pictures of the players sunbathing,

119

sightseeing and sitting by swimming pools, and it was great for Celtic supporters across the Atlantic to have a chance to see their team again, but there was a serious side to it as well.

John Traynor and Tony Griffin in their excellent book *A Season in the Sun* sum it up well:

> The psychology of undertaking such an arduous tour in the wake of a heavy, albeit successful, domestic campaign was brilliantly simple. Jock Stein wanted to build on the achievements of the season just past by fusing the emerging talents of his young players into a unit capable of confronting the challenges which he sensed lay ahead. What better way to weld the team spirit he craved than the combinations of relaxation and discipline, recreation and competition, vacation and vocation which this extended working holiday would inevitably produce? The players would live in each other's pockets for a solid month and would learn to cope with the tensions, both positive and negative, such proximity creates. They would experience the excitement of foreign travel – in many cases, for the first time – together and in the course of travelling that vast continent, partnerships and friendships would be forged and cemented which would later bear fruit both on and off the field. A perfect example of such liaisons is the improbable and enduring bond struck up between genial Bobby Lennox and the fiery Jimmy Johnstone. But above all, they would play together, away from the pressures of a normal season, amidst a variety of locations, atmospheres and standards of competition which would stand them in good stead for the rigours to come.

I shared the goalkeeping duties with Ronnie, sometimes literally in games against local opposition, with Ronnie playing one half and me the other. I played in the 2–2 draw against Bayern Munich

Me in pre-season 1964.

Making a save from Davie Wilson of Rangers.

Getting married to Esther in March 1962.

Greenock 1964: Getting a warning from a policeman for celebrating.

1965: With (left to right) Ian Young, Tommy Gemmell, John Hughes, Bobby Murdoch and the half-hidden John Clark.

A gentlemen's dinner! With (left to right) Charlie Gallagher, Bobby Murdoch, Frank McCarron and Jock Stein.

Hugging my friend and rival Ronnie Simpson after the Scottish League Cup final of 1965/66.

CELTIC YEAR OF TRIUMPH

A "Weekly News" Special
published in co-operation with
The Celtic Football Club

36

1967: The final whistle has just gone in Lisbon. (Left to right) Sean Fallon, Neil Mochan and Bob Rooney are as delighted as I am. But where's Jock?

FIRST TEAM DUTYMEN

Last season's "pool" (left to right) — Hughes, Craig, McNeill, Gemmell, Cushley, Simpson, Fallon, O'Neill, Murdoch, Chalmers, Gallagher, Clark, Wallace, Lennox, Auld, Johnstone.

The squad in 1966/67.

April 5 1969: Celebrating in the Hampden dressing room. We have just won the Scottish League Cup, beating Hibs 6–2.

April 26 1969: We have just won the Scottish Cup, beating Rangers 4–0, and Jim Craig and Billy McNeill are presenting me to the crowd.

With my family
at Butlin's.

Returning to Parkhead many years after Lisbon with (left to right) Jimmy Johnstone,
Bobby Lennox and Bertie Auld.

Still a fan! With (left to right) my grandson James MacPherson, and Susan and Martin, daughter and son of Willie O'Neill.

Me and Esther with our wonderful family, celebrating our golden wedding anniversary in March 2002.

in which things got a little out of hand, with even the normally placid and gentlemanly Steve Chalmers disgracing himself in a brawl and some of his teammates joining in as well. I was particularly singled out for praise for my performance in the final game of the tour against Atlas of Mexico in Los Angeles. Celtic had only twelve fit men but still, with depleted resources, beat the Mexicans 1–0 through a Charlie Gallagher goal. But the "special correspondent" of the *Evening Times* stated that "John Fallon had to make four good saves when his team were under pressure."

There were other, less stressful games and the whole thing was an enjoyable experience, although there was a tactical point to it in the building up of team spirit and the development of the Murdoch and Auld midfield, which would revolutionise Celtic. As well as the bond created between Johnstone and Lennox (they would be seen in future years at railway stations on the way to away games with their arms round each other singing songs like "Roll Over, Beethoven" and "Twist and Shout"), the friendship in the goalkeepers' union between myself and Simpson was cemented.

11

LOOKING ON IN LISBON

Season 1966/67 is well known. The fact that I played only one competitive game, against Kilmarnock, after the League had been well won, does not mean that I did not play a part in the glory of that season. I was an integral part of the squad and was heavily involved in it all, as Celtic emulated the feats of the great men of 1908, 1916 and 1917 by winning every trophy that they entered. Ronnie Simpson, I would have to admit, was outstanding throughout the season, and he totally amazed himself and the rest of the world by being picked by Bobby Brown to play for Scotland in the famous 3–2 defeat of England at Wembley. He was thirty-six, and some writers detected a note of fantasy and fairy tale in the build-up to this game, but Ronnie played and retained his place for the next International.

Every player, no matter how experienced (and it would have been difficult to find anyone with greater experience than Ronnie Simpson) still needs a little support and encouragement. What was highly unusual – possibly even unique in the history of world football – was that Simpson found that his greatest source of support came from the man whom everyone identified as his greatest rival: namely myself! If Simpson had conceded a goal which he felt he might have done better with, then he and I would sit down on the bus home and talk about it.

This team, incidentally, was never described as having a niggardly defence. Goals were conceded – often because the emphasis was very much on attack – and Ronnie Simpson was not like Charlie Shaw in 1914 or Fraser Forster a hundred years later, in 2014, going game after game without losing a goal. A typical score would be something like 5–2, and there was the great game on November 19 1966 at East End Park, Dunfermline, which ended 5–4 for Celtic, and surely Dunfermline had cause to bemoan their luck in that they scored four goals against the eventual European Champions but still lost!

I was a little perturbed, however, to discover that on Monday, October 10 1966, Ronnie Simpson was being given a rest for a Glasgow Cup game against Queen's Park at Parkhead, but that his replacement was not myself but Bent Martin, the young blond Dane who had impressed Celtic while playing against them for Aarhus in last season's European Cup Winners' Cup. He had little to do – the supporters made jokes about "naethin' daen for the Dane" – as Celtic won 4–0. It was his only game for the club, for Simpson returned for the game next Saturday and, to my relief, Martin was transferred to Dunfermline in December, where he became a local hero, winning the Scottish Cup with the Pars in 1968. He was a good goalie, I must admit.

Steps were being taken in Europe as well. Zurich and Nantes were competently dealt with, and even the BBC were beginning to realise that there might be a great team here developing. Liverpool, England's representatives, blew up against Ajax of Amsterdam, thus leaving Celtic the only representative of Great Britain. Sam Leitch in the *Sunday Mirror* dared to suggest that Celtic might even win the European Cup, and was much ridiculed for so doing, but Sam knew what he was talking about. I technically played in those European games, for I was the substitute goalkeeper, something that was allowed in the European Cup of 1966/67.

We even received help indirectly from a bizarre quarter.

Rangers were also doing well in Europe, making progress in the European Cup Winners' Cup, while Everton, England's representatives, had been shown the exit. In a way, this helped to take the pressure off Celtic, and on one occasion in early December, Rangers' success worked very well to Celtic's advantage. On December 6, Rangers, playing very well, deservedly defeated Borussia Dortmund in Germany and returned the following day to a heroes' welcome. They also returned to Scotland to find that their transfer target, Willie Wallace of Hearts, had signed for Celtic, while they were in Germany. Wallace had been contemplating emigration to Australia, according to the *Evening Times*, but he now found himself at Celtic Park on December 7, cheering on his new teammates as they beat Nantes, before making his debut on the Saturday.

Autumn and winter 1966 saw us compared to Perry Mason. Perry Mason was an American lawyer in a drama series shown on BBC television on a Saturday night. Played by Raymond Burr, Perry always managed to get his man off the murder charge even though things looked distinctly pessimistic for his client for most of the show. The defendant was often caught at the scene of the crime holding a gun, but Perry always persuaded the jury that someone else was the perpetrator. Perry never lost. His programme was followed by the news and then the Scottish football programmes. Celtic were usually on either BBC or STV in those days, and at this time they never lost either, so the question was asked: "Who is going to lose first, Celtic or Perry Mason?"

As it turned out, it was Celtic who lost first, but not until Hogmanay, against Dundee United. We had drawn with St Mirren (without the injured McNeill) in early November, then Kilmarnock in early December and Aberdeen on Christmas Eve, but the defeat came as a shock to the system. Ronnie actually had a bad game that day – as he himself freely admitted – looking badly at fault for Dundee United's winning goal as Ian Mitchell rounded him and scored after he had fatally hesitated.

Stein was far from happy, and I began to hope that I would get a game on January 2 against Clyde, or even Rangers at Ibrox on January 3, for Stein was often guilty of knee-jerk reactions to a bad result. (He did in fact drop Willie O'Neill and replace the full back combination of Gemmell and O'Neill with Craig and Gemmell.) In the event, frost postponed both those games. (This might be a questionable decision to modern supporters, but this was before undersoil heating. The weather was sunny and bright and the postponements were tremendous disappointments to all the fans who had travelled some distance to see the games.) By the time of the next game – January 7 against Dundee at Parkhead – Stein had decided to persevere with Ronnie.

The team kept winning, and winning well, and the feeling was beginning to grow that Sam Leitch was right and that this team might even do well in Europe this year. The Scottish League Cup and the Glasgow Cup (a by no means undervalued tournament in those days) were already won – Rangers unaccountably fell at Berwick in the Scottish Cup at the end of January – but more importantly, Celtic kept winning, and had a very important European Cup date against Vojvodina Novi Sad (of what was then called Yugoslavia) approaching in early March. Even though I was not in the first team, I could not fail to be caught up in the excitement of it all. Not only did I retain the enthusiasm of a supporter about it all, but I was always on call too, as it were, for one never knew when Ronnie was going to have a bad game or get himself injured.

Vojvodina were disposed of in dramatic fashion at a packed, excited Parkhead, and progress continued to be made in the Scottish tournaments. The Wednesday before Scotland's famous 3–2 win at Wembley, Dukla Prague, the Czechoslovak army side, had come to Celtic Park and been beaten 3–1, meaning that Celtic only had to defend in Prague. This we did, to achieve surely the best 0–0 draw of all time. Some writers like to say that Celtic chose to defend against Dukla in Prague. In effect we had little choice, for they were a really good side.

Now the first British side to have reached the European Cup final, we flew back to Glasgow that Tuesday night to prepare for the Scottish Cup final against the strong-going Aberdeen on the Saturday. Willie Wallace scored two goals, one on each side of half-time, and Celtic duly lifted their nineteenth Scottish Cup. The League followed the next week in a 2–2 draw at a soggy Ibrox.

And where was John Fallon in all this? In season 1966/67, only one substitute was allowed and only for injuries in domestic football, but the European Cup allowed for a substitute goalkeeper, so I was very much part of the squad. Emotions in such circumstances are difficult, complicated in my case because I was both a friend of Ronnie and a Celtic supporter. So I certainly did not want Ronnie to let in soft goals or to get injured so that I could get a chance, yet I did feel that I wanted to be a part of it more. Outfield players like John Hughes or Charlie Gallagher, for example, who also were not playing in Lisbon, always felt that they had a chance of being picked. Hughes, for example, was a versatile man who could cover for both a centre forward and a left winger, and Gallagher could play in either of the inside-forward positions or even on the wing, whereas I, a specialist goalkeeper, had far more limited opportunities. I depended on something happening to Ronnie Simpson.

But, like everyone else connected with Celtic, I enjoyed Lisbon. With the other reserves, I was given the job of "bagging" the bench that Stein wanted as part of his mind games, and from the bench I watched the agonies of the early penalty but then saw Bobby Murdoch and Bertie Auld take command of the centre of the pitch, Jimmy Johnstone tantalise the defenders and win the hearts of the neutrals and the TV audience, and of course the goals which eventually came from Tommy Gemmell and Steve Chalmers on Celtic's greatest ever day.

Those of us who were alive at the time can recall with vivid clarity just exactly where we were and what we were doing after the second goal went in, even the chap who normally supported Rangers but had changed allegiance for this night and raised his arms in triumph at the second goal, forgetting that he was standing directly underneath his mother's electric lightshade. He was having his hands bandaged by the nurse who lived next door when the full-time whistle went and the good lady was hugged and kissed for one of the few times in her life, and by bloodstained hands.

Those at the ground were gathering at the moat, ready to jump over and invade the field, while most supporters at home, clustered round the flickering and unreliable black-and-white TVs, could not even bear to watch – many hid in toilets and garden sheds or went for a walk round deserted streets. I was on the bench. The final whistle did come – and there is a revealing picture of full-time on the Celtic bench. No Stein, for he had gone for a walk up the touchline to relieve the tension, but Neil Mochan and both Fallons, Sean and myself, were jumping up and punching the air.

There is a true story about my European Cup medal, a bizarre and barely believable one which reflects badly on those who ran the club at the time. Because of crowd problems it was impossible for the whole team to collect their medals. We can all recall the problem that the much buffeted and battered Billy McNeill had getting across the pitch to collect the cup itself. The medals were therefore given to the team at the post-match banquet, twelve of them – one for each of the players and, of course, the substitute goalkeeper, who was included in the twelve. Billy, informally, handed them over.

But then Jock Stein approached me and asked for mine back! I was told that I would be given another one in due course. This did in fact happen but it was a replica medal struck by Celtic themselves in the same way as they have a replica of the European

Cup in the stadium at Celtic Park. So my medal is not a "real" one. My "real" medal was given to no less a person than the chairman, Robert Kelly. Many supporters would have to rack their brains to find out what Bob Kelly did to deserve a European Cup medal.

The return home and the glories of it all passed in a haze, and it was indeed "the best day of our lives", as the words of the song put it, because everyone connected with Celtic walked tall for months and years afterwards. It is often a particular cause of frustration and anger, justified anger, at those who have betrayed Celtic's European heritage when one thinks of 1967 and what it could be for Celtic. It has happened before and can happen again. There can be no excuse for Celtic not doing well in Europe, however much the spineless directorate moan (unconvincingly) about lack of money and claim to be held back by being in a poor league. Such things never stopped Stein, nor the Lisbon Lions.

But to return to the heady days of 1967, I discovered that there was another surprise in store for me – and a pleasant one. Celtic returned to the Iberian peninsula less than a fortnight after the momentous night of Lisbon, this time to provide the opposition for Real Madrid in the testimonial game for Alfredo Di Stéfano, who had personally asked that Celtic provide the opposition. It was a sign, apart from anything else, of how far Celtic had come. Here was the great and normally rather prickly Argentinian, arguably the best player on earth (although not in the opinion of those who had seen Patsy Gallacher), who had enthralled Glasgow in the Hampden European Cup final of 1960 and who had snubbed Celtic when they wanted him in August 1964 now actually asking Celtic to come and play in his testimonial.

In the 1960s, Celtic supporters loved Real Madrid. There were happy memories of their great 7–3 victory in the European Cup final at Hampden over Eintracht Frankfurt in 1960, and Real Madrid had returned to Glasgow to Celtic Park to play in a friendly against Celtic in September 1962. Not only that, but in 1963, when Celtic supporters were badly in need of good news, Real Madrid had done the needful by dumping Rangers out of the European Cup. But now Celtic were playing them as European Cup winners. In fact, it was the 1966 winners against the 1967 winners. Real Madrid had also won the trophy for the first five years of its existence. Even the thought of Celtic being mentioned in the same breath as Real Madrid was a phenomenal thing for those, like myself, who had experienced the bad days.

Politically, question marks might have been raised about this trip. For one thing it was in the middle of the 1967 Arab–Israeli War, and although Spain was well away from the war zone, there might have been problems with aviation. Another thing was that the game was to be played in front of General Francisco Franco, victor of the Spanish Civil War some thirty years ago and responsible for some cruel and vicious repression in the aftermath. He was an unashamed dictator – "El Caudillo" – and a one-time friend of Hitler and Mussolini. More respectably, he was a genuine football fan and lover of Real Madrid, but was he really the sort of man that Celtic should be appearing in front of?

The Spanish Civil War had divided Celtic supporters in 1936. Nowadays, there is little doubt that Celtic supporters, who sing songs like "Viva la Quinta Brigada", are wholeheartedly in support of the Spanish Republic and the heroes of the International Brigades, but in 1936 there had also been the feeling that Celtic supporters should back Franco, for on his side was the Roman Catholic Church, which, to its shame, had chosen to align itself with the European dictators.

But in 1967 any such objections were swept aside in the euphoria that reigned in Glasgow at that time, and the team took up the invitation. Stein, however, would always be reluctant after Lisbon to field exactly the same eleven that played that day. He was occasionally compelled to do so, but wouldn't if he could help it, because he didn't want anyone to say they had beaten the

European Cup winners. He therefore took this opportunity to give some of his fringe players a game. I was one of them, and thus found myself at the Bernabéu in front of 120,000 spectators, playing my second full game of the season.

It was a great occasion. Celtic won 1–0 with a Bobby Lennox goal after some fine play from Jimmy Johnstone. I felt I had a great game – some of my saves can still be seen on YouTube – and if this testimonial was meant to be a win for the home side, or at least a draw, no one told me. I kept a clean sheet. Jock Stein, General Franco, Alfredo Di Stéfano and 120,000 spectators were in agreement that Jimmy Johnstone was the Man of the Match, but the *Evening Times* was very impressed by my goalkeeping. "A Special Correspondent" said, "Vying with Johnstone for top honours was reserve goalkeeper John Fallon, who gave a wonderful display when the Real Madrid sharpshooters were on target. Now Spanish fans are wondering just how good a goalkeeper Ronnie Simpson must be to keep Fallon on the sidelines." Two saves in particular are singled out in Traynor and Griffin's *A Season In the Sun*. One was when "he slipped, but recovered to throw himself athletically across his goal and clutch, not just parry, a point-blank shot from inside forward Serena" and the other "minutes later when he tipped a long shot from [Serena] over the bar".

There was something very Scottish about both the stars of the Celtic side having red hair. Red hair is not at all common in Spain, whereas it is the stereotype of Scottishness in films and TV, not to mention the "See you, Jimmy" tartan hats. Thousands of Madrileños left the Bernabéu that night talking animatedly and excitedly about the two *pelirrojos* (redheads) who done so much to defeat their team. It was not a defeat that caused anyone in Madrid any great heartache, and if it did, they could be consoled by the thought that they had seen a truly great exhibition of football from a team who, like the Barnum and Bailey circus of long ago, could claim to be "the greatest show on earth".

George Aitken of the *Evening Citizen* was effusive in his praise of myself:

> [Fallon is] a goalkeeper of superb quality. Agile and acrobatic, he gripped with a certainty of clutch the very best Real efforts so uncannily that he had the Spaniards shaking their heads in the sheer wonderment of it all, and the Spanish fans on the cliff-like terracing rising from their seats in acclaim. And to think that this outstanding Celt has played only once before in a League match this season! Celtic have no worries about goalkeepers and the first man on the pitch to congratulate Fallon was his inseparable companion at training and on trips – Ronnie Simpson! Fallon accepted the congratulations quietly and began to discuss the two "errors" that he thought he had made in the match. With this sort of spirit going right through the team, Celtic are well positioned to become world champions.

There was one discordant note, and perhaps it indicates the poor relationship slowly developing between Jock Stein and me. It was after the game when I was talking to some journalists, supporters and Real Madrid officials, who were unanimously complimenting me on my performance. Jock happened to be passing, overheard this and said, "That's what he is f***in' paid for!" One hopes that that was some sort of a joke, for otherwise this curmudgeonly, misanthropic and unpleasant behaviour reflects very badly on the man who had done so much for Celtic, Scotland and indeed football itself that year.

It was in total contrast to what Stein said about me for public consumption. He told John "The Voice of Football" MacKenzie of the *Scottish Daily Express*, in the context of what he had achieved this season and how it could not have been done without great reserves, "John Fallon is an outstanding example. We have often been quoted as looking for a goalkeeper. I have always known that John needed only confidence and experience. He has travelled with us on every trip, taking in the atmosphere, sharing in the tension, living with Ronnie Simpson and studying every move his more experienced mate made. He has been a willing pupil and the pay-off came in the last game against Kilmarnock. We can be proud of him." All that seems far better than what he said in private, but then again, Jock Stein, like all men of genius, was himself a contradiction, an enigma and a puzzle.

And so came to an end the momentous season of 1966/67. There would never be another like it, neither for myself nor anyone else.

12

ME, THE SOUTH AMERICAN HERO

If 1966/67 was Celtic's season of glory, the following season was no less momentous. It was not always for the right reasons, but Celtic were seldom out of the news and at the end of the season showed tremendous resources of willpower and determination to overcome all sorts of problems – some of them self-inflicted, some of them not. It was also the season of my personal nightmare.

Often a historian will look back and describe this season as "Fallon's season", but I played only three competitive games of football that season! And what a three! In some ways, I am the man that Celtic supporters will think of when season 1967/68 is mentioned. It ended triumphantly and was the springboard to season 1968/69, when, if anything, Celtic actually played better football even than in 1967 (an ambitious claim). But 1967/68 was the season after the season before, so to speak, and it was one in which character played a part as much as anything.

The title Champions of Europe was by no means an advantage. For one thing, everyone tried that little bit harder to beat Celtic – but that was hardly something to be surprised at; indeed, it was to be expected and even welcomed – for another, it often struck even the most committed of supporters that certain players found this hard to handle, either because they found it difficult to live up to this billing or because they took things, on occasion, rather too easily. A few heads had swollen to a disproportionate and unhealthy extent. Yet Celtic remained a good side, and it was so disappointing, for example, to see exits from both the European Cup and the Scottish Cup at the first time of asking. Admittedly, the opposition in each case was good – but then again, Celtic were the Champions of Europe. A third disadvantage was that being Champions of Europe involved them in a trip to South America, something that did not really do anyone any good at all – with the possible exception, as we shall see, of my good self.

The season began with a 3–3 draw against Tottenham Hotspur at Hampden Park, a game in which Ronnie Simpson was less than totally convincing, but Ronnie maintained his position for the League Cup games in the difficult section which contained Rangers, Dundee United and Aberdeen. Celtic duly qualified in dramatic fashion on a Wednesday night at Parkhead, when they came back from being 1–0 down against Rangers to win 3–1. All the Celtic goals were scored in the last twelve minutes, and the catalyst was the missing of a penalty by Kai Johansen of Rangers, which would surely have killed the game. Johansen, the hero of Ibrox slightly more than a year earlier, was now the villain.

That game was played on the same night as the last episode of a long-running soap opera on TV called *The Fugitive*, in which David Janssen eventually tracked down the killer of his wife. Many people thought that Celtic themselves should have been called "the fugitives" that night in the last ten minutes, for the tired and dispirited Rangers defence had no hope whatsoever of catching the speedy Celtic forwards.

But that game, great though it was, possibly masked a few deficiencies. There seemed little doubt that a few players were now beginning to underestimate the opposition – a fatal condition – and instead of the hunger that had been so apparent in the last two years there was a certain amount of arrogance and complacency beginning to grow in the ranks in the way that certain players, for example, were offhand with supporters and press.

There was also rather too much talk about the money that they had earned and the money they were going to earn. The danger signal went up on September 16 when Rangers beat us 1–0 at Ibrox in the League.

A defeat at Ibrox need not, in itself, be a total disaster – even though some supporters think it is – as long as lessons are learned and the team can bounce back quickly. However much is made of it, it is still only one game out of thirty-four in the League campaign. The important thing is to steady the ship and not to lose other games in its wake. Parkhead history is sadly full of instances of a defeat to Rangers being followed by another defeat to someone else, in sympathy, as it were.

A further and more serious blow came our way when the still self-satisfied Celtic side, in which some members of the defence did not look completely 100 per cent fit, allowed Dynamo Kiev to score two early goals in the first leg of the European Cup first-round tie at Parkhead. Lennox pulled one back, and the team rallied. Now beginning to display once again some Lisbon form, Celtic pressed for an equaliser, but it did not come and Celtic were 1–2 down after the first leg.

Then Jimmy Johnstone, from whom much had been expected and who had produced less than he was capable of, added to Celtic's problems by getting sent off against St Johnstone. He was tackled by Kenny Aird, ironically a former Celtic player, and then Aird was seen lying flat on the turf. "A fist appeared to have been used" is the way that the *Evening Times* coyly put it, but Jimmy's first-half departure meant that Celtic could only draw against the men from Perth.

By the time that the team went to Ukraine for the second leg, it was clear that a few backsides had been kicked, and the team had genuinely bad luck in meeting a poor referee who was clearly influenced by the Kiev crowd. Murdoch was sent off when he fell into the trap of losing his temper and throwing the ball away in disgust. He had been booked previously, and this was rock bottom for the normally so influential Bobby. Then after Lennox had scored, John Hughes did likewise, but the goal was disallowed by the referee. It would have won the game for Celtic, or at least earned extra time, but the fates were against Celtic now, and Celtic departed Europe only slightly more than four months after having been crowned champions.

I was the substitute goalkeeper and watched all these disasters. Ever the team man and ever the Celtic supporter, I was as unhappy as anyone, but I did my best to cheer everyone up, especially those who had suffered their loss of form at exactly the wrong time. However, the main cause was the complacency and lack of appetite which Stein might have done more to counteract with a new high-profile signing, just to indicate that everyone still had to fight for their places. As it was, it was now more and more difficult to convince sceptics in England, for example, that last season had not been a fluke.

But in Scotland, there was a certain amount of compensation. The Scottish League Cup was won, with Celtic back to their goal-scoring best, as seven goals (including a wonderful individual goal from the ever mercurial and quixotic John Hughes) were put past Morton in the semi-final, and five in the final against Dundee, who themselves scored three and would surely have won the Scottish League Cup that day against any other opposition than the determined Celtic. But Celtic had other things on their mind, for that very evening we set out for South America in our quest for the Club World Championship.

Their opponents were Racing Club of Argentina. Celtic had already defeated them 1–0 in the first leg at Hampden on October 18 with a Billy McNeill header. It was a game which revealed the less pleasant side of Argentine football. South Americans are generally charming people, hospitable, kind and generous, as befits people with their Mediterranean origins, but when playing football they are different altogether. Gair Henderson of the *Evening Times* is quite vitriolic about how Racing kicked everything that was not growing on the Hampden pitch and how they punched "like boxing champions". He presciently shudders to think what might happen to Celtic in South America, and frankly, with the benefit of hindsight, it would not have been the worst idea in the world if Celtic had decided to tell the organisers that their trophy was not worth playing for if behaviour was to sink to such depths.

Be that as it may, Celtic won the Scottish League Cup that crisp autumn day of October 28 and then, more or less immediately, flew off to Argentina on a journey that would take sixteen tedious hours. I was there as the reserve goalkeeper. I did not realise how soon my services would be required. The arrival at the ground called El Cilindro (its more common name is La Avellaneda) in Buenos Aires was intimidating enough – the rest of the squad and I were genuinely appalled at the poverty and deprivation that we saw in the environs of the ground, although the stadium itself was very good – but I had changed as substitute goalkeeper and was sitting on the bench when suddenly I was told that I was playing. Ronnie Simpson had been hit on the head by a piece of metal and was bleeding profusely, and this was before the game even started!

I was hunting for a water bottle beside the bench when Bobby Lennox first told me that I was playing, and then I saw Jock Stein hobbling up to me with his characteristic limp, which always seemed worse when he was angry or under pressure, and gesticulating as he shouted, "Don't just stand there! Get on that park! You're f***in' playin'."

There are several unanswered questions about this incident, mainly centred on how the piece of metal managed to get through the iron mesh of the fence erected behind each goal for the very purpose of preventing this sort of thing from happening. There is the distinct possibility that it was thrown from the actual playing area, from a ball boy perhaps, or even a Racing Club reserve. Studies of South American football would not encourage anyone to exclude any possibility.

137

We would surely have been justified in refusing to play – indeed, there was a delay which led a few Argentine radio commentators to speculate that we were going to do just that – but it might have precipitated a riot, and I thus found myself, not having played a first-team game for a long time, getting myself ready, and this was a Club World Championship game. I had little time to prepare and little time to think – possibly not a bad thing in the circumstances – but performed well in extremely difficult conditions. I joke that I could have become a millionaire with all the peso coins that were thrown at me, but fortunately none of them did me any damage, unlike what happened to poor Ronnie Simpson. What, incidentally, one wonders, would have happened if I had been felled in the same way as Ronnie was? There was no other goalkeeper.

Jimmy Johnstone, in his book *Fire in My Boots*, is sympathetic:

> There was only one decision the Boss could make. Ronnie was led off, pale and shaken, and John Fallon was ordered to strip. John looked pale and shaken as he ran on to take his place between the posts. And who could blame him? If that was what the fans could do to intimidate a goalkeeper before the game what would they resort to once the whistle had gone? It says a lot for John that he survived that nerve-wracking experience because he also had to cope with some dreadful abuse from the Racing players.

Clearly not a nice bunch of boys! To their credit, the Argentine newspapers *Clarín*, *El Mundo* and *El Gráfico* condemned this cowardly and thuggish attack on Simpson, but the consensus even among the Scottish journalists and the few Celtic supporters who were there was that Racing deserved their 2–1 win. Everyone, however, was full of praise for my performance – one of the goals looked offside and there was little that I could do with the other one – and the Scottish and neutral observers were similarly

138

happy with the composure of the Celtic players, who played the game in such an atmosphere of intimidation and with genuine concerns about the well-being of Ronnie Simpson. Celtic finished this game with their heads held high, and in full, undisputed control of the moral high ground.

I recall the rough treatment meted out by the Racing players, especially at corner kicks. Everyone in Argentina was astonished that I played without gloves. By the end of the game I had picked up a fair amount of cuts, bruises and scrapes on my knuckles. I should have worn a suit of armour! Humberto Maschio, the inside forward of Racing Club, echoed that when he told the famous Celtic historian Tom Campbell years later that he thought that I was a very courageous goalkeeper.

According to Bob Kelly, Celtic made an attempt to have the game declared null and void because of the incident involving Ronnie Simpson. Celtic had a point, but Racing's counterargument was a bizarre and yet successful one. They claimed that it didn't really matter: Simpson was not missed, because his deputy John Fallon had played so well.

The Argentina game itself was tough, as anyone who had seen the Hampden game might have suspected that it would be, but it was nothing like as bad as the play-off game in Uruguay would become. The referee in Buenos Aires had been brave enough to award Celtic a penalty (converted by Tommy Gemmell), and although he found life difficult, no one could reasonably accuse him of serious bias or incompetence. The irony was that on the away-goals rule Celtic would have won and gone home, but these were not the conditions under which the game was being played, and a third game in neutral Uruguay three days later was decreed.

Mr Kelly, who had been a reluctant traveller after the Hampden game, now evinced a desire to go home, even if it meant withdrawing from the competition. In retrospect this might have been the right decision, but Mr Kelly was talked out of it by the other

139

directors and by Jock Stein. They all shared his apprehension but felt that as long as they were in this distant continent, they might as well see this out, for good or bad. After all, the title Champions of the World meant a great deal. And the fact that the game was in Uruguay seemed a good thing.

Uruguay was then sometimes described as the Switzerland of South America in that it was, in comparison with other countries, a haven of peace and security. It was a country that was seldom talked about in Scotland, although everyone was aware that Uruguay had beaten Scotland 7–0 in the 1954 World Cup, in Switzerland. To counteract the general ignorance of South America, Celtic had arranged a friendly match against Uruguay's best club side, Peñarol (the reigning Club World Champions) at Celtic Park in early September and had beaten them 2–1 in a fine and very sporting game of football. It was generally felt, moreover, that although the Uruguayans were on the same continent and spoke the same language as the Argentinians, they had no reason to love an Argentinian football team.

There was, however, one factor which united all South America in 1967: there was a hatred of Great Britain. Arguably this still exists in the twenty-first century. There were good historical reasons for this, going back well over a century and involving the Falkland Islands, or Las Malvinas, but in football there was a specific issue on which South Americans were all united and that was their resentment that Great Britain should be allowed four nations in the World Cup. They felt that there should be one team called Great Britain. This attitude possibly reflects a more general South American paranoia and inferiority complex about Europe. There is certainly a strong feeling against North America and the USA in particular, and as Europe (at least the western half of it) tended to side with the USA in geopolitical affairs, anything seen as Europe-based tended to be looked upon with suspicion and mistrust.

In addition, and more immediately and more recently, there

140

was the World Cup of 1966, and in particular the quarter-final in which England beat Argentina in what were seen in South America (and, ironically, Scotland) as unfair circumstances. There was thus a definite anti-British feeling in South America, which, to the frenzied mind of a South American football player and supporter, transcended such rational factors as Scotland and England being two separate countries as far as football was concerned. The words "Inglaterra" and "Inglés" were often used when "Great Britain" and "British" would have been more appropriate. The Argentinian fans were even less likely to appreciate that, in any case, the supporters of Celtic Football Club were the least likely people in Great Britain, or indeed the world, to align themselves with England's football team or even the British crown. The situation was replete with paradoxes and ironies.

Be that as it may, we crossed the River Plate to Uruguay. To describe the third game, on November 4, in supposedly neutral Uruguay as a nightmare is an understatement, and no point can be gained by minimising what some Celtic players did in retaliation. Ronnie Simpson was still struggling with his head injury, and I was still in the team, this time, however, having a couple of days to get used to the idea. The team arrived to find a huge bare patch down the centre of the field, and once more there would have been justification for the team refusing to play there, for the pitch would have disgraced many Scottish junior teams. But play we did, going out first to wave a Uruguayan flag at the crowd to get them onside before realising that the crafty Argentinians had done it first.

The details are well known about the sendings-off and other things (there is an excellent book called *Tears in Argentina* by Tom Campbell), but I was one of the few Celtic players to emerge with any credit. I felt I had a fine game and I was well reported in the South American press, referred to as *el pelirrojo* (the redhead) who kept the score down to only 0–1. Jock Stein did not agree, however, shouting at me for losing the only goal of the game – a goal from

141

some distance, which detached observers unanimously agreed was well out of my reach.

The truth is that we failed to keep cool under tremendous provocation, and that the referee was appallingly weak, with frankly not a clue how to deal with the situation. Some of the excesses perpetrated on Jimmy Johnstone in particular were unbelievable, and although some of the dismissals of Celtic players were harsh, others weren't. Indeed, several others might well have been sent off as well. The whole affair, played back with relish and obvious enjoyment by the BBC, reflected very badly on Celtic, and it possibly would have been a great deal better if we hadn't gone to Uruguay in the first place. As for myself, I was relieved to get home in one piece (like the rest of the party) but was astounded to find out that I, like everyone else, was being fined £250 by the club for my part in the fracas.

This punishment, draconian and severe, stunned football, with people like Bertie Mee, the manager of Arsenal, amazed and shocked, as was the rest of the sporting world. It would have to be said that in 1967, £250, although not insignificant, would by no means leave Celtic football players out of pocket, but it seemed to be particularly unfair on me, as I had been called in at short notice and not even committed a foul. It would have been fair enough to mete out this punishment to those who did, so obviously, disgrace the proud reputation of the club, but I, the goalkeeper, was completely innocent.

Two postscripts to the affair perhaps highlight the difference between the cultures of the two continents. One was that the Argentinian players were all willing to shake hands and swap jerseys after the game, and the other was that the South American press in the days and weeks to come did not stress what a dreadful game it had been. They hailed Racing Club as *campeones del mundo* (champions of the world), and praised their own players, and one or two Celtic ones (especially myself), but merely mentioned the *espulsados* (sendings-off) as if it were a matter of course and did not really matter, as long as their team had won the cup. This was in direct contrast to the notoriety that Celtic earned throughout Europe and to the strong, even unfair, action taken by the Celtic directors against their own players. The money went to charity, it was stressed by Mr Kelly.

It would be a long time before anyone at Celtic could honestly claim to have recovered from this awful experience. It was not the sort of thing which one could draw a line under and move on. As far as I was concerned, however, this was only part one of the horror story of winter 1967/68. Worse was to come, but for the moment in the months of November and December with the team not playing well but still grinding out results, I was back in the reserves with Ronnie Simpson returning to the first-team goal.

13

MY NIGHTMARE

I was particularly disappointed not to be playing in the first game after the South America fiasco. The fact that Simpson played a game for the reserves on the Thursday night before the first-team game gave me some hope, but the reserve game was merely used to give Simpson a trial to test his fitness. The first Scottish League game after the return was played in archetypal Scottish conditions in pouring November rain at Broomfield, Airdrie, on November 11. Celtic won 2–0, with good goals from Jim Brogan and Bobby Murdoch, and were given a great reception from their fans, not least Ronnie Simpson, who ran onto the field still wearing a plaster over his head wound. Many people felt that having a game off might have been a good idea for Simpson, especially as Celtic had a capable deputy in myself, who had done so well in South America.

The team, showing a great deal of character, limped to Christmas without impressing too many of their supporters. The 2–0 victory over Raith Rovers at Stark's Park at the end of November was described as "Celtic's worst ever victory", but there was also a particularly thrilling 5–4 win over Dundee at Dens Park in the middle of December. New Year's Day saw a good 3–2 win for Celtic over Clyde at Shawfield. This maintained Celtic's title challenge, but Rangers, playing consistently in spite of having sacked their long-serving manager Scot Symon, replacing him with David White from Clyde, were still two points ahead. Other teams had, perhaps predictably, fallen by the wayside, victims of chronic lack of investment and the fanatical desire to sell their talent for money. Celtic were happy with their 3–2 victory at Shawfield, but unfortunately Ronnie Simpson sustained a rib injury and was ruled out of the all-important Old Firm game at Parkhead on January 2. Was destiny calling on me again?

In fact, I had been meant to play in the Clyde game on New Year's Day, but Ronnie, although suffering from a knock, was given the nod. As it was, I then travelled to Celtic Park on January 2 without knowing for definite whether I was playing or not. I was told in the snooker room about an hour before the start of the game that I would be donning the yellow jersey.

Simpson's misfortune was my opportunity. It was hardly quite as dramatic as my sudden elevation to the goalkeeping spot in Argentina, but it was no less challenging. It was a tall order to step out of the reserves into a 75,000 crowd at Parkhead for a game which Celtic really had to win to bring themselves level with Rangers. I would not have been human if I were not nervous. The game was even more crucial than most Old Firm games in the context of winning the League, for a credible challenger had failed to emerge from the other teams in Scotland. Aberdeen, Dunfermline, Kilmarnock and maybe Dundee United would have their odd moments of glory, but everyone knew that the League title of 1968, like so many other years before and since, would go to either Celtic or Rangers.

The weather was pleasant enough, and the crowd were well behaved, but Celtic, showing a welcome return to good form, were extremely disappointed that the game ended in a 2–2 draw. In fairness, it must be mentioned that there were other factors involved, notably the repeated fouling of Jimmy Johnstone by Rangers defenders, who, as the shrewder members of the press noticed, took it in turns to dish out the raw meat to avoid bookings and sendings-off. It was a well-thought-out tactic of new manager David White and reflected no credit on anyone at Ibrox.

That said, there is no escaping the conclusion that this game was my greatest nightmare. I made two horrendous mistakes that allowed Rangers twice back into the game, and they have haunted me for the rest of my life. Gair Henderson in the following day's *Evening Times*, in an article entitled "Biff, Bang and Blunders", said:

> If Ronnie Simpson's stand-in plays for another ten years, it is a safe bet that he will never feel as miserable as he did yesterday when the final whistle sounded and the Rangers players hugged each other with delight. [Rangers] had done little to deserve a draw and it may have been sheer inactivity that caused Fallon to allow one shot from Willie Johnston to trundle through his legs and that other from Kai Johansen to roll under his body as he dived and missed the harmless shot, which shocked the 75,000 crowd.

My mistakes twice allowed Rangers to equalise. Celtic had scored first from a deflected free kick from Bertie Auld, then had taken the lead late in the game thanks to a lovely goal from Bobby Murdoch. Only three minutes were left when Rangers scored their second equaliser, and the Ibrox fans now realised that they had maintained their two-point lead at the top of the League and only sixteen games remained, none of them against Celtic.

It is difficult to put into words my agonies that night and for the next few weeks. Jock Stein would have blamed me anyway for most goals being lost, so there was not much hope of forgiveness or understanding there, and both Tommy Gemmell and Bobby Murdoch are on record about their resentment that I apparently went around the dressing room after the game with some sort of insouciance, combing my hair and whistling. But insouciant I was not. It was surely the loneliest, most desperate time of my life.

Two things made it worse. The team themselves, still not over the South American fiasco, went out of the Scottish Cup at the end of January to Dunfermline, and, worse than that, I myself was out of the team, apparently now forever. I would not play again that season, so I did not get any chance to redeem myself or to show the fans what I could do. A free transfer seemed to beckon.

Some fans were completely unforgiving. The veteran supporter who had disapproved of my "thumbs up" gesture to the fans at Arbroath in 1959 positively gloated over my misfortune, but he was not the only one, as supporters took their frustration out on me. One always has to be suspicious of such claims as "Celtic supporters are the best in the world". It is frankly not true, for anyone who has watched Celtic for some time has heard men like Steve Chalmers and John Hughes, and even giants of the game like Jimmy Johnstone and Kenny Dalglish, subjected to the most dreadful abuse on occasions when things were not going well for them. In the early days of 1968, my many fine performances were ignored and forgotten about as the support turned viciously on me, inflicting all sorts of agony on myself and my family.

It was, after all, simply a bad day with two bad mistakes. Had I been an outfield player, my errors would not have been so prominent or pointed – indeed, they might not even have been noticed at all, and I might have been able to recover and nullify my errors – but a goalkeeper has no such means of escape. At the end of the day, they were simply mistakes, and anyone who has not made a mistake has never lived. I had chosen the worst possible day and the worst possible opponents. My more sensitive teammates said little – they knew what I was going through – and my fellow goalkeepers would sympathise, but there was no getting away from the fact that I had given every sign of having lost the League for Celtic. It was so unjust, so undeserved.

Years later I discussed the matter with Peter Latchford, who expressed sympathy with the Kai Johansen goal in particular, which was one of those "head-first" dives that goalkeepers find difficult. Other goalkeepers, like Billy Ritchie of Rangers, were publicly supportive, and goalkeepers generally knew what I was going through. One recalls the Scotland v England game at Hampden Park in 1976 when the usually excellent Ray Clemence allowed a half-hit trundler from Kenny Dalglish to go through his legs. I was by no means alone. In addition, on at least three occasions a Scottish goalkeeper has been pilloried by the Scottish and English press for losing an International at Wembley. One thinks of Fred Martin of Aberdeen in 1955, Frank Haffey of Celtic in 1961 and Stewart Kennedy of Rangers in 1975. Kennedy tells the story of years later when he was playing (brilliantly) for Forfar Athletic, and the lonely voice of a cretin on the terracing behind him at Shielfield Park, Berwick, started singing "Wembley! Wembley!" There is no escape for a goalkeeper.

At least one manager sympathised with me. This was George Farm, then the manager of Dunfermline Athletic. Farm was normally brusque, outspoken, tough-talking and not afraid to tell his players to dish out the rough stuff, if necessary. But he had been a goalkeeper himself, capped for Scotland, and he had vivid memories of the 1953 English Cup final. This game was famously won by Stanley Matthews, but earlier in the game a couple of howlers from Farm had allowed Bolton Wanderers to take the lead. Farm had more reason than most to be grateful to Stanley Matthews.

The more respectable and compassionate journalists also sided with me and sympathised. John MacKenzie, the "Voice of Football" in the *Scottish Daily Express*, was widely suspected of having Rangers sympathies but, like Gair Henderson, could not really afford, for circulation reasons, to be completely anti-Celtic, and he wrote this lengthy piece to try to reassure Celtic and myself. It was called "Let's Be Fair To Fallon" and MacKenzie said:

148

John Fallon committed the major sin on Tuesday of letting Celtic down in a game against the arch enemy – Rangers. It would be a crying shame if this excellent young goalkeeper, who has served Celtic so well in the past, should be made to suffer for his tragic lapse. John knows that he let his mates down. He slipped up not once but twice in the one game that matters much more than all the rest. And he has suffered real torment since that shot from Kai Johansen slipped under his body into the net. Fallon is a real Celt, a good servant who has waited patiently for his chance, kept in the shadow of that great veteran Ronnie Simpson.

MacKenzie continued:

But I saw Fallon, as a young player, turn in a fantastic performance for Celtic in Bratislava a few years ago. I watched him bring the house down in Madrid last summer in the Di Stéfano benefit game, with as fine a goalkeeping performance as that great San Bernabéu Stadium has ever seen. In November I suffered with him as he was thrown into the cauldron of the World Club Championship [*sic*] game against Racing Club, after Simpson had been felled with a missile before kick-off. Fallon always seemed to come into the team for the big ones. He never let the team down. Like all goalkeepers he made mistakes . . . and when a keeper slips there is no one behind him to cover up. But more experienced goalkeepers than Fallon have slipped up . . . and his great friend Ronnie Simpson is the first to admit that he has let some daft ones through himself.

He then advised the Parkhead legions:

Celtic supporters were angry at the way the vital point was lost . . . angry that a game that looked won against

149

their age-old rivals was thrown away. But let them too have sympathy for their deputy goalkeeper. Weeks of reserve football waiting patiently for the big one is not the best preparation for the big, vital occasion when it comes. The Celtic fans have often shown their big-heartedness in the past – forgiving mistakes and encouraging players who have come through a bad spell. John Fallon needs their help and sympathy now.

MacKenzie was right. It is like an actor on stage. Any actor, however talented and experienced, is a liar if he claims that he has never forgotten his lines or been late for an entrance. A test batsman, be he Brian Lara or Don Bradman, will now and again miss a simple one and be bowled first ball. A World Chess Champion will now and again, through oversight, lose his queen or leave his king vulnerable. Andy Murray has frequently missed the most simple of smashes. It is all about being human. Never was the old aphorism more appropriate: "To err is human; to forgive is divine." The trouble is that very few football fans are anything vaguely like divine. Some of the abuse that has been directed at me hardly deserved the term human. Amazingly, some older supporters still keep it up.

There was one historical Celtic parallel, but it was a long time ago, in the 1890s. It concerned the great Dan McArthur, arguably as good a goalkeeper as any subsequent ones. Dan was well known for his courage and agility, particularly the former in those days when goalkeepers had little protection from charging and barging. Dan had won two Scottish Cup medals, in 1899 and 1900, but the 1901 Scottish Cup final was Dan's nemesis. Already looking at fault for a couple of the Hearts goals, Dan was despondent when the team were 3–1 down. But then Celtic, inspired by men like Sandy McMahon, fought back, and with minutes remaining turned things round to make it 3–3. But then, in the very last few seconds, Dan

150

fumbled a shot and Hearts scored with the rebound. Poor Dan, and poor Celtic.

The team, without me in the early months of 1968, won League games, but so too, infuriatingly, did Rangers. Now expecting a free transfer at the end of the season, I kept playing in the reserves or travelling in the team bus and supporting the side from the stand, cheering good saves from Ronnie Simpson and acting like a normal supporter without anyone knowing the trauma I was going through. But I simply had to "work through it". A propaganda victory came when Rangers withdrew from the Glasgow Cup, ostensibly because they had too many fixtures. Unlike Celtic, they were still in Europe and the Scottish Cup. But that excuse cut no ice in Glasgow, where Celtic supporters were convinced (and Rangers supporters too in their weaker moments) that the real issue was that Rangers were afraid of Celtic. The phrase used was "crappit it". They had been astonishingly lucky to beat Celtic at the New Year. But Rangers still kept winning League games, often narrowly and luckily.

There was one happy event, however, and that was when Esther gave birth to our fifth child, and the only girl of the family, in February. In early March, however, Stein let it be known that he was interested in signing another goalkeeper. It seemed to be curtains for me, but when the *Scottish Daily Express* let it be known that the goalkeeper in question was the Yugoslav Internationalist Zlatko Škorić, Jim Paterson quoted Stein as saying, "Even if I sign this goalkeeper, Fallon stays with us. A club of Celtic's size requires three top-class goalkeepers, and as far as I am concerned, Fallon stays here." I was glad to hear that and for my part insisted that I was still quite happy at Parkhead: "I love being here and as long as they are happy, then I am too. I shall continue to try and win a regular first-team place."

As winter turned to spring, all that Celtic could do was win their games and hope Rangers would lose. But Stein realised the value of propaganda. Celtic were, after all, still the European Cup holders from the previous season. We were not Champions of Europe for nothing. The orders were to play our best attacking football, impress the neutrals and the media, and allow the pressure to build on Rangers. Rangers, with a new and inexperienced manager, would eventually crack, if Celtic played well enough. How this comes about, no one can tell, but it is certainly true that if one member of the Old Firm plays particularly well, the other will oblige by blowing some of their games. One supposes things like "auto-suggestion" or simply "mental weakness".

Celtic did play very impressively, as winter slowly and reluctantly gave way to spring, with very fine away wins at St Johnstone, Dundee United, Hearts and Aberdeen. The Dundee United victory at Tannadice was a significant one. Celtic won 5–0, knowing that Dundee United would be sufficiently upset to raise their own game for the visit of Rangers the following midweek, given the massive "panning" that they were likely to receive from the manifestly pro-Celtic local Dundee press, spearheaded by Tommy Gallacher, son of the legendary Patsy Gallacher. This indeed happened, and Rangers, travelling to Dundee United "like a man on his way to the dentist", in the words of a supporter, dropped a point at Tannadice to reduce the leeway to just one point. With a bit of luck, United might have won, and the good people of Dundee who had seen both Old Firm teams at Tannadice were in no doubt at all about who was the better side.

The action now moves to the night of Wednesday, April 17 1968, when three matches were being played – Celtic were playing Clyde in the Glasgow Cup final at Hampden, Rangers were at Greenock Morton in the Scottish League, and Celtic Reserves were playing Raith Rovers Reserves at Celtic Park. In front of less than a hundred spectators, I played for Celtic Reserves. (For some first-team games I was taken to watch in case Ronnie had a mishap; other times I played for the reserves.) The reserves duly won 2–1, but no one really bothered too much about that, least of all myself, whose mind was on other things.

A ball boy kept coming to talk to me and tell me the progress of the other two games. Good news came from Hampden, where Celtic beat Clyde 8–0, and even that could have been a great deal better if we had not taken the foot off the gas at half-time, when we were 7–0 up. This was, of course, the same Glasgow Cup that Rangers had withdrawn from – or, as less kind people said, run away from. The Glasgow Cup was no longer the mighty tournament that it had been before the Second World War, but it was still another piece of silverware, won by a truly devastating Celtic performance, arguably as good as any in the Stein era.

But, good though it was, that was not the best part of the night for me. I was still at kick-off time the villain of the piece and was running the risk of going down in history as the man who gifted the League to Rangers at the New Year. Celtic still had to play Morton at home in the League and then to go to Dunfermline for the last game of the season. Rangers were at Morton that night, then had to go to Kilmarnock before facing Aberdeen at home. Neither side had an easy task, but the gap was now only one point in Rangers' favour, assuming they won at Greenock. Rangers were now, however, clearly cracking under the psychological onslaught of many great Celtic performances. In theory, how Celtic were doing in another city and in another tournament had nothing to do with Rangers. In practice, it did – and, of course, in Glasgow football culture, still does.

Rangers had exited the Scottish Cup in March to an ordinary Hearts team at a dangerously overcrowded Tynecastle, then in the Inter-Cities Fairs Cup went down over two legs to Leeds United. Everyone knew, however, that who had really beaten them in both competitions was Celtic, the ever-present green and white spectre which whispered words of depression and dismay to the Rangers players in their weakened mental state, reminding them of Lisbon and the European Cup, mentioning Berwick and

Nuremberg of last year, and emphasising the cowardice of pulling out of the Glasgow Cup. Their heart of hearts told them that they had been lucky to get that draw from Celtic Park at the New Year.

I was told at half-time that Morton were 2–0 up, then soon after half-time it was 3–1. There was no radio commentary at Cappielow (BBC radio coverage in Scotland was poor in 1968), but the English-based Radio 2 gave score flashes from time to time, and the loudspeakers at both Parkhead and Hampden now broadcast the news to keep spectators informed. (There was also my sympathetic ball boy, who was getting very excited as well.) The games that these same spectators had paid to watch now played second fiddle to the mighty events at the Tail of the Bank in that most dismal yet in some ways most vibrant of Scottish towns, Greenock. Greenock and its football team had no reason to love Celtic, but they didn't like Rangers either.

In the second half Rangers scored to make it 3–2, and then again to make it 3–3. That would have been enough to give Celtic the initiative, but it was as well for the weaker of the Celtic following, or indeed myself, that we did not see the frantic and hysterical barrage on Morton's goal. But Morton, with a packed defence and containing one or two unashamed Celtic supporters among them, held out with their Danish star Preben Arentoft (who would later be transferred to Newcastle United) outstanding.

Celtic were now effectively in the lead, given our vastly superior goal average. There were still two games to go, difficult ones, but at least the strain had been taken away from me. If Celtic lost the League now, I would no longer be the only one to blame. With Glasgow now in a ferment of excitement, 51,000 appeared to see Morton at Parkhead. Morton were given a heroes' reception for Wednesday night but then showed that their effort was no fluke and held Celtic at 1–1 until, in the very last minute of the game, Bobby Lennox, to the delight of the spectators, scored off his shin with a miskick to give Celtic the victory. Rangers had been similarly lucky at Kilmarnock, winning by the same 2–1 margin, so Celtic still retained their narrow advantage.

And then Rangers' arrogance once again let them down. The same contemptuous behaviour which had spurned the Glasgow Cup came to the fore in their refusal to postpone their game at Ibrox against Aberdeen the following Saturday. This meant that they were in opposition to the Scottish Cup final between Dunfermline and Hearts. What effect this had on their players we cannot tell, but once again Celtic seized the moral high ground, with Stein taking his players publicly to watch the Scottish Cup final, while Rangers' game was given second billing. To the horror of their fans but to the delight of the Celtic players, myself included, Rangers blew up against Aberdeen, losing 2–3 – their only defeat of the season – and Celtic won the League.

I was relieved, but I was lucky to avoid a free transfer. For this I have to thank Chairman Bob Kelly, who talked Stein out of the idea. There was to be a short tour of America, and Stein intended to leave me at home, taking only Ronnie Simpson, with the intention of recruiting another goalkeeper for the new season, but Kelly advised against that idea. I was indeed taken across the Atlantic. It was a very short tour, more of a holiday, with only three games, two against AC Milan and one against the Mexican side Necaxa.

Stein, duplicitous and manipulative as ever, gave Hugh Taylor of the *Daily Record* to understand that I would be playing in one or other of the glamour games against AC Milan. He said: "John must get his chance again. But I think it's best for him if it's away from Parkhead. There are too many bitter memories at home. I have not lost faith in him, however. I never have. It was always my intention to let him fight for a first-team place. In New Year and Toronto he has a better chance of regaining his confidence and he'll play for part of one of the games at least." This must be regarded as a piece of hypocrisy, and in the event it wasn't even true. Simpson played in both the Milan games (a draw in New York and a victory in Toronto) and the only time that I was called upon to play was in Mexico when Simpson was injured and had to be substituted.

But I was still considered good enough to be on the retained list for the 1968/69 season. It was one of the few occasions where "the chairman knew best" – an especially ironic episode in Celtic history, perhaps, given the reasons that Jock Stein had been brought to Celtic Park in the first place in 1965.

But, for me, the bottom line was that my Celtic career was still to continue. Indeed, my finest hour had yet to come.

14

BORN AGAIN

I began the 1968/69 season with an uncertain future. I had almost been given a free transfer in the summer and did not seem to have any great hope of displacing the evergreen Ronnie Simpson in the goal. In addition, Celtic had recruited a young Ayrshireman called Bobby Wraith with a view, perhaps, to making him the long-term replacement to Simpson, while Stein kept threatening to look for still more goalkeepers. In general terms, however, the atmosphere at Celtic Park remained upbeat and optimistic.

The season started with Celtic, as the previous year, in the same League Cup section as Rangers. We beat them twice, but in the second of these victories, at Parkhead, Simpson picked up a slight injury and thus I was given two games against Morton and Partick Thistle, both comfortable wins for the accomplished Celtic side of that time, as we qualified with ease for the quarter-final of the Scottish League Cup. I was hardly troubled in either game.

Simpson then recovered and I returned to the reserves. Ronnie kept playing well, celebrating his thirty-eighth birthday and still being picked for Scotland. It was while he was playing for Scotland against Austria that he picked up a leg injury, and I found myself back in the team against Arbroath at Gayfield, on November 9. It was actually Sean Fallon in charge that day, for

Jock Stein had gone to Yugoslavia to have a look at Red Star Belgrade that weekend, who were due at Parkhead in the European Cup the following Wednesday. Indeed, it was wondered whether I was merely playing against Arbroath to rest Simpson for the big European game.

I thus returned to the ground on which I had played my second ever game for Celtic some nine years previously, and played impeccably as the team won easily 5–0. Simpson's leg did not heal as quickly as anyone would have liked, and thus I found myself between the sticks for the Red Star game, arguably one of the best games of the Stein era. It also continued the pattern of me being suddenly called in at short notice for a vital fixture, but that, I suppose, is likely to happen if you are the reserve-team goalkeeper, and at least I had a few days to get used to the idea this time.

This was, of course, the game in which Jimmy Johnstone was given the incentive to do well, and did so. Jimmy was chronically afraid of flying – a serious problem in the new age of European and transatlantic travel – and struck a bargain with Jock Stein that if Celtic were four up in the first leg then he wouldn't have to go to Belgrade for the second leg. Those with an eye to the melodramatic often say that this deal was struck just before the start of the game, or even at half-time, but this is not so. It was common knowledge and had been highlighted in the press a few days before.

Such preferential treatment didn't always endear Jimmy to the rest of his teammates, some of whom experienced similar problems, but the fact that Jimmy was, on his game, the best football player in the world meant that his neurotic behaviour tended to be taken a little more seriously. This does not in any way negate the fact that he played a brilliant game at Parkhead that night, teaming up with Bobby Murdoch to defeat the Yugoslavs 5–1. Nor does it negate the fact that whole team played superbly.

I also felt had a good game that night, as I often did against European teams. I had no chance with the Yugoslav goal and had a couple of good saves in the first half but was virtually a spectator in the second half as I watched, along with the other 67,000, the way in which Jimmy tore apart the Red Star side, running off the field shouting, "I'll no need tae go! I'll no need tae go!"

Neither he did, but the rest of the Celtic side did go a couple of weeks later to Belgrade, where we earned a 1–1 draw and qualification for the next round. The outcome might have been different if goals had been scored early in the game, but only once was I beaten in the first half and that was when the ball hit the bar. I also had a great save from Jovan Aćimović. Thereafter, the Celtic defence and myself grew in confidence as the game fizzled out in a large stadium before a tiny crowd. Wallace scored for Celtic late in the game, and Red Star even later in a goalmouth scramble, but by then the tie had been won.

The game was all over by mid-afternoon Glasgow time and the team were home later that night. Three days later, Celtic, at Easter Road – where we frequently turned on our best performances in the late 1960s – proved, if anyone had ever doubted it, that we were a class act. Perhaps it was the fact that Hibs themselves were also a good football team, but games between Celtic and Hibs at that time were invariably great football matches. On this occasion, with Celtic down 1–2 to the fine Hibs side with only quarter of an hour to go, "it was as if Jock Stein had pressed a switch in the dugout", as the BBC TV report said, and Celtic suddenly turned it on and won 5–2 in breathtaking style. I felt that I had a good game that day as well, several times saving in the first half, particularly from my old friend Joe McBride, who had recently joined Hibs.

This was fine Celtic stuff, but then came midwinter, hard pitches and three rather unsatisfactory draws, and then, worse still, a defeat at Ibrox by Rangers in the New Year. The three draws on hard pitches against Falkirk, Kilmarnock and Airdrie were perhaps disappointing for the fans, but they reflected no discredit on me, for two of them were shutouts. Try to imagine, however, what my feelings must have been as the game against Rangers approached with the ever-present thought of the previous New Year hanging over me. This time, though, on a day that was far worse for Celtic than a year previously, I myself emerged with a great deal of credit.

New Year's Day itself was good. The announcement of the knighthood given to Chairman Bob Kelly might have been greeted incredulously by those supporters who remembered how little more than five years ago there had been street demonstrations against him, but the 5–0 win over Clyde was a fine performance, and I was only called upon to make the occasional save or take a pass back as the team demolished our east-end neighbours in a dazzling performance.

However, Ibrox the following day was a different matter. There was a rumour that Ronnie Simpson was going to be coming back soon, and Stein was very keen on the idea of him playing at Ibrox, if at all possible, so that the events of last New Year would not be repeated. Both goalkeepers were brought to Ibrox and Ronnie was given a fitness test. Sadly for Ronnie, he was not quite match fit, and Jock was reluctantly persuaded that he could not play. His words to me, however, were a little short of a ringing endorsement: "You get f***in' ready, and no' like last year!" Moreover, my boots were at the very bottom of the hamper, a clear indication that I was by no means in the forefront of Celtic's thinking for this game.

Yet I had a good game. I was given a hard time by the Rangers crowd and players, who never failed to remind me of last year at Parkhead, but five times John Downie of the *Glasgow Herald* sang the praises of John Fallon. That in itself tells a tale, in that Rangers were able to put more pressure on the Celtic defence than it used to. As it turned out, the game was settled by a disputable penalty, but it is also true that we failed to exert sufficient domination to turn things around, and for the second New Year in a row the blue half of Glasgow was considerably happier than the green one. Following the three draws in December and now the defeat to Rangers, we were in a midseason slump.

Yet Celtic were still in the lead over Rangers in the League race, and nothing was as yet lost. The year 1969 seemed to offer a great deal, for, apart from the Scottish League, the Scottish Cup and the European Cup, the Scottish League Cup had still to be played for, and Celtic were in the final, which had been postponed because of a fire in the Hampden stand in October only a few days before the final was due. Serious challenges and great opportunities to redeem myself now beckoned for me, but would I be able to hold on to my place now that Ronnie Simpson was approaching full fitness?

I played against Dunfermline Athletic on Saturday, January 4 at Parkhead. It was a game that Celtic simply had to win in order to bounce back from the New Year defeat by Rangers, and we did, but the 3–1 win was a curiously lacklustre performance. Once again I was highly regarded in the press, and the Celtic fans were given a boost with the news that Rangers had dropped a point in an exciting but nasty game at Rugby Park, Kilmarnock.

Stein had dropped Jimmy Johnstone for the Dunfermline game, to make a point presumably about his perceived poor performance in the New Year's Day game. Stein had no injury worries for the next game against Aberdeen, at Pittodrie, but I was deeply disappointed to discover that I was being dropped in favour of Ronnie Simpson. I felt I had done well enough, but it was back to the reserves. The press stressed that I had had seven shutouts in thirteen games and was by no means a failure, and the general feeling was that Celtic, in view of their heavy programme to come in the early months of 1969, were giving both goalkeepers match practice. Other teams would often watch Celtic with admiration for and envy of the fact that we had two goalkeepers of such calibre.

Ronnie stayed in goal for the month of January, but then the beginning of the end of his long and remarkable career came on Wednesday, February 12 at Shawfield in a Scottish Cup tie against Clyde. It was a dreadful 0–0 draw on a frozen and barely playable pitch. (The game had been postponed on the Saturday, but it was little better on the Wednesday night.) Early in the game, Ronnie was injured as he dived at the feet of a Clyde player (ironically, it was young Jimmy Quinn, a Celtic player on loan to Clyde and grandson of the great Jimmy Quinn of blessed memory) and after seventeen minutes had to withdraw. Tommy Gemmell took over in goal for the rest of the game and Bertie Auld came on as a substitute. It was a bad day for Celtic, who were unable to force a victory, but the severity of Ronnie's injury, a badly dislocated shoulder, effectively meant that I would now be in the Celtic goal for the rest of the season, whether my manager liked me or not.

Continuing my tradition of being thrown in at the deep end, my first game was in the San Siro against AC Milan in the European Cup quarter-final. The press carried a story that Simpson was not going to Milan and that my deputy would be young Bobby Wraith. This may have been an attempt to split up what Stein saw as an unhealthy friendship between Simpson and myself, but on the other hand he can hardly be blamed for his decision. It made little sense to take an injured man when a substitute goalkeeper was required in any case. It would have been nice to have Ronnie with me, though.

Saturday's Scottish League match had been postponed, but then Celtic flew to Italy to find conditions little different from the harsh Scottish winter. It doesn't snow all that often in Milan, but it did that night of February 19, as Celtic excelled themselves and exceeded all expectations to gain a 0–0 draw. It was not the greatest game of that season, but both goalkeepers, Fabio Cudicini and myself, were singled out for praise: me for a great save in the very first minute and then another one just prior to half-time, before Celtic came more into the game in the second half. It was a fine

162

defensive performance, and I was lavishly praised in the press. Jock Stein added his opinion: "I was also very pleased with John Fallon, who has not had a great deal of practice recently. Lack of active work has more effect on keepers than outfield players."

An odd thing happened before this game, an interesting one in view of the current obsession about diet in the hearts and minds of some modern managers. On the night before the game, the players came in to the dining room of the hotel to discover the tables laden with lovely Italian pasta made by the chef, who had at one point worked in the culinary department of AC's great rivals Inter Milan. Jock Stein was less than impressed, however, stating that he would have preferred his men to have been given chips.

Stein was a traditional Scottish miner who saw nothing wrong with a fatty diet. His obsession and paranoia about alcohol are well known, and he was clearly unhappy about both his goalkeepers, Simpson and myself, enjoying the occasional cigarette, but there was never any restriction on diet. It simply was not an issue with him, unless you were Bobby Murdoch, who had a serious and recurrent problem with his weight. Two other stories are told about dietary habits. Bobby Jeffrey, who played intermittently for Celtic and earned recognition at Scotland Under-23s, once amazed everyone in a restaurant by asking for "mince and tatties", whereas on the other end of the spectrum, a member of the Celtic squad of a marginally higher social class than the others, earned a certain amount of ridicule by asking for a prawn cocktail.

Sadly the European adventure came to naught when AC Milan visited Celtic Park on March 12. Again, it was a close match with little between the teams other than the bad mistake by Billy McNeill which allowed the Italians to score the only goal of 180 minutes. It happened within the first quarter of an hour, when McNeill breasted down a throw-in but took his eye off the ball, and Pierino Prati seized his opportunity to run on and score. I was not to blame – most newspaper reports give me a lot of credit for my part in this game – but Celtic could not quite convert the number of half chances that came our way and, to the immense disappointment of the 75,000 crowd, we departed the European Cup at the quarter-final stage.

Often, however, one can define the calibre of a team by its ability to fight back from adversity and to recover from a disastrous result – if a defeat to AC Milan could be described as a disaster. By the time that we met Milan, we had already reached the semi-final of the Scottish Cup and had progressed in the League. We had beaten Clyde comfortably enough in the replay of the game in which Ronnie had been injured and then faced on March 1 a very tight match at Parkhead against St Johnstone. Celtic scored first and with ten minutes remaining were a comfortable 3–1 up, until Henry Hall scored with a fine header, and the Saints then made it very tough for us as they pressed for an equaliser. But I kept my nerve, coming out with confidence for high cross balls, and I saved a low shot near the end, and no replay at Muirton Park was necessary.

Three weeks later we reached the final of the Scottish Cup with a good win over Morton at Hampden after the Greenock men, through Allan McGraw, had had the temerity to score first. This was the game in which Celtic appeared in all white and came out first, thereby fooling some of our spectators at the top of the East Terracing, who thought that this was Morton! On that same day, Rangers put Aberdeen to the sword at Celtic Park in the other semi-final, and thus the third Old Firm Scottish Cup final of the decade was set up.

It was, however, Muirton Park, Perth, which saw the beginning of Celtic's best ever month. April Fools' Day, a pleasant spring evening, saw Celtic two goals down at half-time to the excellent Perth side of Willie Ormond. This looked as if it were going to be a severe setback to our ambitions of retaining the Championship, but if ever the phrase "that's what champions are made of" meant anything, it did that night at the venerable old Muirton ground. I had no chance with either of the two goals scored against me in the first half, both of them scored from a distance, and for a long time in the second half I was busy enough to have it suggested that Celtic were in for a severe beating. Things had not been helped with a bad injury to John Hughes (who had a tendency to get injured at that ground) early in the game.

But the last quarter of the game saw us simply turn it on, playing the brilliant football of which we were capable and leaving the Perth locals and the large Celtic following alike bewildered at how the game had turned. First Willie Wallace pulled one back and then Tommy Gemmell hit a goal out of nothing through a ruck of players, and then, with time running out, Harry Hood got the winner after Wallace hit a Murdoch lob onto the post and Harry was there for the rebound. Some people would call that lucky; others called it inspired football.

This was breathtaking stuff, but it was only the start. The sunny Saturday of April 5 1969 saw the first cup final of the season, the League Cup final postponed since October because of the fire at Hampden. This was a good break for me, because I would probably not have been in the team if the final had gone ahead on its original date. The opponents were Hibs, a team also renowned for their attacking football and simply hoaching with talent, as a glance at their team line-up would indicate: .

Hibs: Allan, Shevlane and Davis; Stanton, Madsen and Blackley; Marinello, Quinn, Cormack, O'Rourke and Stevenson

Celtic: Fallon, Craig and Gemmell; Murdoch, McNeill and Brogan; Johnstone, Wallace, Chalmers, Auld and Lennox.

Referee: W. Syme, Glasgow.

Many supporters (there were 74,000 of them present that day) rate this particular game as the best example of pure Celtic attacking football in the Stein era. It is an ambitious claim to make, but on that fine spring Easter Saturday, Celtic simply tore the Edinburgh men to shreds with three goals in the first half at the Celtic End of the ground and three goals in the second half at the Mount Florida End. Hibs scored a couple of late, irrelevant goals. "Celtic's Easter Parade" trumpeted the *Evening Times*, with Gair Henderson finding it difficult to pick out any Celtic player as being better than the others, except "of course Jimmy Johnstone". In truth, Bertie Auld was immense, Lennox was fast and became the second Celtic player to score a hat-trick in a League Cup final after Billy McPhail, and even Jim Craig got a goal at the end. The disappointment at losing to AC Milan was now paid back. Yet, if anything, it made it all the more difficult to accept, for a team playing like we did were clearly world-beaters.

I felt that my part in this was by no means minimal. Twice, with the score at 2–0, I saved difficult shots from Peter Marinello, who was giving Tommy Gemmell a hard time, and then early in the second half, when Hibs came out to attempt a spirited recovery, I saved in quick succession from Marinello, Cormack and Stevenson. Shortly after this, Lennox scored a fourth for Celtic, and the game was effectively over with thirty minutes to go. Glyn Edwards in the *Glasgow Herald* has no doubts about my contribution: "Fallon, often criticised, finally won the hearts of the sceptics with three wondrous saves at a critical time of the match."

It was a day on which it was great to simply be a member of this superb team. It was not bad to be a supporter either. The sight of Billy McNeill lifting the League Cup for the fourth successive time (it was Celtic's sixth triumph in that competition overall) was a tremendous lift after the Milan heartbreak. It was a day which really did not need any more good news, but we were celebrating in the dressing room when we heard that Dundee United had defeated Rangers 2–1.

"The Huns goat bate two-wan" was the news that reached the supporters as they stood in the queues for the trains at Mount

Florida Station and in fact Dundee United's victory over Rangers at Tannadice strengthened Celtic's position at the top of the League. It was one of these days when one wonders if there is some kind of telepathy which affects players a hundred miles away. It happened in 1968 when Rangers eventually buckled under the effect of great Celtic performances elsewhere. It now happened in 1969 as well. Celtic had in the past often been accused of accepting a "slave mentality" to Rangers. Now it was clearly happening the other way round.

The *Scottish Daily Express* on the Monday quotes Jock Stein as saying about me: "I am very pleased with John. He asked for no favours in his comeback bid and has merited his success." Praise indeed from someone who praised seldom! I myself, who had slightly injured my shoulder during the game and was doubtful for the next game, was quoted as saying: "I am playing with great confidence at the moment and that is what really matters." Jim Rodger confirmed that I had had some tremendous saves, and adds: "He was not afraid to give his defence 'stick' when they slipped up and became careless in the closing stages", surely a sign of increasing confidence, for I had now experienced both of Rudyard Kipling's two great impostors: "triumph" and "disaster".

Because of my injured shoulder, I finished the League Cup final in a certain amount of pain. But I was able to collect my first ever Scottish League Cup medal, and although there was a certain amount of doubt about whether I would miss Wednesday's game against Falkirk, I rallied enough to take part and gritted my teeth through the pain, and the team won 5–2.

Rangers folding at Tannadice meant that Celtic were now five points ahead with five games left. As it turned out, the League was won in anticlimactic circumstances. We drew with Airdrie on Saturday, April 19, then on the Monday at Kilmarnock struggled again for a 2–2 draw, this time being indebted to a late Tommy Gemmell equaliser after a performance which was hardly

167

League Championship-winning stuff. But the following night, Dundee did the job for us when they beat Rangers at a half-full Dens Park. It would have happened anyway, but it would have been nice to see the title won in more triumphant circumstances. Nevertheless, another medal had come my way, even though Rangers had won both Scottish League games against Celtic.

There remained the Scottish Cup final, Rangers' last chance of a trophy this season. The game was equally balanced, historically, for both sides had won the trophy nineteen times, but current form clearly favoured the Parkhead side. But there were other factors as well – indeed, there was a "Stein" factor in each side. Jock, of course, was the manager of Celtic, determined to win a domestic treble as he had done in 1967, and possibly all the more committed to the idea following the heartbreak of the departure from Europe a month earlier. Rangers' "Stein" factor concerned their centre forward Colin Stein (no relation to Jock), who had been bought from Hibs earlier in the season. He could certainly score goals but had an unfortunate propensity to get himself sent off.

He had been suspended for his latest misdemeanour – a silly kick at a Clyde player in the last minute of a game which Rangers had won 6–0 – but a half-hearted attempt was made by a few glory-hunting journalists, who even involved a Morton director, to get the suspension delayed so that Stein could play in the Scottish Cup final, which should, of course, be a "showcase" (we were told) and would be enhanced by his presence. Rangers themselves, for a while, went along with this daft notion, which would surely have destroyed the very credibility of Scottish football, before seeing the madness of it all and dropping the idea.

No such tantrums were thrown when Jimmy Johnstone was suspended for us. This was an accumulation of offences, usually retaliation, but Celtic accepted their punishment and got on with it, bringing in young George Connelly. John Hughes had also not recovered from his injury sustained at Perth on April 1, so Celtic had problems with their forward line, if one could honestly describe George Connelly and Bertie Auld as less than adequate substitutes.

I faced this game well aware that my performance a year past January had not been forgotten, but also with a new-found confidence following what I had done after my return to the side in February. I did, after all, now have two medals this season already, but the Scottish Cup would be a great bonus. Yet in spite of this buoyancy and the general optimism pervading the side, I would not have been human if the events of January 2 1968 did not keep recurring in my mind.

Both teams went off to the Ayrshire coast to prepare for the big game, Celtic to Troon and Rangers to Largs. Rangers made a rather premature announcement that the Scottish Cup would be brought back to Ibrox for some sort of victory parade on the Saturday evening. It was, of course, a propaganda stunt designed to make everyone assume that they were going to win. Yet it was amateurish and ill-thought-out, and has been compared to Hitler's projected victory parades in London and Leningrad. They might have got away with it in the old days of the early 1960s, when Celtic gave every impression of being afraid of them, but under Jock Stein it was a different matter.

Some newspapers tipped Rangers, and a certain amount of money went on for them at the bookmakers. Their supporters were upbeat and determined. They had lost the Scottish League but were still in the Inter-Cities Fairs Cup, where a date with Newcastle United beckoned in the semi-final. They had good players, on whom they had spent a small fortune by the standards of the 1960s: Andy Penman, Alex Ferguson, Dave Smith and Örjan Persson, in addition to their International defenders Ron McKinnon and John Greig, that tough, determined character, not to mention Kai Johansen, who had won the Cup for them in 1966.

But there was no getting away from the fact that we were the champions and had recently shown in the League Cup final just how well we could play. "Mind you, they won't be three goals up at half-time in the Scottish Cup final like they were in the League Cup final," said the *Scottish Daily Express* on the morning of the game – a prediction that would come back to haunt the writer. It was admitted that Celtic could be ruthlessly determined and professional when we needed to be but could play with a great deal of panache and flair as well.

Scotland often confuses religion and football, it is said, and most sensible people now accept that religion should be kept out of football. But this did not prevent even such a person as the Moderator of the General Assembly of the Church of Scotland, a man who told everyone that he was a Motherwell supporter, admitting on TV that watching Celtic in the League Cup final was the way that football should be played. Some Rangers supporters saw this as treason.

As the bus headed to Hampden that day, what was going on in our heads? Amidst all the jokes and banter, all the speculation of what was going to happen in the English Cup final to be played the same day between Manchester City and Leicester City, and all the pretended sangfroid and "we'll be all right", there was the undeniable realisation that this was a match which ranked only marginally below Lisbon, in which I had been a substitute, and Buenos Aires, in which I had played. The "Fallon factor" of January 1968 had been mentioned in the press now and again in the build-up, but only in the context of the nerves, which would affect other players as well. It was certainly something of which I was well aware. But there was also a confidence in the team which permeated through to me as well.

Jock also got the tactics dead right. George Connelly and Bertie Auld, the two replacement wingers for Jimmy Johnstone and John Hughes, were told to stay on their wings and as close as possible to the halfway line. He said this because he knew that Rangers liked to man mark, and therefore Kai Johansen and Willie Mathieson would stay as close to them as possible, thus leaving the Rangers central defence of John Greig and Ron McKinnon exposed to the thrusts of Wallace and Chalmers, and, in particular, the speed of Lennox. This disorientation of the Rangers defence was certainly a factor in the errors they would make and the goals they would concede.

There would be only a few less than 134,000 in the Hampden arena that day. This was only the seventh Old Firm Cup final. Celtic had won only twice in 1899 and 1904, whereas Rangers had won their first Scottish Cup against Celtic in 1894, then the occasion of the famous Meiklejohn penalty of 1928 before the two more recent and still painful ones of 1963 and 1966. Rangers had the better recent cup final pedigree, but there was also a more tragic precedent in 1909 when the Scottish Cup had to be withheld after the Hampden riot. Given the general behaviour of football crowds in the late 1960s, no one ruled that one out either.

The teams were:

> Celtic: Fallon, Craig and Gemmell; Murdoch, McNeill and Brogan; Connelly, Wallace, Chalmers, Lennox and Auld.
>
> Rangers: Martin, Johansen and Mathieson; Greig, McKinnon and D. Smith; Henderson, Penman, Ferguson, Johnston and Persson.
>
> Referee: J. Callaghan, Glasgow.

Celtic won the toss and chose to play towards our own fans at the King's Park End of the ground. As an aside, the *Evening Times* tells that the coin used was a new hexagonal coin, which in 1971 would become the new fifty-pence piece when the country's coinage was decimalised. I ran to the Mount Florida End to endure the jeers of the Rangers fans, but even before my nerves had settled, events at the other end of the ground took over.

Within a few minutes, Celtic were ahead. A corner was forced, taken by Lennox, and McNeill headed home. Rangers had

171

committed the cardinal sin of nobody going up with McNeill and compounding the felony by failing to man the right-hand post. It was a free gift, but that must not in any way take anything away from the way Celtic took the opportunity. Film footage of the aftermath is revealing. Alex Ferguson, the man detailed to watch McNeill at corners, is seen holding his head in his hands (maybe "I should turn to management rather than playing" was going through his head) while John Greig is angrily pointing at the right-hand post and asking Kai Johansen, the hero of 1966, why he had not been *in situ*.

The game now turned nasty (the *Glasgow Herald* uses the word "spiteful"), with Rangers going all out for an equaliser, and one particular charge on me by a man who is now a household name all over the world, Sir Alex Ferguson, does not get any better the oftener one watches it on YouTube. But I held firm, with one or two good saves, one in particular from Örjan Persson, as Celtic rode out the storm, until the couple of minutes before half-time when first Lennox and then Connelly took advantage of further Rangers defensive errors to put Celtic three up.

Three weeks ago, we had gone in at half-time three goals up in the League Cup final against Hibs. "Aye, they'll no' be going in three goals up against Rangers" was the conventional wisdom before the game and was mentioned, as we have seen, in the press. Oh, no? Jock had to work hard to calm everyone down and persuade us that there was still a second half to go through. It would be a torrid forty-five minutes.

I was relieved that for the second half I had the Celtic supporters behind me, for the Rangers fans at the other end turned nasty and invaded the field, some of them claiming, improbably, that they simply wanted to go home. The Glasgow Police did not swallow that and sadistically pushed them back onto the terracing to watch more of the game. By this time, we had scored again through Steve Chalmers, and the game finished with me making a great save from Willie Johnston, which lead to an unwarranted

172

and waspish comment from Glyn Edwards of the *Glasgow Herald*: "Nor did it matter a hoot that that Fallon brought off a superlative save from Johnston in the dying minutes – except for the fact that it could only have convinced the Celtic contingent in the crowd of 132,000 that the goalkeeper can now be trusted implicitly." There was still a corner of the Celtic support that barracked me, even in that cup final. I enjoyed waving to them at the end.

Some of this was barely believable, and does little to support the view that Celtic fans are the greatest in the world, but it was only part of a campaign by some so-called Celtic fans never to let me forget my disaster of January 2 1968. Things had been shouted at me near my house in Blantyre by the sillier elements of the Celtic support, who dispensed pearls of wisdom like, "We hate John Fallon!" There is no way of reasoning with or talking to that kind of mentality – the Scottish educational system does have its failures – and one can also mention similar treatment being given to other Celtic players.

The most spectacular was perhaps Steve Chalmers. One recalls a day at Tannadice Park in May 1963 (astonishingly, only four days before the Scottish Cup final replay) when Chalmers was having a shocker on the left wing. The criticism of Chalmers by a section of the support lacked any reason or rational thought. It was sheer vitriol and filth delivered by louts, and hardly likely to improve the play of Chalmers either in this game or in the imminent cup final. Oh, but how we would have loved to see the facial expressions of the ignorant when the same Steve Chalmers, four years later in Lisbon, scored the goal which won the European Cup!

It is to be emphasised that such behaviour, although more widespread than one would like, was not universal, and for most Celtic supporters my redemption was welcomed and greeted with joy. I was officially presented, as it were, to the Celtic End by other members of the team at the close of the game and then the team went up to get the trophy. No lap of honour was possible after the Scottish League Cup final of 1965 when Rangers fans had invaded the field in an apparent fatuous attempt to steal the League Cup. But the Celtic team in 1969 passed the Scottish Cup back to one another, each player earning a cheer like a "Hail Caesar" in the arena of Ancient Rome, and I was given as great a cheer as anyone. After that, felt I was walking on air or even flying as the team travelled to the Royal Stuart Hotel to celebrate. It was, by some distance, the best day of my playing career. My resurrection was complete.

Rodger Baillie, the respected journalist of the *Sunday Mirror*, wrote the first of the *Playing for Celtic* books in 1969. He sums the Scottish Cup final up thus:

> It would not be a Cup final without heroes. Celtic had two of them. George Connelly, drafted into the first team for his first full match since October and playing as if he had never been out . . . And 'keeper John Fallon, who for so long looked as if his career was going to be fatally affected by the disaster of the 1968 New Year game against Rangers. I liked the way Jim Craig and Billy McNeill rushed to him at the end and presented the 'keeper to the crowd . . . a nice touch.

Hugh Taylor in the *Daily Record* echoes these sentiments:

> Although the final had too many niggles, too many nasty moments, it will never be forgotten by John Fallon, who has surely at last come out of the shadows and was a magnificent goalkeeper against the team which not so long ago seemed to have ruined his career. And it was a great example of Parkhead camaraderie when defensive colleagues "presented" him to the fans at the end for the ovation that he deserved. For John was a Celt who played a great part, one save in particular being vital. It was from

174

Persson at a stage when Rangers were going fiercely for the equaliser. Fallon stopped the ball – and probably turned the whole tide of the game.

I myself gave a quote to Alec "Candid" Cameron of the same *Daily Record*. Cameron says that as goalkeeper I had one of the best games of my career and then I said, "When we're not in the team, we're hoping that the man who is has a great game. That's why we do so well." I knew, of course, what I was talking about in saying this, and was, as much as anything, here alluding to the great help that I received from Ronnie Simpson in the build-up to the game.

The team had won a domestic treble in April. It was astounding. Three medals in three weeks! But then, just to deter anyone from getting too carried away, there was a small blip and Celtic were cut down to size. On the Monday afterwards, we played our second-last League fixture against Morton at Parkhead. The trophies were displayed in the centre circle before the game, and each player, myself included, was given a round of applause from the triumphant 34,000 crowd. Then everyone settled back to watch the football.

Within ten minutes, the Celtic defence, admittedly without Craig and Brogan from Saturday's team, had conceded three goals. Sheer complacency and lack of concentration was the cause. The team eventually rallied and made a game out of it but still lost 2–4 to a Morton side who earned a few cheers from the Parkhead crowd. Stein was furious at such a performance, which ultimately did not matter in the slightest but did show what could happen when the team took our foot off the pedal. We then finished off the season by beating Dundee 2–1 at Dens Park in what was a better game of football.

Summer 1969 was a great time for Celtic supporters to be alive, although there was a dreadful Home International series in which Scotland went down 1–4 to England at Wembley. I even began to entertain a few thoughts about a Scotland cap, and to this day I am of the belief that I would have been chosen to play for Scotland in one of the four games played that summer – against the three other British countries and then a World Cup qualifier against Cyprus – had Jock Stein, by using his influence over the gentlemanly but malleable Bobby Brown, not spitefully prevented my selection.

There was an additional factor: I was eligible, through my grandfather, to play for Eire as well as Scotland. Charlie Gallagher had already done just that, and apparently the Eire team made a few enquiries about my availability. Once more, I believe, Jock Stein blocked any move. Such things are hard to prove, but I remain convinced, and in this respect I was backed up by a respected journalist, the late James Sanderson. Why did Jock do this? Why did he feel that he needed to do this? The season was over, and any injury I sustained would have healed up by August. It was, I am convinced, sheer spite.

In the event, Scotland had a shocker against England in the Wembley International, and the Celtic community would certainly have experienced a few moments of angst when they watched on their TV screens AC Milan win the European Cup that year by beating Ajax 4–1 in Madrid. That so easily could have been Celtic. It would have been no injustice, for the Celtic team in 1969 was good enough. I remain proud to have been part of it.

15

THE BEGINNING OF THE END

For Celtic fans, including myself, the 1969/70 season simply could not come quick enough. April 1969 had been the best single month in the history of the club, and there seemed no reason at all why last year's success could not be repeated. Not only that, but everyone was aware that it was only one mistake that had deprived the team of a chance to get to the European Cup semi-final, and there was an anxiety to prove to everyone that summer 1967 had been no fluke. There were those who argued cogently that the team in 1969 was at least the equal of 1967. It is interesting to note in passing that although the European Cup exit was almost entirely due to an error by Billy McNeill (you could also argue that John Clark as the "sweeper" might have been better placed), there was no intense persecution of McNeill, as there had been of me in 1968. But in any case, my performances in 1969 had redeemed me to a considerable extent.

Rangers in 1969 had brought back Jim Baxter. Baxter had left them in 1965, a departure which had done neither of them a great deal of good. Baxter had played for Sunderland and Nottingham Forest but had attracted more attention for his off-field activities than for what he had done on it. Rangers, of course, had clearly lost out in a big way to Stein's Celtic, and Baxter, apart from one spectacular and famous performance for Scotland at Wembley in

1967, had failed to impress in England. His return to Ibrox, much heralded to fool the gullible, did have a look of desperation about it, and it soon became obvious from the pictures that appeared in the pro-Rangers *Scottish Daily Express* and other papers that the name "Slim Jim" was no longer very appropriate.

At Celtic, I shared the general euphoria. I knew that I had done well in the glory month of April and that I had in particular distinguished myself with my courageous display in the Scottish Cup final, making myself a hero in the eyes of most of, if not all, the support. Some people might have suspected that Ronnie Simpson would be given a free transfer in the summer, thus bringing to an end an astonishing career of a quarter of a century, but he was kept on. However, when the season opened in August 1969, it was myself who was in the goalkeeping spot, and I was determined that I was going to keep it that way. Gair Henderson in the *Evening Times* in his eve-of-season preview stated that Jimmy Johnstone was out of the Celtic side for the game against Airdrie because he was not yet back in favour, Jim Craig was still injured, and Ronnie Simpson was "no longer first-team choice as goalkeeper" and gave way to "his great friend John Fallon".

Ronnie had yielded his position in a pre-season friendly at Carlisle on August 2. The team lost, and I was brought on in the last few minutes with instructions to kick the ball out down the field in front of the wingers (bizarre instructions, perhaps), but I was then retained for a thrilling 1–1 draw with Leeds United at Parkhead on the following Tuesday. I made "not a semblance of a mistake", according to the press, and was retained now in the goal.

For the third year in a row, Celtic and Rangers found themselves in the same League Cup section with Airdrie and Raith Rovers, both of whom were capable of pulling off a shock against the big boys and relished the big crowds but did not really expect to win the section. Celtic's season opened with an excellent 6–1 defeat of Airdrie before 40,000 at Parkhead in the typical Glasgow weather for that time of year: warm sunshine interspersed with heavy showers of rain. It was one of John Hughes' best performances, with one goal in particular where he waltzed through the whole defence to score remaining long in the mind.

But that evening's edition of the *Evening News* has Gair Henderson urging Scotland manager Bobby Brown to "cap" Fallon. I am described as the goalkeeper with "the flaming-red hair but the ice-cool temperament" who had not put a foot wrong in the pre-season games: "Having seen him in action against St Etienne in France, Carlisle United and Leeds United, I can give this first-hand report on his performances – not only was he a dead-safe goalkeeper: he was an inspiration to the players out in front of him."

"Fallon," said Henderson, "is still haunted by his double blunder of eighteen months ago, but there is no man in the world who has never made a mistake", and he thought that Bobby Brown, Scotland's manager, would do well to watch me in detail. Brown would not be drawn on his plans for Scotland, but there was a plethora of good goalkeepers around, such as Jim Cruickshank of Hearts, Donald Mackay of Dundee United and Tommy Lawrence of Liverpool, and his mind was still open.

Henderson then highlighted how well I performed in the pre-season of 1969: "In the three games he made at least a dozen saves look ridiculously easy . . . he did not drop one ball in the 270 minutes and he proved himself worthy at cutting out the dangerous crosses that came over not under the crossbar but at that dangerous distance – six or seven yards out." Jock Stein seemed to agree, although there is an element of damning with faint praise: "Fallon is keeping Ronnie Simpson out of our team, and until he was injured last season, Simpson was Scotland's first choice as goalkeeper. So Fallon must be in top-class form." It was not quite a ringing endorsement, but then again Jock was not always given to such things, even with his acknowledged geniuses, Bobby Murdoch and Jimmy Johnstone.

Yet there were still those who were not pleased with me. Peter Black in the *Weekly News* singled out a few Celtic supporters in my village of Blantyre who were quite happy to describe their bus as the "We Hate John Fallon" bus. Peter Black was happy to use words like "morons" and "cretins" to describe such people, and in truth it always is difficult to deal with the ignorant, who are apparently oblivious to the harm that they can cause to someone's wife and family. Sometime later a letter appeared in the *Celtic View* from a Mr Frew of the Kinlochleven Celtic Supporters' Club "in the corner of the Highlands", who deplored this attitude and told how even after the 1969 League Cup final against Hibs, a "fan" was roundly abusing me. But then Mr Frew said, to nobody's surprise, "he had had too much to drink".

The 1969/70 season was off to a good start for both myself and Celtic with the game against Airdrie, but Rangers and Baxter awaited at Ibrox on Wednesday night. The game was a disappointment. We got off to a good start with a goal from Harry Hood, but that was as good as it got. Bobby Murdoch was badly injured and his presence in midfield was sorely missed. In addition, one or two players chose to have an off-night and Rangers were allowed back into the game. I could not really be blamed for the loss of the first goal, when Örjan Persson was given too much room by some slack marking, but I would have to take a share at least of the collective blame for the second goal. Celtic were still coming to terms with the psychological effects of the first goal when a free kick from Jim Baxter found John Greig at the edge of the box. He then headed the ball across the penalty area and Willie Johnston on the other side of the goal headed home.

It was a goal scored at the Celtic End of the ground, and to those behind that goal it looked bad. Some immediately blamed me for it all, but there were others who could have cut the ball out as well. Celtic then rallied and tried to get back into the game, which they had thrown away, but without the injured Murdoch it was too much, and Rangers held out for a 2–1 win.

But this was not the end of the story. A week later the tables were turned. Celtic had beaten Raith Rovers by some distance on the Saturday with me hardly troubled, and then Rangers came to Parkhead on Wednesday, August 20. This was a remarkable game. Once again I would have to admit that it preyed on my nerves, with the added dimension that this was my first game at Parkhead against Rangers since the horrors of January 1968, but this time it was the other goalkeeper, the luckless German Gerhardt Neef, who made the mistake and allowed Tommy Gemmell to head home the only goal of the game. It was improbably claimed and sung that "he scored it with his nose", in a reference to Tommy's fairly obvious facial feature. Although delighted with the victory, I could spare a thought for my counterpart in the Rangers goal.

For my part, I thought I had an excellent game, with at least one good save and otherwise radiating command. But this was the game when Rangers felt that John Hughes should have received his marching orders after an incident with a Rangers player who probably did not help his cause by making a meal of it. It was, however, an example of how refereeing breaks were now going in Celtic's direction, when for years we had claimed that we did not get a fair deal. On this occasion all sorts of things happened – incredibly, the fact that the referee, Mr Callaghan, had an Irish name was brought into it, and that was by journalists who should have known a lot better – and Callaghan was later suspended for his error. It was clear that accepting defeat gracefully was not yet part of the Ibrox psyche.

There was also that night an example of the primitive nature of football coverage on BBC TV. The game was apparently dead-locked at 0–0, then with a Rangers player rushing in on goal and me coming out to narrow the angle, the picture suddenly faded. There was a brief apology that they couldn't show any more because of technical problems, but they also announced that Celtic had won 1–0! There were those who saw some sort of conspiracy here (admittedly there were historical precedents for the BBC being reluctant to show Celtic successes against Rangers), but the whole thing was just sheer incompetence.

This game was also the start of a prolonged Rangers collapse that season: Baxter was out injured (he had never really been fit) and the pressure now began to mount, spearheaded by Willie Waddell (who had his own reasons, in that he wanted the Rangers manager's job for himself) in the *Scottish Daily Express* on their young manager David White. Perhaps predictably, they blew up against Raith Rovers three days later, and Celtic qualified with ease.

I then had a couple of good games against Aberdeen as Celtic qualified for the League Cup semi-final with a goalless draw at Pittodrie and a narrow but deserved 2–1 win at Celtic Park after Aberdeen had taken the lead. I was particularly pleased with my performance in the Pittodrie game, being only once beaten by a header which rebounded off the bar, and although I had my moments of uncertainty in the first half at Parkhead when the team were under pressure, I rallied well, and once the team had gone ahead, the whole defence showed great composure when Aberdeen pressed hard in the last few desperate minutes.

The League campaign, however, did not get off to the best of starts. Celtic, with their eye on Europe as well, suffered two narrow but disappointing defeats in successive weeks, against Dunfermline at East End Park and then Hibs at Parkhead. However, in the next game Harry Hood scored the only goal to beat Rangers at a wet Ibrox. The Dunfermline game saw a goal conceded when a ball bounced off my body on the way to the net, but there were other people who were responsible for the defeat as well, notably Willie Wallace, who got himself sent off. The Hibs game was lost in the last minute, and the Celtic defence collectively had to take the blame.

But Stein irrationally blamed it all on me, as he often did with his goalkeepers. He started looking for someone else (and making it obvious that he was doing so as well) and in the meantime did all he could to encourage the return of Ronnie Simpson. Simpson was given a game on October 4 against Raith Rovers. Stein was emphatic in the *Evening Times* that I was not being dropped but was being given a rest in view of the fact that I had been playing two games per week since the start of the season. Also playing that day, incidentally, was a "bright young boy" called "Kenneth Dalgleish" [*sic*] who had impressed in the reserves.

Ronnie Simpson played well that day (the team won 7–1) against Raith Rovers, but I returned for the following game, the League Cup semi-final against Ayr United. It was a Celtic horror story, a 3–3 draw after extra time in which we were lucky to get a replay, needing a dodgy penalty from the ever controversial referee J.R.P. Gordon. "Dalgleish", described eccentrically as a "red-headed boy" by a colour-blind journalist (whose spelling was not all that hot either), was impressive, but the loss of three goals once again threw Stein into a rage, and the goalkeeper was changed yet again.

This was described as a shock decision in the press. As it happened, Simpson's comeback game was also his thirty-ninth birthday. I had originally been selected for the game and duly walked into the dressing room after having had my walk on the pitch. To my astonishment, I saw that Ronnie's boots had been laid out for him and that he was sheepishly preparing to get changed. I had been dropped and Stein hadn't even had the courtesy to tell me.

The crowd sang "Happy Birthday" to Ronnie that day of October 11 1969, and because Billy McNeill was ill with flu, Ronnie was made captain for the day. (Clearly, Stein and Simpson had come far since the days when Simpson felt that Stein didn't like him at Hibs.) Yet his next game turned out to be his last. This was the semi-final replay against Ayr United. Over 47,000 turned up on a Monday night (a tribute to Ayr United and their manager, one Ally MacLeod) to see another good game in which Celtic, although having lost an early goal, were edging towards a 2–1 victory when Ronnie Simpson dislocated his shoulder saving from Ayr United's Alex "Dixie" Ingram. Tommy Gemmell went into goal for the remaining twelve minutes, and Celtic were mightily relieved to hear the final whistle, which put them into the Scottish League Cup final for the sixth successive year.

Naturally I was more than a little upset at the injury to my friend, even though it opened a door of opportunity for me, but I was not the only goalkeeper watching the game in the Celtic party in the Hampden stand that night. A man called Evan Williams was there, and the following day he signed for the club. Not everyone would have heard of Evan Williams. He had played for Third Lanark without having become a household name, then he had gone to Wolverhampton Wanderers and was now out on loan to Aston Villa. In conditions of the greatest secrecy while pretending to be interested in other goalkeepers, Stein had had him watched, and now he signed him on as a cover for Simpson (who could not really go on for very long in any case) and for myself, whom, increasingly, Stein did not seem to trust.

Williams was given a game in a Glasgow Cup game on Wednesday against Clyde. It proved little. Some thought that he might have done better with Clyde's only goal, but it was a very quiet game as Celtic's youngsters won 4–1. It so happened that the next game was the Scottish League Cup final on October 25, ten days later. This was because Scotland were playing West Germany in the World Cup on the following Wednesday, October 22, so Celtic's first-team game against Dundee United on the Saturday, October 18 was postponed.

The Scottish League Cup final was against St Johnstone, a team for which Celtic and Stein had the greatest respect. On more than one occasion in recent years the Saints had given Celtic a great deal of bother. Bobby Murdoch is on record as saying that, next to Rangers, St Johnstone were the most difficult team Celtic had to play in the Celtic glory years. Managed by Willie Ormond, once of the Hibs "Famous Five" forward line, the Perth side were in their first ever national final. It would be true to say that the Fair City was far from being a hotbed of Scottish football, with more interest paid there to curling and cricket (Perthshire were arguably Scottish cricket's best side in 1969), but on October 25 1969, the whole of Perth mobilised to go to Glasgow to see this game.

It would have to be said that they had the backing of most of Scotland, and even a few of the weaker Celtic fans were heard to say that it would not be the world's greatest disaster if St Johnstone were to win the Scottish League Cup. They were a difficult team to hate, they had nice supporters (including a very high percentage of women and children) who did not ape Rangers fans and sing unpleasant songs about anyone's religion, and it would do a great deal for football in Perth if they were to win.

But sentiment played little part in the Celtic make-up. Celtic were going for their fifth League Cup win in a row: we had not really had the best of starts to the season and we wanted a trophy. Apart from creating a record number of seven wins, Celtic would have the additional and unprecedented distinction of having won the trophy twice in the same calendar year, for the previous final had been played some six months ago, in April.

Stein might have played Williams in the goal for the Scottish League Cup final but decided to play for safety and to go, however reluctantly, for myself instead. It could be described as a comeback game for me, and it was also a comeback for Bobby Murdoch, who had been out of the side for a spell trying to deal with his weight problem at a health farm in England. Bobby Lennox had failed a fitness test, but there was still Bertie Auld, and Harry Hood and Tommy Callaghan were to be given their first taste of a cup final for Celtic. Jimmy Johnstone, at that point neither in full fitness nor in full favour with Big Jock, was named as substitute. (He would, in fact, play virtually all the second half after Chalmers was injured.) No one, however, was prepared for

185

the bombshell that Stein was to drop in another area of team selection.

The bombshell was Tommy Gemmell. Tommy had been sent off on the Wednesday night while playing for Scotland against West Germany for taking a deliberate kick at a West German player, in retaliation for some persistent fouling. Stein considered this a sufficient embarrassment to the club to drop him from the Scottish League Cup final three days later. There was more than a suggestion, though, that Stein was looking for an opportunity to leave him out. Big Tam was certainly not the sort of a guy who would suffer from lack of confidence and perhaps Stein felt that he needed to be taken down a peg or two. The crowd were under the impression that Gemmell must have suffered some kind of a knock and were unaware of the real cause. Indeed, Tommy himself did not know he was not playing until he entered the dressing room and saw young Davie Hay getting ready to take his place. Gemmell, as had happened to me several times, was not only being dropped; he was being humiliated as well.

There was really no rhyme or reason for this. If it had not worked, Stein would have been classed as being monumentally stupid. He was lucky that he had an adequate replacement in the clearly talented Hay, and, as Gemmell himself would often say, Stein might not have been quite so principled and moral if the opponents in the Scottish League Cup final had been Rangers rather than St Johnstone. As it was, the rest of the team, myself included, were deprived of the sometimes talismanic presence of Big Tam, who clearly relished big occasions like cup finals.

Be that as it may, 73,000, at least a third of who seemed to be supporting the Saints, saw the following teams take the field under the benign tutelage of referee J.W. Paterson of Bothwell:

Celtic: Fallon, Craig and Hay; Murdoch, McNeill and Brogan; Callaghan, Hood, Hughes, Chalmers and Auld.

St Johnstone: Donaldson, Lambie and Coburn; Gordon, Rooney and McPhee; Aird, Hall, McCarry, Connelly and Aitken.

The game was a fine one on a crisp autumn day, and Celtic won 1–0 thanks to an early Bertie Auld goal. St Johnstone played well, proving that they deserved to be in the final, and if it hadn't been for several good saves from me, one in particular near the end at the Mount Florida End of the ground from St Johnstone's centre half Rooney, they might well have earned at least a replay. They were given a generous reception from a relieved Celtic support at the end of the game.

Jim Parkinson, in the following Monday's *Glasgow Herald*, said that St Johnstone's goalkeeper Jim Donaldson was "erratic" and sometimes ran out of his area to join in the general play but that

> his edginess was in complete contrast to Fallon in the Celtic goal. [Fallon] was confident and relaxed, and it was because of his masterly save from Rooney near the end that the game did not require to go into extra time. St Johnstone's players and officials feel that Fallon more than anyone else deprived them of the cup, or at least a replay in the first major cup final. I would confirm that the red-haired goalkeeper had several saves, but the man who caused the most trouble was the revitalised Murdoch . . .

Gair Henderson in the *Evening Times*, clearly an admirer of myself for some time, confirmed that I played very well and went into overdrive about my late save from Rooney: "Fallon's save was of the kind that brings teammates round to pat the goalkeeper on the back – and that is always a first-class reference." He did stress, however, that this was no easy final for Celtic, but that they deserved their win – just.

Hugh Taylor of the *Daily Record* talked highly of St Johnstone and said, "They might have got an equaliser, if it hadn't been for two superlative saves near the end by John Fallon, who must surely now have done enough to prove to the critical that he is a top-flight goalkeeper."

For me, 1969 simply kept on getting better. I had now won four medals in that year to add to my Scottish Cup medal in 1965, and I seemed to have reinforced and strengthened my place in the Celtic side. I was very aware, however, that stern tests lay ahead, not least in the European Cup, where the mighty Benfica were coming to Glasgow in mid-November. I was equally aware that Stein would not have signed Evan Williams as a goalkeeper if he did not intend to deploy him at some point.

Celtic's European Cup campaign had begun with a couple of games against Swiss champions Basle. We had won comfortably enough, drawing 0–0 in Switzerland and winning 2–0 at Celtic Park. I had played in both games, had a couple of good performances and had generally impressed the larger audience that watches European football. The first game, in Basle, could have been a shock because of general sloppy Celtic play, even though I made a "whole series of fantastic saves", according to Gair Henderson in the *Evening Times*, to earn a 0–0 draw. And he was even less impressed with Celtic in the game at Parkhead. The team made it difficult for themselves, he said, with a seeming desire to score spectacular goals, and there were a few defensive errors while "Fallon made two saves but did not look all that comfortable". This remark should be seen in the context of the general defensive malaise all around me rather than my own inadequacy. Be that as it may, everyone heaved a huge sigh of relief at the full-time whistle, and I was now looking forward to the difficult test against the Portuguese champions.

November 8 saw a really bad day at the office for Celtic as Hearts came to Glasgow and, in a real coupon-buster of a result, beat Celtic 2–0. The first goal was a fluke from an impossible angle, but the second was one of those goalmouth scrambles

188

which always reflect badly on the goalkeeper in the eyes of both the fans and the manager if they are looking for a scapegoat. But it was simply a bad day. In view of the imminent arrival of Benfica, youngsters like Lou Macari and Kenny Dalglish were deployed and, frankly, they struggled against the rugged, determined and experienced professionals of Hearts. Tommy Gemmell returned after his contretemps with the manager, but it did not really look as if peace had been restored, for a transfer request was still on the table. In any case, everyone had their minds on Benfica.

Benfica had the great Eusébio with them and were full of excellent players, but November 12 1969 was one of our greatest ever European matches, with 80,000 in attendance at Celtic Park on a typically wet Glasgow November night to see a tremendous 3–0 win for Celtic. Stein's pragmatism in swallowing his pride and deploying Tommy Gemmell was vindicated when Big Tam scored one of his great goals. Willie Wallace and Harry Hood scored the others, but I was as big a hero as anyone. I had a difficult save from a Eusébio header at a vital stage of the game, when the score was still 1–0. Celtic's great 3–0 result deserved all the praise that was heaped on us by the press and media, and not least the ever-chivalrous Eusébio himself.

It was a different story some two weeks later in Lisbon. The game was remarkable for several reasons. It did not kick off until 9.45 p.m. Scottish time, so many morning newspapers did not know the final score and outcome. For a spell, neither did anyone else in the stadium, for Benfica scored their aggregate equaliser with the last kick of the game (after an inordinate amount of injury time) and the referee promptly took the players off the field without clearly indicating whether a goal had been scored or not. Therefore no one was really sure whether we had won or whether extra time was to be played.

Extra time was played, however, and neither of the two exhausted teams were able to produce a winner. Then, in an anticlimactic atmosphere, rightly criticised in both the Scottish and the Portuguese press, Celtic won on the toss of the coin. Penalty shoot-outs may have their critics as a way of resolving drawn games, but they are better than that!

It was a remarkable night, and I was praised by Gair Henderson in the *Evening Times* for two great saves, but my manager was less than impressed, blaming me for the loss of some of the goals. This was an opinion emphatically not shared by the press, who all tended to agree with Gair Henderson. Nor was Stein's idiosyncratic opinion shared by the great Eusébio himself. The Portuguese ace talked to John Blair of *The People*. He was full of praise for Celtic, and at one point singled me out: "I had one shot in the first half which would have beaten most of the keepers in Europe, but somehow he flew across the goal to save. Had that one gone in, the spin of the coin would not have been necessary." It was felt by most observers that at least two of the goals were lost through a certain amount of what could be called "showboating" by Tommy Gemmell and Bertie Auld, who might have been better advised to defend sensibly and "boot the ball up the park" if necessary rather than try to show off.

John Blair then went on to say that that Eusébio's endorsement was a tremendous boost for me, who always seemed to be "the target for the knockers". One of my knockers was sadly the man who held the manager's chair at Celtic Park, but his criticisms were tempered at this point. I kept my place, for the time being at least, with clean sheets against Morton, St Mirren and Dundee. As winter strengthened its grip in December, the team won 4–1 at St Johnstone, then on the following Wednesday night turned on a magnificent display to beat the strong-going Dundee United 7–2 at Celtic Park. This performance earned praise from everyone, with phrases like "the Green machine" used frequently. Jimmy Johnstone was singled out, but there were no failures, certainly not me, who had had no chance with one of the two goals conceded, and the other was a penalty kick.

But on Saturday, 20 December, I played my last game for some time. It was a 3–1 win at Celtic Park over Kilmarnock. The game was played on a hard pitch in freezing-cold conditions and was marred by a bad injury to Kilmarnock's Frank Beattie. It was the day of the famous gesture of Jock Stein, who threw his overcoat over Frank Beattie as he was being stretchered off. It was a particularly fine gesture, given the history of Celtic v Kilmarnock games, which had not always been pleasant in the past few years, but Jock was not always as generous to his own players.

I did not have a bad game that day. I may have made one or two minor errors of judgement, but there was nothing in my own performance nor that of the team to suggest that I was about to enjoy a period of enforced leisure and that it was to be the beginning of the end of my time at Celtic Park.

Over 30,000 fans turned up in the fog at Celtic Park for the Partick Thistle game on December 27, for what was the last game of the 1960s, to discover that Evan Williams was in goal and not John Fallon. No reason was given, and none was really asked for, as everyone was simply dazzled by the Celtic machine, which turned itself on at full tilt and beat Thistle 8–1. Williams had little to do and kept his place for the New Year's Day game against Clyde and the all-important game against Rangers on January 3. He played well in both games, a shutout on both occasions, and kept his place for the rest of the season.

I did play a game at Dens Park, Dundee, on April 6, after the Scottish League was well won and when we were preparing ourselves for the Scottish Cup final and the European Cup semi-final later in the month. I thus missed a very active time of Celtic's history, as the team beat Fiorentina and Leeds United to contest the European Cup final on that awful night in Milan where, quite frankly, the team underestimated their Dutch opponents and became complacent after scoring first. Feyenoord equalised straight after Gemmell had given us the lead and then clinched the trophy for the first time just a few minutes before the end of extra time. I had also watched from the stand a month earlier as

Celtic lost the Scottish Cup final to an Aberdeen side who deservedly brought something to cheer about to a part of the country which had been deprived for so long – but were helped in doing so by some dubious refereeing by Mr Bobby Davidson of Airdrie.

The two major disappointments of spring 1970 could not reasonably blamed on Evan Williams or poor goalkeeping. Indeed, Evan himself looks back on his European Cup final with a great deal of happiness and felt that he had a good game. The faults lay elsewhere. And yet, were there really all that many faults?

Historians have quoted Charles Dickens – "It was the best of times; it was the worst of times" – about 1970. It was odd for supporters to have seen their team win two trophies out of four, to have seen their team hailed as the best in Great Britain after the defeat of Leeds United and the second-best team in Europe for reaching their second European Cup final in four years, and yet to feel so devastated by the events of Milan. Partly it was due to the effects of inflated expectation – undeniably, both supporters and players thought that the job was done and the European Cup was won after defeating Leeds – but there was something else as well. Certainly there was a feeling that some heads had swollen to unacceptable proportions, but there was also the feeling that the good times had gone and that big changes in personnel were about to happen. And where would that leave the second-choice goalkeeper?

But if 1970 was not a happy time for me personally, it was not a happy time for Celtic either, as we went on a rather pointless and unhappy tour of North America. I was included in the party. Had Celtic gone on this tour as the Champions of Europe, there seems little doubt that it would have been a great success. As it turned out, it was a hideous failure. No one really wanted to be there; everyone simply wanted to go away and lick their wounds after the traumatic disappointment of Milan.

We players also committed one major public relations gaffe.

The day after our defeat in Milan, and before we set out to the Americas, we announced the formation of a syndicate to control, regulate or maximise our earnings. To our supporters, some of whom had impoverished themselves to go to Milan to see a dreadfully substandard performance, this was distinctly tactless, to put it mildly, and did little to dispel the idea that the players were only in it for the money. Some of the players were distinctly upset by the abuse they received from some supporters, but it was a lesson in the fine distinction between success and failure, and also how, if you are going to receive the big money, you really must produce the goods.

Part of the deal was that any sponsorship deal for an individual player was to go into a pool. It was not a bad idea, for it emphasised the idea that everyone was in it together, a form of wealth-sharing so that no one player was seen as being more important than any other. It included sponsorship for wearing a given type of football boots, but there were unanswered questions. Did it, for example, include what the manager himself earned for his writing in the *Sunday Mirror* (a weekly column ghostwritten by Rodger Baillie)? There were a few grey areas, and a certain amount of resentment.

Then the tour itself saw some extraordinary, depressing and worrying happenings. There were delays in getting there, then the only game that had any significance at all was the first, a 0–2 defeat by Manchester United, one of the goals being a Billy McNeill own goal. Jimmy Johnstone was allowed not to go because of his chronic fear of flying – something that was deeply resented by the other players. Many players found it hard to hide their unhappiness, and then Jock Stein suddenly abandoned ship and went home in the middle of a game in Toronto.

Admittedly, the game was a farcical one, with the Italian team Bari staging a walkout at one point, but it was odd behaviour nevertheless from the Celtic manager and led many people to think that it was the precursor to a resignation. In fact, Stein would claim that he had to go home to sort out a contractual problem with Jimmy Johnstone, who was causing trouble back in Scotland. It may be that Stein himself was not well. He certainly took the loss of the European Cup badly and may have had a guilty conscience about several things, notably the choosing of the team. In any case, it would be hardly surprising if a man of his energy and commitment, not to mention his unhealthy shape, did not show a few signs of burning himself out after the intensity of five and a half seasons in charge of Celtic. It was probably true that there was never a day when his name was not in the newspapers.

Meanwhile, Gemmell and Auld were sent home from America by acting manager Sean Fallon because of the example they were showing to young players like Kenny Dalglish, and the whole thing became an utter shambles, dragging the name of Celtic even deeper through the mire. I played in some of the games against lesser opposition and certainly did not disgrace myself, but the whole tour was something that Celtic and I could well have done without.

The future, so bright even six months ago, now seemed obscure and uncertain, but there was at least an excellent World Cup to watch on TV. Some still argue that the 1970 Mexico World Cup was the best of them all, and there was certainly some great football played, by the Brazilians in particular. It was a shame, however, that Celtic were no longer mentioned among the really great teams of the world.

I, at least, was blameless in the distressing events of the spring. I could have indulged in a certain amount of *Schadenfreude*, the rejoicing in other people's misfortunes, but I was far too much of a Celtic supporter to do that. Most Celtic supporters recall summer 1970 as an unhappy, worrying time, with the future very gloomy and unclear. Yet we were the second-best team in Europe. In any case, I still had my playing career and the chance, admittedly now diminishing, to win back my place.

194

16

THE SEASON AFTER MILAN

The new season of 1970/71 opened with me in the goal. Evan Williams had injured himself in a pre-season friendly with Carlisle United, and I found myself in goal for the high-profile pre-season friendly against Malcolm Allison's Manchester City at Hampden Park before a large crowd of 62,000. It was a goalless draw – always a good result for a goalkeeper – and the *Glasgow Herald* talked highly of my performance, mentioning a couple of good saves from Francis Lee. Malcolm Munro in the *Evening Times* was convinced that this performance showed everyone that Celtic could cope with the English First Division (Manchester City were the current holders of the European Cup Winners' Cup, and had won the English League as recently as 1968) and he singled me out for my performance, asking the question: "Have you ever seen a keeper picking them out of the air the way that he did?"

Celtic should have won, and Stein, the traumas of the early summer forgotten, or at least put on the back-burner for a spell, was sufficiently pleased with my performance to put me in the side for the opening fixture against Hearts at Tynecastle in the Scottish League Cup. We won 2–1 in a tight game, with me by no means to blame for the Hearts goal, but then on the Monday night after that, in the Glasgow Cup final (delayed from the previous year), a youthful Celtic side beat Rangers 3–1. However, Evan Williams was back in the goal and stayed there for Wednesday night's game against Clyde, which was won 5–3 in a very entertaining display of attacking football by both sides. The newspapers talk of "defensive frailties", and clearly Stein must have thought that Williams was due another rest, so I found myself back in the goal for the visit of Dundee United on the Saturday.

This one was a 2–2 draw, with Celtic winning 2–1 until the last minute. The *Evening Times* reminded me that I had the misfortune, late in the game, to dislocate my pinkie; I had to have it pushed back in by trainer Bob Rooney. This may or may not have been the cause of Dundee United's late equaliser, "with half of the crowd already streaming down London Road", as the *Evening Times* put it, but it was certainly the end of my involvement in the first team for some time. Apart from a trip to Kokkola, in Finland, for a European Cup game (Celtic having comfortably won the first leg), I did not play a game again until late November. Evan Williams was playing very well in the goal, even on the terrible day in late October when Celtic lost the Scottish League Cup final to a new and revitalised Rangers, making it the third Cup-final loss in the calendar year of 1970.

A glance at the teams chosen in the early part of the 1970/71 season will show no consistent pattern. Players seemed to be chosen on a whim and suddenly dropped for no apparent reason, and no one really had any idea what the next team would be. This might perhaps indicate (and it often looked like that at the time) that Stein was struggling after the Milan defeat. The opposite is the case. In fact, a new and different Celtic was beginning to emerge, and Stein was assessing who he wanted and who he could discard. The goalkeeping position was no different from any other in this respect.

My reappearance was a sudden and unexpected one. Celtic had dropped a point on November 21 to Falkirk in a 0–0 draw.

Stein told all the newspapers on Friday that Jimmy Johnstone had been dropped (Stein did this sort of thing now and again, just to show who was the boss) but made no mention of any change in the goalkeeping position. The first time the 25,000 Celtic fans realised that I would be playing instead of Williams was when they reached the ground. Whether Williams had a cold or an injury or was just dropped I can't remember, but it was myself in the goal. I played very well in the comfortable 3–0 win over St Mirren, being commended in the *Sunday Mail* for an "excellent save" from Knox and then Hamilton, and some "fine anticipation". The *Evening Times* on the Monday after the game made the odd but significant comment about a "new, vociferous Fallon".

Both goalkeepers were named in the squad to travel to Tannadice Park for the next game, on December 5, but it was myself who was given the nod. I conceded one goal, but it was an odd one – an own goal from Billy McNeill, who simply miskicked and sliced the ball past my bewildered gaze. But Celtic won when Dundee United returned the compliment by conceding an own goal themselves! In this game I pulled off one marvellous save which amazed both Jim Blair in the *Evening Times* and two of the Dundee United forwards: a shot from Kenny Cameron was deflected, and I had to do a "back-flip in mid-air" to tip the ball over the bar. "Even the ranks of Tuscany could scarce forbear to cheer", as Thomas Babington Macaulay might have said in his *Lays of Ancient Rome*. The *Dundee Courier* tells us that Alan Gordon and ex-Ranger Davie Wilson gave me their personal round of applause. Celtic's eventual victory set things up nicely for next Saturday's game, the visit of the strong-going Aberdeen to Celtic Park.

Newspapers built this one up, calling it a "virtual title decider" – in December, oblivious to the fact that the season had still not reached the halfway stage. The *Evening Times* even compared it to "Joe Frazier v Cassius Clay", the two foremost heavyweights of the day. There was a touch of hyperbole in this, of course, but nevertheless it was an important game, and a huge crowd of 63,000 obviously thought so. I was once again in the goal.

Aberdeen had developed into real challengers to Celtic, possibly replacing, temporarily at least, Rangers. Buoyed up by their Scottish Cup success of April (however fortuitous and dependent on quixotic refereeing decisions), the Dons were well managed by Eddie Turnbull, an old adversary of Stein from the days when he was a member of Hibs' Famous Five. The Aberdeen team had a few good players in Martin Buchan, Joe Harper, Jim Forrest and Arthur Graham, and were now mounting a credible League challenge to Celtic. This game at Celtic Park would be a stern test of their credentials.

Aberdeen won 1–0 in a tight encounter. I was not to blame for the goal any more than anyone else in the Celtic defence was. It was one of those dreadful goals when the ball floats over the penalty area and one forward heads on for another (in this case, Joe Harper) to score. I also had a couple of good saves, and one would have thought that I had done enough to earn a permanent place in the team. But to everyone's surprise, Evan Williams was back again in the goal at Somerset Park for next week, and effectively I was out again for the rest of the season.

The year 1970 thus finished badly for Celtic. Three cup finals had been lost to Aberdeen, Feyenoord and Rangers (I had not been involved in any of these three disasters) and now it appeared that Celtic had lost the League, if one could believe some of the press. They had certainly fallen behind to an excellent Aberdeen team, who operated a very efficient offside trap and were now playing as a good team which had been built and welded together by the crafty and knowledgeable Eddie Turnbull. It may be that Jock dropping me was emotionally motivated. All managers need scapegoats, and Stein, who had never really liked me all that much in any case, saw perhaps in the changing of goalkeepers a way in which the mob could be pacified. In truth, neither Evan nor myself were outstandingly better than the other. I was possibly more agile and better at the difficult shots, whereas he was marginally better at cross balls and the more mundane tasks.

Possibly there was no rational thought behind it, and it was all done on a whim. On one occasion, after my brother Pat had died, I returned to Celtic Park to be told that I was not playing in the next game because I was not "mentally attuned". When I protested that I was in a fit condition for the game, Jock persisted and said that I wasn't. This attitude contrasted with that of one of Stein's illustrious predecessors. In 1915, after both Jimmy McMenemy and Joe Dodds had lost a brother in the Battle of Loos, Willie Maley consulted them, and when both said they wanted to play, he agreed and put them in the team for the Glasgow Cup final of 1915 against Rangers. The team won comfortably.

The fans were becoming restless. Years of virtually unbroken success seemed to be coming to an end, as Stein kept chopping and changing in an attempt to find a settled team. In fact he was rebuilding, with quite a few of the old guard either having already gone elsewhere or heading in that direction. And it was beginning to look as if I too was going to be leaving my beloved Parkhead very soon.

17

DISASTER STRIKES

I was, of course, distressed by all this, but it was difficult to see any way back. Indeed, my Celtic career was now over. It came about in a particularly distressing way. I suddenly became aware in January 1971 that my hip was giving me problems. It seemed a normal wear-and-tear sort of thing, by no means uncommon among professional football players, and it apparently happened in my house rather than on the football field. It seemed a routine, if very painful, problem, but there was more to it than that, for I never seemed to be getting any better and I was beginning to lose weight. Moreover, the injection I got every four hours for the pain did not seem to help.

I feel to this day that I owe my life to a Dr Wang, who lived in Uddingston. Dr Wang felt that I had not been diagnosed properly and had another look. He diagnosed septicaemia rather than merely some damage to the sciatic nerve. One does not need to be a genius to work out that this was not only painful but very dangerous as well. But following Dr Wang's diagnosis and a new regime of treatment, everything improved within a week. However, it would be a long time before I was likely to play professional football again.

I still resent the grudging visit paid to me in the Bon Secours hospital by Jock Stein. Stein was never a great hospital visitor to his own players. (It was a different story when it came to supporters who were ill, though, rather than a player.) Like Bill Shankly, Stein apparently saw injured players as a nuisance, for they were not contributing anything to the club. It was Sean Fallon who visited me regularly. He knew how ill I was and suggested ever so tactfully to Jock Stein that a visit to me in hospital might be no bad thing. Jock duly went, but all I recall him saying in those short and uncomfortable few minutes was "Get a haircut!"

I thus missed what turned out, eventually, to be a very good season for Celtic. Yet it was a season scarred by the Ibrox disaster of January 2 1971, when sixty-six Rangers supporters were killed on Stairway 13 while leaving the stadium after a very exciting Old Firm game in which both sides scored late in the game to earn a 1–1 draw. Some were crushed to death; others lost their footing and were trampled on after crush barriers and barriers down the side of the stairway buckled and gave way because of the pressure of the crowd. This tragedy dominated everyone's thinking during the month of January, and it was a long time before football could become football again. The only – very small – positive was that it did help to a certain extent, and only for a limited period, to bring the two communities together.

Celtic's much-changed team kept winning, but a clear indication that we were simply not good enough for the European scene came in March when we exited the European Cup to Ajax Amsterdam. The season finished well for Celtic, though, with a Scottish League and Cup double. Sheer perseverance eventually wore down Aberdeen, but it was not until Celtic gained a hard-earned point at Pittodrie on April 17, followed by Aberdeen blowing up at Falkirk the following Saturday, that Celtic could be sure of the title. Then in the Scottish Cup final, it needed two games to get the better of Rangers. Evan Williams played through all this, seldom distinguishing himself but always doing well enough. In the meantime, I, now well on my way to a total recovery, could only watch as a supporter rather than a participant.

· A clear indication that things were changing came in the last League game of the season. The League was already well won, but Stein decided that the Lisbon Lions should have one last appearance together in the game against Clyde on May 1. It was the week before the Scottish Cup final and there was more than an element of propaganda in all this. It attracted 35,000 spectators to a Celtic Park then in the throes of having the main stand redeveloped, and the team went on to beat Clyde 6–1, but I had to sit and watch Ronnie Simpson come out with the team. He couldn't play because he had now officially retired and was no longer registered, so he had to withdraw before the game began and was replaced, not by me but by Evan Williams. I was less than happy about that, for I had been the substitute goalkeeper.

It was a time for nostalgia, but it also meant that a few players would soon leave – Chalmers, Clark, Wallace, Gemmell and Auld would all leave within the next few months – as a new Celtic was about to emerge. And where did it leave me, now nearly thirty-one, just recovered from a serious, crippling injury and still, in any case, failing to regain the confidence of my all-powerful manager, who had now rejected an offer from Manchester United and had clearly decided to stay with Celtic? Only a fool would have predicted any sort of future for me at Celtic Park.

18

JOCK STEIN

By early 1972, it was becoming apparent to all concerned that time had run out for me at Celtic Park. Although I had now totally recovered from my injury and illness of a year ago, it was clear that I would never reclaim my first-team spot, which was now held by Evan Williams. I was never even remotely considered for a game in the early part of the 1971/72 season and was in danger of becoming Parkhead's forgotten man.

As far as Celtic were concerned, autumn 1971 was characterised by the catastrophic defeat in the Scottish League Cup final to Partick Thistle. The 1–4 scoreline was barely explicable and surely brought about by a combination of Celtic complacency and a determined effort by Alex Rae's Partick Thistle. Although Billy McNeill missed the game because of a muscle strain and Jimmy Johnstone was taken off injured, little credit can be given to Celtic on that occasion other than their good sportsmanship and the excellent behaviour of the fans, who applauded the Partick Thistle players, particularly the known Celtic supporters in their team. Partick Thistle had not won anything for fifty years – when Jimmy McMenemy was playing for them in 1921 – so it was hard to be jealous. It was easy for Celtic fans, however, to be angry at the lacklustre performance of their own team.

The public side of Celtic was all magnanimity and good

humour, but Stein's behaviour indicated serious hurt and anger. He was often prone to knee-jerk reactions, but on this occasion he excelled himself. His plunge into the transfer market to buy Dixie Deans from Motherwell is well documented, but he also moved on the goalkeeping front. Clearly the luckless Evan Williams had to carry the can for at least some of the goals – I was not the only goalkeeper to be blamed for everything – and, although I was still available and might have hoped for another run in the team, Jock signed another goalkeeper, Denis Connaghan, from St Mirren on the following day. Connaghan went immediately into the team for the game against Dunfermline on the Wednesday night.

Ironically, Connaghan had been at Parkhead before but had left because of the perceived surfeit of goalkeepers, but his arrival now brought the total number of goalkeepers at Celtic Park to five! In addition to Evan Williams and myself, there was also Gordon Marshall Sr, signed in the twilight of a brilliant career, mainly with Hearts, and an Irishman called Tom Lally signed in the close season of 1971. It was a fair bet that I was now fifth out of five.

Worse than that was the total and apparently irretrievable breakdown in the relationship between Jock Stein and myself. I was never one of Stein's favourites in the way that McNeill, Murdoch and Lennox were (and even in a funny way Jimmy Johnstone, for whom Stein was always prepared to go the extra mile), and now the two of us hardly spoke. Stein had been in my house on one occasion, trying to persuade me to go elsewhere: a few intemperate exchanges had taken place, including the some-what amazing description of me as a "bigot" by Jock Stein, as well as the bald statement that "the fans don't want you and I don't want you"! Esther had, on that occasion, intervened and had politely but firmly shown Jock the front door, a humiliation that Jock would not forget.

We have already seen that Celtic supporters, like any

supporters, can turn on one of their own. We have seen how so-called supporters turned on me after that awful day in January 1968, and it is now time to turn our attention to Jock Stein and the myth that Celtic's playing staff, management staff and everyone else were always happy under Jock Stein. One cringes when one hears bland statements like "happy, family atmosphere", and they really have to be addressed.

In the first place, most people's families are not always happy, but in any case, happiness was not always an ever-present phenomenon at Celtic Park in the years 1965 to 1972, when Jock Stein and I were both there. The other Fallon, Sean "The Iron Man", the assistant manager, comes out of any review with a great deal of credit, as do men like Neil Mochan, Jim Steel and Bob Rooney. They are often praised for the "bridge building" and the "picking up" that is necessary sometimes, when egos have been bruised and personas have been deflated, often after a blasting from the Big Man, who was not always as nice, as tactful and as diplomatic a man as he is depicted, and whose public relations with the fans and the press were always second to none.

It has to be said – and it is difficult sometimes to point the finger at a man like Big Jock, who did so much for the club – that there were times when Jock was poor at man-management. I am far from the only one to say such things. Charlie Gallagher, the late John Cushley and, in particular, John Hughes give similar assessments, the pattern seeming to be that the eleven who actually won the European Cup in 1967 were lauded to the skies and, on occasion, had excuses made for the occasional fall from grace, as happened in the case of Bertie Auld, Tommy Gemmell (even after they had been sent home from America in 1970) and, repeatedly, Jimmy Johnstone, whereas the fringe players tended to be belittled and even persecuted.

Funnily enough, although he maybe did not trust me (or goal-keepers in general) on the field, Jock did trust me with his car.

205

Sometimes Stevie Chalmers was similarly favoured, but more often it was me. Jock was very proud of his Merc and very few people were allowed near it, but now and again, if we were at Seamill Hydro, for example, he would throw me the keys and tell me to go and fill it with petrol, or even if we were playing at Parkhead or Hampden, he would tell me to take his car to the ground from Seamill so that he could pick it up after the game. He would travel in to the game on the bus with the players, presumably to better supervise some possible miscreants or rebels.

I felt I was privileged to be allowed to do this, and he also trusted me to grab the bench at Lisbon so that Helenio Herrera couldn't get the best seat. Yet he still had this idea that some people had to be made a fool of, sometimes publicly.

Why this was so is hard to explain. Stein was always very good at encouraging youngsters like Dalglish, Hay and Danny McGrain. He was well rewarded for that in that such players paid him back with good performances, and yet he fell out, unnecessarily, with Davie Hay, causing him to leave for Chelsea in 1974, and the whole truth about the Dalglish transfer in August 1977 has yet to come out, in spite of many efforts to find out what actually happened. Stein was certainly a key factor in Dalglish's sad departure, and there seems little doubt that Stein himself realised this, for his managership of Celtic never recovered. Some have even suggested that Jock suffered some kind of nervous breakdown in that awful season of 1977/78, and nervous breakdowns are often triggered by guilty consciences.

All this has to be balanced against what Stein actually achieved with Celtic. Frankly, it was a managerial record that is difficult to parallel anywhere else in the world in terms of sheer success in trophy winning, and his achievements are all the more remarkable when one considers where Celtic were in January 1965. Had Stein not appeared in early 1965, Celtic would have sunk more and more, and their vast support would have found something else to do with their Saturday afternoons. Celtic would have remained the great underachievers of Scottish football. As it happened, little over two years after the arrival of Stein Celtic were a major world power and would remain so for a fair time.

So why did a man of those achievements and such obvious ability feel that he had to persecute so many of his players? Was it something to do with his background? Was he really insecure and unsure of himself, and therefore felt that he had to bully others? Certainly, to a supporter, he was always genial, even jovial, but then again he was very aware of and was frequently quoted on the need to be nice to fans, saying that they were the life's blood of the game and that "without fans, football is nothing". Why, then, was he so different in his treatment of some of his players?

His mining background was tough. One hears a great deal of romantic stuff about miners being "the salt of the earth". This is not necessarily always the case, as anyone who has ever lived in a mining community will tell you. Yes, it is a community, and yes we all look out for each other, especially in hard industrial times, and we all hate the Tories and, in the old days, the owners, but within that community, there are conflicts, jealousy, disputes, drunkenness, crime and violence.

In Stein's case, his footballing life was complicated by the undeniable fact that Celtic were not the original darlings of his family, yet he had been associated with Celtic since 1951. Possibly he felt that he had to prove himself repeatedly and this had a great effect on him. In addition, in spite of all the trash that one reads about other managers, as a rule, nice men don't make successful managers. There must be a nasty, ruthless streak some-where, but that is true of every walk of life. Successful business-men, headmasters, prime ministers rarely get there because they are nice people. Yet one can surely be ruthless, determined and committed without being spiteful and nasty.

It was often said that he had a particular problem with

goalkeepers. (The reverse is true as far as centre forwards are concerned, for in that respect everything he touched seemed to turn to gold – for example, Joe McBride, Willie Wallace, Harry Hood, Dixie Deans, Kenny Dalglish.) Some have dated this to the 1955 Scottish Cup final, when Johnny Bonnar's ghastly and uncharacteristic error allowed Clyde a late equaliser and deprived Jock of his second Scottish Cup medal. And although the paths of Jock Stein and Dick Beattie never really crossed to a huge extent at Parkhead, Stein, by nature a gambling man, would have been totally aware of the rumours of match fixing.

It is one of life's supreme ironies, however, that even if Stein did have a problem with goalkeepers, it was a goalkeeper that made him. This was the extremely painful (for Celtic supporters) occasion of the Scottish Cup final replay of 1961. The man who won the Scottish Cup for Dunfermline that night was, without doubt, Eddie Connachan, the Celtic-supporting, unassuming chap from the East Lothian mining community whose boyhood hero was Willie Miller of his beloved Celtic. Time after time Eddie defied the Celtic forwards in that Mount Florida End goal, then Dunfermline ran up and scored halfway through the second half and then again almost at the final whistle. As the gloom of darkness symbolically descended on Hampden Park at the final whistle, Stein's white coat gleamed like a beacon as Connachan was chaired off by his mates. It was a goalkeeper who made Dunfermline that night, and he also made Stein.

Stein's relationship with Ronnie Simpson was complex, and it is probably true that he came to trust and possibly even to like Simpson, who was such a transparently nice man and had a wealth of goalkeeping experience behind him. Stein would eventually leave Simpson to take charge of the goalkeeping side of things. But, leaving me aside for the moment, no other goalkeeper lasted long under Stein. Evan Williams, Denis Connaghan, Ally Hunter, Peter Latchford, Roy Baines and others all had their moments of glory, but Simpson remains the only Celtic goalkeeper who could honestly say that he won and then retained Stein's trust between the sticks. Ironically, Jock's last ever signing in 1978 was a goalkeeper, an Irishman called Pat Bonner.

I will always claim that Stein's criticisms of me were unfair. A particularly good performance against the likes of Benfica in 1968, Manchester City in 1970 or Dunfermline in the "springboard" cup final of 1965 were much lauded in the press and among the fans but glossed over in the dressing room, whereas defeats were often laid solely at the feet (or hands) of John Fallon. The Club World Championship defeat to Racing Club is a case in point. Stein felt that I could have saved the only goal of the game, but that is not an opinion likely to be shared with anyone who consults YouTube to have a look at it. But then again, defeated managers can be quite irrational. It is a reflex to blame someone, and the goalkeeper is always the likely target. In this respect, fans can be distressingly similar.

The late Bob Crampsey, the respected journalist and broadcaster, had this to say about an incident between Stein and myself: "I still think that John Fallon was a superb goalkeeper technically, but I happened to be at the training ground at Barrowfield one day when John was in goal. He was performing heroics, but then Stein came out onto the track from the dressing room, and Fallon just turned into a wreck." Yes, he could have that effect on anyone.

19

MOTHERWELL AND MORTON

Winter 1972 was a pretty severe one, and it was also the time of the first miners' strike, won handsomely by the miners. The end of January saw Bloody Sunday in Northern Ireland, when the British Army gunned down some peaceful protesters. On the field Celtic were doing well, following their dreadful performance in the League Cup final against Partick Thistle. The team did not sustain another defeat until nearly the end of the season, and fans and press were now beginning to be impressed by young Kenny Dalglish, who teamed up well with Dixie Deans and Jimmy Johnstone to score goals galore. Denis Connaghan and Evan Williams were doing well enough in goal, but I was indeed "the forgotten man" of Celtic Park.

It was Motherwell who rescued my now somewhat moribund career. At the end of February, manager Bobby Howitt found himself with a goalkeeping crisis on his hands. Billy Ritchie, the ex-Rangers veteran, was out with a broken leg, and Keith MacRae had broken his wrist. Time was of the utmost importance, for Motherwell had a Scottish Cup replay against Ayr United in the offing, scheduled for the afternoon of Wednesday, March 1. The miners' strike was still in progress and restrictions on the use of electricity meant that floodlights could not be used in the evening.

On Monday, 28 February, Stein had seen me at training but had said nothing. Then my great friend Bobby Murdoch approached me and said that he had heard a rumour about Motherwell being interested in me. I thought no more about it. Football grounds are always full of rumours. I then went home after training and had hardly entered the house when Jock Stein was at the door. The conversation was tense and difficult, but eventually I agreed reluctantly to leave Celtic Park and to go to Motherwell.

Thus on Leap Year's Day, Tuesday, 29 February 1972, Dixon Blackstock in the *Evening Citizen* announced that John Fallon had joined Motherwell. The deal was settled "around breakfast time" (something that does not seem to square with my own recollection, but what was meant was that *Stein* agreed to the deal at breakfast time). Financial arrangements had been agreed to the mutual satisfaction of both Motherwell and Celtic, and I myself was delighted to get the chance of first-team football for the first time in over a year. I joined my new teammates for a training session later that morning, and I would apparently be between the Fir Park sticks for the cup tie the following afternoon, because, as the *Evening Citizen* put it, "the normal 14-day signing rule for Scottish Cup ties does not apply to goalkeepers", and even Jock Stein himself, keen presumably to rid himself of me, had telephoned SFA Secretary Willie Allan to confirm that I could play in the replay against Ayr United. Everything looked fine.

But the snag was that this was a replay, and Rule 10 Paragraph 4 stated quite clearly that only players who had been eligible at the time of the first game could play in a replay, whether goal-keepers or not, and therefore I could not play against Ayr United. Basically, not for the first nor last time, the SFA had made a mistake. It was not on the same scale as the Jorge Cadete howler of 1996, when Jim Forry, for reasons best known to himself, failed to register the Portuguese player and was eventually sacked. But it was still very disappointing for both Motherwell and myself. However, I turned up at Fir Park and had a word or two of encouragement with young Tom Burns, who was now drafted in to the Motherwell side, before taking my seat in the stand.

Burns had an unfortunate start, conceding an early goal when he collided with a defender and a harmless ball sailed into the net, but he soon recovered and had some very fine saves, diving on one occasion at an opponent's feet to save a ball, and Motherwell rallied to beat Ally MacLeod's Ayr United 2–1. Malcolm Munro of the *Evening Times* describes Tom Burns (with a touch of hyperbole, one feels) as a "young March lion" for his part in earning the Steel men a quarter-final tie with Rangers, but it was myself who was in the goal for Saturday's game at Dens Park, a 0–2 defeat in snowy Dundee.

It was at least something for me. No goalkeeper, indeed no football player, likes long periods of inaction. I would, of course, have preferred to be in the first team for Celtic, but that did not seem to be possible any longer in the circumstances. At least with Motherwell, I had the chance of first-team football in the short term. I was thirty-one and knew that I could not go on forever, but I was determined to give it a go, for Motherwell, a team with a great tradition – they had won the Scottish League in 1932, the Scottish Cup in 1952 and the League Cup in 1950/51, as well as many near misses when Sailor Hunter was their manager – but whose recent past had rarely got above the mediocre.

The 0–2 defeat in Dundee was by no means a pleasant occasion for me, but I had a far better game the following week, when, virtually on my own, according to some accounts, I earned Motherwell a goalless draw against a good Hearts team at Tynecastle, with Nick Scott of the *Sunday Mail* talking about "the redhead ex-Celt" being in great form. But the big game for Motherwell that spring was the appearance of Rangers at Fir Park to play in the Scottish Cup quarter-final, on March 18. It was Rangers' last realistic chance of a domestic honour this season, and David Bowman in the *Sunday Times* told how thousands of Rangers fans arrived well before the match to jeer me. He added sadly that "the collective hatred of this man proved what the afternoon was all about" for so many of those louts.

It was a fine game, however, with Rangers scoring first, then Motherwell equalising and then going ahead. Inside the last ten minutes, Motherwell, with myself in great form and feeling confident, were holding Rangers out. I had a great save from a fierce John Greig drive, and with Rangers now desperate, a goal came from a "route one" goal. Rangers' goalkeeper Peter McCloy kicked the ball from one penalty area to another. It caught everyone by surprise and two Motherwell defenders managed to get in each other's way as the ball came to Colin Stein, who, without ever having total control of the ball, managed to hook it into the net, giving me no chance.

It was a devastating blow, and I never really forgave the Motherwell defenders, who, I felt, gave me little support. As often happens in such circumstances, Motherwell went to Ibrox for the replay on the following Monday night, nine days later, with a death wish hanging over us and folded to a 1–4 defeat. I had one bad mistake when I dropped a ball and conceded a goal but otherwise played well. It was a sad night for Motherwell, and I would not stay at Fir Park for very much longer.

I had been interviewed by Peter Black in the *Weekly News* on the Friday between the first game and the replay, and said that the "sherricking" that I got from Rangers fans didn't bother me. They didn't really dislike me, I claimed, and told the story of how when I returned to my pub after the 2–2 game there were four Rangers fans bedecked in red, white and blue from top to toe and they congratulated me on my performance. I then went on to say that playing for Motherwell meant that football was no longer a matter of life and death, as it had been with Celtic, and that I could settle down and enjoy my football. I emphasised this point by saying, "There was a time when the thought of meeting Rangers twice within nine days would have unsettled me, but not any more" – a clear indication of how difficult I had found coping with the tension before an Old Firm game, and also perhaps a feeling of being "demob happy" as the end of my career approached.

The defeat at Ibrox probably taught me a little about life at a provincial club, and how important it was, financially, for a team like Motherwell to get a good cup run. I now realised as well that at the age of nearly thirty-two I could not go on playing forever. I played once against Celtic as a Motherwell player, on Saturday, 22 April 1972 at Celtic Park. There was a certain piquancy about my return – some supporters cheered me, others booed and Jock Stein ignored me altogether, as I shall explain – but that particular day saw bigger issues for Celtic fans. The Scottish League had been won on April 15 at East Fife, but the previous Wednesday, April 19, had been the night of the infamous Dixie Deans penalty shoot-out against Inter Milan in the European Cup semi-final, when Dixie had been the only player to miss a penalty.

That was painful enough, but for me it had its own embarrassment as well, for that was the night that I was refused admission to Celtic Park. This came about when Bill Peacock, the man at the door, told me, "Sorry, John, but I have orders not to let you in the complimentary gate." There were no prizes for guessing who had issued the orders, and it seemed to be a little piece of revenge for his being asked to leave my house by Esther some time previously. I told Bill where to go, and I was not a happy bhoy that night. On the Friday I received a phone call from Celtic Park to say that Jock Stein wanted to talk to me, but when I got there it was actually Sean Fallon that I met, and nothing really came of it.

On the Saturday, of course, I arrived with the Motherwell party, and Big Jock was standing there to do the welcomes. I cheekily asked if I could get in, laughed and just walked past him. Dixie Deans, the pantomime villain of Wednesday night, played that day and was given his own cheer when he touched the ball (although some idiots booed him) and then when Celtic were

214

awarded a penalty, the crowd shouted for Dixie to take it. Dixie demurred and Bobby Murdoch slammed the ball past me. Celtic won the game 5–2 before a crowd of 30,000. I felt I had played well enough and it was nice to see my old friends again. As a Celtic supporter, I had been upset at their disappointing defeat in Europe, but I also enjoyed their 6–1 defeat of Hibs in the Scottish Cup final two weeks later, when Dixie more than redeemed himself with his hat-trick.

By then I was no longer a Motherwell player. I played in their last game of the season, a 1–1 draw with East Fife on Saturday, April 29 in front of a miserable crowd of 3,500 when I made what the *Evening Times* was compelled to describe as one of the season's biggest blunders under the heading: "What a Boob by Fallon". It gave East Fife their draw as I dropped a simple cross ball which seemed to bounce off my chest. The *Evening Times* announced laconically on the Monday: "Fallon has been given a free transfer by Motherwell."

That might well have been the end of my senior career. Indeed, I felt that it was. In 1972 I was past my sell-by date, but I had had reasonable success, having been at Parkhead during the unusual decade of the 1960s, when the club knew both the heady wine of triumph and the bitter, acerbic taste of defeat. I had definitely seen both sides of the game of football, and my short interlude at Motherwell was a not uninteresting postscript to my career.

But there was something yet to some. Jock Stein tried to persuade Davie McParland of Partick Thistle to sign me, but when Davie phoned and admitted that Thistle were not a rich club, I turned him down, saying that I was not a charity case. I was slightly more receptive to Morton, however, and it came about thanks to a goalkeeping crisis at Cappielow. Morton were not without their Celtic connections, for Eric Smith was their manager, and former Lisbon Lions Steve Chalmers and John Clark were playing out the last games of their distinguished careers at Greenock. The goalkeeper was Roy Baines (who would in later years play for Celtic as well), but he was badly injured and carried off in the first game of the season as Morton lost 1–5 to Stranraer in the Scottish League Cup.

This necessitated a recall for Erik Sørensen, now in his second spell with the club and concentrating more and more on coaching duties. Sørensen played on the Wednesday night in a 0–0 draw with Partick Thistle, but, as luck would have it, he too was injured and Morton were now left with no recognised goalkeeper. Rather than try their luck with an unknown youngster from the junior ranks, and presumably on the suggestion of Chalmers and Clark, Morton turned to me. I was glad to help out on a match-to-match basis.

I played four games for the club, losing to a penalty kick in a 0–1 defeat at Central Park, Cowdenbeath. I then kept a clean sheet in a 0–0 draw against Partick Thistle at Cappielow, this game being described brutally by the press as "dull" and "uninteresting". But a 0–0 draw usually says something about the goalkeeping, and I also played well in the next game, at Stair Park, Stranraer, when the team won 3–1 in that southern outpost of Scottish football.

Morton now had an outside chance of qualification for the League Cup quarter-finals, but our 7–2 victory over Cowdenbeath at Cappielow was not quite enough, and Morton lost out by one goal to Stranraer. This was my last game in senior football, for Sørensen returned from injury in time for the start of the League programme, and my services were now no longer required.

I would have dearly loved to play when Celtic visited on September 9 1972, but I have to be content with an honourable mention in the programme: "There is no shortage of goalkeepers at Cappielow these days. Erik Sørensen, Roy Baines and John Fallon are all available. John Fallon has done well by Morton in their time of crisis, taking the place of Baines and Sørensen when they were on the casualty list." Nevertheless, the playing career of John Fallon was now at an end.

216

Years later, however, I did play in the Hal Stewart testimonial game in 1980 for Morton Stars v Lisbon Squad members. It was light-hearted stuff and finished 0–0, as I remember. There had to be a winner, so it went to penalties, and I saved four of them. As I left that night and we passed Benny Rooney's office, I saw Big Jock there with some of the Lisbon Squad. He said something to me and I replied by saying, "Jock, you wouldn't know a goalkeeper if you saw one." Yes, it was a bittersweet relationship that I had with that man. No one could deny his knowledge of football or what he achieved for Celtic, but his man-management skills left a lot to be desired, even down to his spiteful omissions of me from the photographs of the Lisbon team, which contained only the eleven who actually played. I felt that I was officially a member of that team and, to be fair, there were a few photographs of the squad taken later, but I was the substitute goalkeeper and should have been included.

My exclusion from Celtic Park lasted until big Billy McNeill came back in 1978. He had heard that I attended some home games paying my money at the turnstiles. He invited me to Celtic Park one day and gave me a ticket and a pass for the area behind the directors' box. This lasted until I went back into full-time management of my pub and couldn't attend all home games, but to this day I have a free seat for life at Celtic Park.

20

LIFE AFTER FOOTBALL

There comes a time in every football player's life when enough is enough, and that is when it is becoming obvious that the body will take no more of the stern demands of professional football. It is one of the less appealing aspects of a football player's career. It is a fine career when one is fit and well, but it does not last very long. Other jobs can last until someone is in his sixties or even older, but a football player has a lot less than that, unless he feels that he can become a coach or a manager – and these jobs are notoriously stressful and seldom last for very long.

The trouble is that spending the best years of your life as a professional football player does not really equip you all that well for life outside. In my case there was the apprenticeship that I had served at Foden's, but by the time that I gave up the game in 1972 I did not feel inclined to go back to that trade. A feature on me in a *Weekly News* colour supplement in 1966 showed a picture of me under a car bonnet and said that I might like to open a garage one day. But I had been away from it for too long, more or less a decade, since I went full-time in 1963. Football was very much my life. In any case, a motor mechanic's job was a dirty, greasy one.

Financially, of course, a professional football player with Celtic is always likely to have a considerably higher income than most people. It was before the days of the gross disparity in wealth and the silly money that is given today, often to players who are manifestly struggling to cope with the demands of the game, but nevertheless, in 1972 I had a good standard of living, playing for a successful Celtic team with loads of bonuses and so on, although there were less and less of them after I lost my permanent place in the team. I was, therefore, not a poor man, although I was aware that my money would not last forever.

I had several thoughts. I might have gone to Canada, but at that time Esther was not well. I turned down a job in South Africa as a coach, and also one in New Jersey. I could have gone to Cyprus as a coach as well, but in 1974 war broke out there between the Greek and Turkish Cypriots, one of a long line of periodic and (to British eyes) pointless struggles for supremacy between two communities who took a long time to realise that cooperation might be a better idea.

So it was to the traditional haunt of the ex-football player that I turned – the licensing trade. It could be a poisoned chalice, this one, for one is sometimes too close to the drink of which Jock Stein disapproved so much. Alcohol is always a temptation, and it was no secret that quite a few of my contemporaries had major problems with drink. It is a particular problem when one is oneself the licensee. At least one ex-teammate of mine, sadly no longer with us, who entered the licensing trade once his career was finished sadly admitted to some of his fans, "I was my own best customer."

I had no such problems, however, when I leased the Central Bar in Blantyre, which I soon renamed Fallon's Bar. I was "mine host" there for a few years before a fire which started in adjacent premises badly damaged the pub and the place was closed down.

I am now retired, living happily with Esther, with none of my family too far away from me. I play golf, go to most Celtic games and am always delighted to reminisce about my playing days and goalkeeping.

Celtic are a team famous for having good goalkeepers. Prince of all is, of course, John Thomson, the lad from Fife who captured the hearts of the Glasgow public before his tragic end in 1931, but there were also the great Dan McArthur and Davie Adams of the old days.

After Adams came Charlie Shaw, the man who looked like everyone's favourite uncle, who was much loved by the fans in the years of the Great War and immediately after. He was immortalised in the Rangers song to the tune of "The Red Flag": "Charlie Shaw never saw where Alan Morton put the baw". What a compliment that was to the great and gentle Charlie, who seldom conceded goals, and therefore Rangers made a great fuss about it when they did.

Adams and Shaw were fortunate to have a great team in front of them, and the phrase that Celtic were "ten Internationals and Charlie Shaw" did have a ring to it. It was also literally true sometimes, the idea being that Charlie would never get a chance to play for Scotland (he did play three times for the Scottish League on either side of the Great War) because he never got a real opportunity to show his talents for Celtic. During the war, Celtic had such a great side that soldiers would receive letters telling them that Charlie had gone home for his tea one day in the middle of the second half and nobody noticed. Sometimes he even wandered round the park and asked the other goalkeeper if he needed a hand to keep Jimmy McMenemy and Patsy Gallacher out. Another tale was that he had a girlfriend who was an actress at the Empire Theatre and he would often be seen heading along the Gallowgate with flowers in his hand, having told Alec McNair: "Keep an eye on things for me. I'll be back in a bit."

After Charlie went to the USA there came Peter Shevlin, and he was replaced by the young man from Fife called John Thomson. It is always tempting, of course, in the wake of tragedy to exaggerate the qualities of the deceased, but Thomson's deeds need no exaggeration when stern critics like Harkness, Maley, Struth and Meiklejohn were all convinced of his value.

When John Thomson died, Celtic brought a man from Canada to fill his place. This was Joe Kennaway, one of Celtic's best, who played a great part in the success achieved by them in the last years before World War Two. After the war was the great Willie Miller, who had loads to do because he was the custodian of a very bad Celtic team. He was like Charlie Shaw in reverse. Then came George Hunter, Johnny Bonnar (whose Coronation Cup heroics must be balanced with the horrors of the 1955 Scottish Cup final), Dick Beattie (a colourful and controversial character who sometimes sported an orange jockey cap) and then Frank Haffey, whom I, of course, replaced.

I hope I have already made clear the remarkably good relationship which existed between myself and Ronnie Simpson. There was an age difference about ten years, and in a sense we were never really rivals, for I was always waiting for Ronnie to retire. In any case, Ronnie had a wealth of experience, which he had gleaned from a lengthy career, including the 1948 Olympic Games and two English Cup medals with Newcastle United, as well as his years with Queen's Park, Third Lanark and Hibs. I learned a lot from him.

Of more recent vintage, I think highly of Craig Gordon and Artur Boruc, both of whom I rate higher than Fraser Forster. In days gone by, of course, I hero-worshipped Willie Miller, and greatly admired George Hunter and also Johnny Bonnar, who apparently always said "I goat my hand tae it" or "I nearly goat my hand tae it" as appropriate, when he conceded a goal.

I always thought Dick Beattie was a flashy character, but I was genuinely surprised when the details emerged of Beattie being involved in the match-fixing case when he was at Portsmouth. When with Celtic, Dick did have two very high-profile bad games – the 1956 Scottish Cup final against Hearts, and the 1957 Scottish Cup semi-final replay against Kilmarnock – but no evidence was ever produced against him, nor against Bobby Evans, although there were rumours. On the other hand, Dick endeared himself to the Celtic fans with a seven-fingered gesture after the 7–1 defeat of Rangers in 1957.

Frank Haffey, whom I understudied for several years, I rate as a flamboyant character who greeted a bad game with a shrug of the shoulders. But inside, Frank hurt after a bad defeat for which he was to blame, and he certainly, in spite of apparently taking it in his stride, was distressed by the 9–3 game at Wembley. His error ten days later in the Scottish Cup final replay was more serious from a Celtic point of view, but it was late in the game and, as Celtic were already one goal down, was the goal which confirmed the loss of the Scottish Cup to Dunfermline rather than the goal which actually lost the Cup. Nevertheless, Haffey was confronted by angry defenders like Crerand, McNeill and MacKay for not doing better.

As for Ronnie Simpson, I look back on him with genuine affection – an odd emotion, perhaps, for a man who kept me out of the team. Ronnie was a great penalty-box man, and certainly the Jungle could clearly hear his call of "Mine" when a ball came across, and he was also wise enough to calm down the wilder elements of the team. One remembers often a quiet word in the ear of Billy McNeill when Billy seemed to be on the point of losing the plot, and in the 1965 Scottish League Cup final the Celtic End was in no doubt about who the real captain was in those frantic last few minutes. Celtic had scored with two John Hughes penalties in the first half. Rangers then got a fortuitous own goal when John Greig and Ian Young collided. That goal was scored in front of the Celtic End, where stood 50,000 anxious hearts. Eight minutes of hysterical Rangers pressure remained, but Simpson took charge. We all thus got a great view of his leadership and command of the situation. Calling upon all his experience, Ronnie gave orders, pointing, gesticulating and banging his fist into his other hand to keep the defence together and see Celtic through.

I often felt that if Ronnie had a weakness it was his inability to stop shots from a distance. He was a good goalkeeper for the penalty box, but a sudden shot from a distance, like the notorious goal of Kai Johansen in the 1966 Scottish Cup final replay, would often catch Simpson out.

Another goalkeeper at Parkhead for a short time before he moved to Dunfermline was Bent Martin. He was good, except that he didn't like diving in the mud. This would appear to be a serious disadvantage in Scotland, and perhaps it is not surprising that he never broke through to the first team at Celtic Park. He did well for George Farm at Dunfermline, however.

I would not be human if I did not feel that I was a shade better than Evan Williams, the man who displaced me, but Williams did not last long either as Celtic began to change goalkeepers with devastating regularity. The funny thing was that none of them were actually all that bad: Ally Hunter, Denis Connaghan, Peter Latchford, Roy Baines and eventually Jock Stein's final signing Pat Bonner.

I think highly of Bonner, as I do of most of Celtic's goalkeepers, men like Gordon Marshall Sr, Rab Douglas and Jonathan Gould. And I have a special word for Allen McKnight, who, like myself, languished in the reserves until he was suddenly called upon to do the honours in the Scottish Cup final of 1988 against Dundee United when Pat Bonner was injured.

Goalkeeping is an art that changes. I came just when shoulder-charging was going out. The game was all the better for the demise of that piece of thuggery – a look on YouTube at the FA Cup finals of 1957 and 1958 can be a shocking experience – but for most of my career, certainly the early part, the ball was a heavy brown one. Generally, therefore, it did not swing in the air. It was far too heavy for that, and in any case, the heavy rain of the average Scottish winter ensured that it was permanently weighed down in mud. Often the heavy ball is blamed for the prevalence of dementia and other brain disorders in men who headed it a lot. It was only when I played in Europe, in particular a game against Valencia in autumn 1962 in the Inter-Cities Fairs Cup, that I realised that a lighter ball could swing in the air and deceive goalkeepers.

I have my own ideas about the way the game should be played. I am a passionate believer that a team defending a corner kick should always have a man well up the field, so that if the goal-keeper wins the ball he is in a position to throw it to a man who can then have a run at the opposition goal. I say this because Celtic in my day often deployed Stevie Chalmers or Bobby Lennox for this purpose, and it was remarkable how often a goal would come from a counter-attack springing from a corner kick for the opposition. It all depends, of course, on the goalkeeper winning the ball and the attacker being a good and willing runner, but the two gentlemen mentioned, Chalmers and Lennox, were just that.

"Zonal marking" has become an in-phrase over the past few seasons. I disagree with this. Far better the "take a man each" philosophy of the old days, with one full back covering each post at corner kicks and never passing the ball across the penalty area. The boot up the park should never be totally despised, although it is, of course, better if you can be a little more constructive and develop an attack out of defence. But I do like the famous quotes of "Sunny Jim" Young of the 1900s and 1910s: "Face the ball, Celts" and when facing a free kick or a corner, "Tak a man apiece!"

A goalkeeper should always, literally and metaphorically, be on his toes, never more so than when facing a penalty kick. A penalty kick should, of course, be scored, and very few people will blame the goalkeeper if he does not save it. If he does save it, however, he immediately becomes a hero. I always believed that nine times out of ten a penalty-kick taker would be inclined to kick the ball across his body, meaning that a right-footed player would be likely to hit the ball to the goalkeeper's right and a left-footed player would hit it to the goalkeeper's left, but you could

224

never go 100 per cent by that. The man's run up would sometimes give you a clue, as would the angle that he was coming from, but the main thing always was to watch the ball, in the same way that if you are playing with a dog or a cat with a ball, the animal will always keep its eye on it. The important thing too was to make up your mind which way you were going to go and to dive at the very moment that the ball was being kicked. The key thing is correct anticipation.

Training for goalkeepers was far different in my day from what it is now. There was no specialist goalkeeping coach, although occasionally there were special sessions for the goalkeepers taken by Stein himself. These were little more than brutal shot-stopping sessions, with the ball being driven at the goalkeeper from all angles, and although Bent Martin earned a little ridicule and scorn for being reluctant to dive in the mud at training sessions, I had a little sympathy with him in the sense that the training jerseys were not always washed as often as they could have been and were often left to dry still caked in mud.

On other occasions, Ronnie and I would play in training games, but as outfield players. This was to encourage us, presumably, to dribble and kick when required, but Stein always believed that the six-yard box was the goalkeeper's and that hands should definitely be used there. I learned that when going up for a cross ball a goalkeeper should stick his knee out to prevent a challenge from a forward, and that when punching a ball the elbow should be bent for similar reasons but also so that I could get more purchase on the ball.

Speed in forwards, I believe, is a great thing. While Chalmers, McBride and Wallace were no slouches, they were nothing like as fast as Bobby Lennox, who would surely have won the Powderhall Sprint on New Year's Day if he had not been playing for Celtic at the time. Similarly, young Jimmy Quinn – grandson of the great Jimmy Quinn from Croy of the Edwardian era – was very fast. Unfortunately young Jimmy, occasionally played hideously out of position at left back, kept picking up injuries and his career never really developed.

The biggest problem that I see for Celtic, particularly at home, is when so many mediocre Scottish teams come to Parkhead and "park the team bus" inside their own penalty area. This is nothing new, but in my time Celtic tended to have the guile of Johnstone, the craft of Murdoch and the speed of Lennox to solve this problem. The answer is still the same: to get behind the defenders, to reach the dead ball line and then to cross a ball accurately for the centre forwards to do the needful. There is always the unexpected, which can produce devastating dividends sometimes.

It took a long time for Celtic to appreciate that "parking the team bus" was a recognised skill of the game which they should practise occasionally as well. Much was made of the European Cup semi-final in Prague in 1967 when we came out with a defensive formation with only Steve Chalmers up front. To a large extent we had little choice, for Dukla Prague were no bad side, but I wish that Celtic had been streetwise enough to do that at the Nep Stadium in Budapest against MTK in 1964.

Looking back on my career, I think with fondness about the goalkeepers who were my opponents. I remain a paid-up member, as it were, of the goalkeepers' union, and would always make it my business to seek out my opposite number and have a chat about goalkeeping and other matters. There was nothing new about this, and the story is told elsewhere in these pages about the day at Parkhead in the late 1920s when, because light was failing, half-time was held in the field to save time. Four groups were spotted: Willie Maley was haranguing the Celtic men, Hearts manager Willie McCartney was doing likewise with his men, the referee was talking to his two linesman – and the two goalkeepers, Jack Harkness and John Thomson, good friends even though they were rivals for a place in the Scotland team, were sitting on the ground together drinking their tea and discussing the art of goalkeeping. (It was not even beyond the realms of possibility that they were bitching about their respective managers!)

This tradition continued and, to my delight, I found that I got on well with George Farm, the manager of Dunfermline Athletic. Not everyone liked Farm's brusque and unsympathetic approach to some of his players, nor the brutal, uncompromising style of play which characterised the Pars in the 1960s, but Farm had been a goalkeeper and could understand what we were going through. Farm had been the goalkeeper of Blackpool in the famous Stanley Matthews FA Cup final of 1953. He had not had a great game that day, even though Blackpool eventually triumphed. This was possibly why Farm publicly sympathised with me when I went through my horrors of New Year 1968.

Scotland was blessed with many good goalkeepers in the 1960s, and I think a lot of men, like Willie Whigham of Falkirk, "Tubby" Ogston of Aberdeen, Donald Mackay of Dundee United, Jim Cruickshank of Hearts, Willie Wilson of Hibs, and Billy Ritchie and Norrie Martin of Rangers. Goalkeepers are indeed a breed apart, and we generally got on well together, not least because we could never foul each other. We are at the other end of the field and only see each other before the game starts, at half-time and when the game is over. We are literally a breed apart!

At one point I used to do the tours of Celtic Park, something that I enjoyed very much, apart from the fact that it took too long. I loved talking to supporters and answering their questions. I recall on one occasion Martin O'Neill, when he was the manager, coming up and joining one of my tours, saying afterwards how much he enjoyed listening to my history of the club. He then asked me to take some of his friends on another tour!

A sour note was struck once and led to a slight rift between myself and some of the Lisbon Lions. The eleven players who played on May 25 1967 were all invited to a celebration twenty-five years later at Seamill, in May 1992. A film was made and subsequently shown on TV. At one point, Jim Craig asked them to remember that they should not forget people like Joe McBride, Charlie Gallagher, John Hughes, Willie O'Neill and myself, who were part of the squad but did not actually play. Bobby Murdoch and Ronnie Simpson agreed, and I felt particularly that I should have been part of it because, after all, I was not only in the *squad* but actually in the *team*, for I was stripped and could have been used as substitute goalkeeper. (In 1967, a substitute goalkeeper was the only substitute allowed in the European Cup.)

I then received an irate phone call from Joe McBride, wondering why we were not at the celebration. Joe, of course, was a special case as well, for he would surely have been in the team had it not been for his sad injury sustained at Pittodrie on Christmas Eve 1966. Eventually I was appointed a spokesman for the "rebels" to approach Willie Haughey, who arranged such things, at the club. An issue was also raised about the photographs. There are loads of photographs of the team which won the European Cup, some of whom have eleven players, others fifteen or sixteen. I eventually got some sort of promise that we would be included in the future, but it still irks me that I had to ask the question.

A bizarre accusation was laid against me that I had allowed my European Cup medal to be used for the striking of a replica. (My European Cup medal took a bit of acquiring, as you may recall from a previous chapter.) Unbeknown to my accuser, my medal was actually on show at Celtic Park and someone else's medal was being used for that purpose. This was a rather heated argument, and I was never really supported by the rest of the squad and was told that I would not be invited to other functions or golf outings.

But my being *persona non grata* may have had something to do with what happened one year at the Carrick Loch Lomond. It was a four ball, and I had on my team my friend Robert McLarrie, a bank manager and a BA pilot. And we won! I was never invited back the following year to defend it, though.

228

I continue to be a committed, even obsessive, Celtic supporter. I seldom go to hospitality at Parkhead, because, as I tell them, I prefer to live among the fans. I attend every home game and most away games as well. I hold court to a loyal band of followers outside the superstore and the pools office ("my office", as I like to call it) before every home game, talking to everyone and shaking hands with these huge goalkeeper's hands of mine. Often I have my grandchildren, James, Lloyd and Monica, with me. Esther and I are always willing to attend supporters' functions all over Scotland and even in Ireland and the USA. My opinions about players are sincerely, if volubly, expressed. I am, above all else, a Celtic supporter.

I enjoy standing in "my office" beside the pools office and talking to my friends from Cleland, Fraserburgh, Kirkcaldy, Ayrshire, Newcastle, Dundee and of course Ireland. And what do we talk about? More or less everything, including the odd reference to Sevco, Deadco or whatever they are called these days. Not that I miss them! And then along comes "Free State" Charlie McGinley, camera in hand. He is snap happy and must have hundreds of photos. Then there is Tommy Stevenson, who, if he had played, would have been complete wreck, for he is so worked up before a game. Then there is Wardie Jim, Big Frannie and Wee Frannie, who is a real jack in the box, and Paul the Tim, whom we call a stalker because of his ability to get on Facebook with some of the players. Then there are the Govan Bhoys, who discuss and dissect every game.

Away games? We go with my grandchildren, sometimes picking up George and Maxi in Edinburgh, and then we head north. One law that we have is no tunes or songs before the game, but after the game my grandchildren play the Celtic songs.

Friends? I have loads of them, with the common theme of supporting Celtic. I have friends in Ireland, from Derry, Belfast, Galway, Drogheda, Cork, Donegal, Sligo; some Geordies, from

Newcastle; and even further afield, in Canada, Australia, Malta and the USA – and that is even before I begin to think about Scotland and Glasgow. In particular, I would like to single out Charlie "Free State" McGinley, Andrew Milne of the *More Than 90 Minutes* fanzine, Nigel from the Celtic Fanzone, Joe McHugh, Celtic Video Web, Jim Ward, Martin Gilmour, Gerry, Big Mervyn, Martin Walsh, Seamy Darragh, Hilly from St Margaret's in Drogheda, Mick from Derry, Seamus Kennedy from the Abbey Guest House in Derry, Phil and Ann, the Agnew family, Patrick Rollink and Kevin McShane.

They are all Celtic to the core, and so am I. I am so proud to have been part of this huge family for so long, and to have played my small part in handing down a tradition to the future. It is in the Fallon genes.